The Return of Technology's Timeless Tool

Divination, oracles, seership, alchemy—these words have provoked scoffs and fear for centuries. Today, the growing partnership between ancient mysticism and modern science brings validity and acceptance to many divinatory tools and techniques. In no area is this more evident than in crystal technology.

As transistors and computer chips, crystals are at the heart of tools in the communication field. As personal communication devices, crystal balls and crystal bowls are multi-purpose instruments of transformation. Both allow individuals to access, amplify, and project energies not normally available. Still, with all of their popularity, there has been little practical information on their applications and use.

Now, anyone can utilize crystal balls and crystal bowls in one of their most prized roles. *Crystal Balls & Crystal Bowls* takes these mighty instruments of divination out of the realm of the occult and places them in the hands of the people for empowering personal use. Join author Ted Andrews as he uncovers all the aspects of crystal science and mysticism in this authoritative guide to *Crystal Balls & Crystal Bowls: Tools for Ancient Scrying & Modern Seership*.

About the Author

Ted Andrews is a full-time author, student, and teacher in the metaphysical and spiritual fields. He conducts seminars, symposiums, workshops, and lectures on ancient mysticism, focusing on translating esoteric material to make it comprehensible and practical for everyone.

Ted is certified in basic hypnosis and acupressure, and is involved in the study and use of herbs as an alternative path in health care. He is active in the holistic healing field. Trained in piano, Ted also employs the Celtic harp, bamboo flute, shaman rattles, Tibetan bells, the Tibetan Singing Bowl, and quartz crystal bowls to create individual healing therapies and induce higher states of consciousness.

Ted is a clairvoyant and works with past-life analysis and synthesis, aura interpretation, dreams, numerology, and the tarot. He is a contributing author to various metaphysical magazines, with published articles on various topics including Occult Christianity, Working with Our Angelic Brethren, and the Metaphysical Mirrors within Our Lives.

To Write to the Author

If you wish to contact the author or would like more information about this book, please write to the author in care of Llewellyn Worldwide and we will forward your request. Both the author and publisher appreciate hearing from you and learning of your enjoyment of this book and how it has helped you. Llewellyn Worldwide cannot guarantee that every letter written to the author can be answered, but all will be forwarded. Please write to:

Ted Andrews
c/o Llewellyn Worldwide
P.O. Box 64383, Dept. K026-4, St. Paul, MN 55164-0383, U.S.A.
Please enclose a self-addressed, stamped envelope for reply, or $1.00 to cover costs.
If outside U.S.A., enclose international postal reply coupon.

Free Catalog From Llewellyn Worldwide

For more than 90 years Llewellyn has brought its readers knowledge in the fields of metaphysics and human potential. Learn about the newest books in spiritual guidance, natural healing, astrology, occult philosophy, and more. To get your free copy of *Llewellyn's New Worlds of Mind and Spirit*, send your name and address to:

Llewellyn's New Worlds of Mind and Spirit
P.O. Box 64383, Dept. K026-4, St. Paul, MN 55164-0383, U.S.A.

Crystal Balls & Crystal Bowls

Tools for Ancient Scrying & Modern Seership

Ted Andrews

1996
Llewellyn Publications
St. Paul, Minnesota 55164-0383, U.S.A.

FIRST EDITION
Third Printing, 1996

Cover photograph by Russell Lane
Interior illustrations by Anne Marie Garrison
  (pp. 43, 66, 77, 109, 110, 114, 126, 127, 130, 134, 148, 167, 220)
Interior photos by Margaret K. Andrews
Editing and interior design by Connie Hill

Special thanks to Cedric and Carol Wise,
Crystal Distributing Co., Inc., Houston, Texas

Library of Congress Cataloging-in-publication Data
Andrews, Ted. 1952–
    Crystal balls & crystal bowls : tools for ancient scrying & modern seership /
Ted Andrews. — 1st ed.
        p.   cm.
    Includes bibliographical references and index.
    ISBN 1-56718-026-4
    1. Crystal gazing. I. Title. II. Title: Crystal balls and crystal bowls.
BF1331.A54   1994
133.3'22—dc20   94-44921
                                                                          CIP

Llewellyn Publications
A Division of Llewellyn Worldwide, Ltd.
P.O. Box 64383, St. Paul, MN 55164-0383

Dedication

To Vinnie Gaglione
to clarify the difference
between balls, bowls, bulls, and bowels.
Many thanks for your support.

Other Books by the Author

Simplified Magic
Imagick
The Sacred Power in Your Name
How to See & Read the Aura
The Magical Name
Dream Alchemy
Sacred Sounds
How to Meet & Work With Your Spirit Guides
How to Uncover Your Past Lives
Magickal Dance
Enchantment of the Faerie Realm
The Occult Christ
Animal-Speak
The Healer's Manual
How to Develop and Use Psychometry
How to Heal with Color

Special Acknowledgement

A special thanks to Crystal Distributing,
7320 Ashcroft, Suite 303
Houston, Texas 77081
Telephone: 713–774–3200
Fax: 713–774–3224
for their assistance in supplying materials for the cover photo.

Table of Contents

PART TWO
Song of the Crystal Bowl

Photographs and Illustrations

Part One

Mysteries of the Crystal Ball

Chapter One

Divination & Seership

Through the beaded curtains of the doorway you see a woman seated at a small round table. In front of her rests an object covered with a black silk cloth. By its shape you know it must be her crystal ball. An empty chair is opposite her, waiting patiently for you to occupy it. The fragrance of an exotic incense teases your senses while relaxing you. The lighting is dim, but not dark. The room seems alien and mysterious.

The woman raises her head and smiles at you, and in that moment your impression of the room shifts. It now seems warm and inviting. She greets you with a soft gentle voice and motions toward the empty chair, inviting you in. You hesitate briefly, and then step through the curtains.

You pause just on the other side. For an instant you feel as if you have crossed a threshold into another dimension. The feeling passes, and as it does, you take a moment to study the room. On one wall are books of astrology, tarot, and subjects which you don't recognize, but which seem mysterious and intriguing. Behind the woman is a large poster of tarot cards spread out in various designs.

The lamp overhead is soft, giving enough light to see everything clearly without glaring. On a table in the corner to your right is a rich blue cloth, upon which are laid crystals and stones of different colors and sizes. A candle burns softly, and in front of it a stick of incense perfumes the air as it slowly burns. Somehow you know that all of this is not necessary. The decorations serve no purpose other than to be effects in which the woman finds enjoyment.

You turn your attention back to the woman. Her smile is still soft and patient. She seems to know that you are anxious, and she allows you time to familiarize yourself with the surroundings. She knows that the more relaxed you are, the easier it will be to divine for you.

You take the seat, and she extends her hand, introducing herself to you. You begin to feel more comfortable and relaxed. She tells you briefly of herself and her background. You find yourself surprised that she is so normal. All of your preconceptions begin to melt away.

You tell her it is your first time for anything like this, and again she smiles, and her expression becomes more playful.

"Well, it won't hurt too badly," she says, her eyes twinkling. "Very seldom is there any bleeding or permanent scarring, and bruises usually go away within a week or two."

You both laugh, and she removes the black silk cloth from the crystal ball in front of her. Before you is a crystal globe about six inches in diameter. You are surprised to see that it is not perfectly clear, and you mention this to her.

"The crystal ball does not need to be perfectly clear. Most balls that you have seen displayed in this manner were of glass and not true quartz crystal. There are some who would never think of using anything but a clear ball, but the balls come in different sizes and different degrees of clarity. One is no better nor worse than another."

She then moves the ball closer to you, and asks you to place your hands upon it, to stroke it, and to focus your attention upon it.

"Keep your eyes fixed upon the ball. It will hold your attention and help relax you even more. You will imprint it with your energy. The ball will take your energy and form it into different patterns and forms. As I gaze into it, the forms will begin to appear. At times I see only images and symbols, while at other times I may see whole scenarios.

"Sometimes the images appear in the ball itself. Sometimes they appear in my head as I gaze into the ball. One way is neither better nor worse than the other. It just varies from time to time. Whatever I see—whether in my head or in the ball—I will describe just as I see it. After I have described the scene and images, I will go back and tell you exactly what that means to you, for you, and about you."

The ball at first is cool to the touch. Gingerly, you trace its texture and form with your fingertips, and then you cup it in your hands. It feels alive, but you are not sure if this is really true or if you are imagining this because of the atmosphere and your own preconceptions. As you stroke it softly with your hands, it begins to warm. You feel a warm, soft sensation rising up out of the ball and tickling your hands—like static electricity. You are amazed at how it makes you feel.

The ball draws your eyes into it, as if trying to absorb you—or at least some part of you. You are amazed at the shifting light patterns and rainbows that reveal themselves as the light of the room is reflected and refracted. The different planes and occlusions within the ball give it a depth and appearance that truly seems out of this world.

After several minutes, the woman reaches out and places her hands upon yours on the ball, and then she gently lifts your hands from it. You draw them back to your own lap, and yet you still feel them tingling. She moves the ball back toward herself, and leans forward. Her eyes take on a soft gaze and she begins to speak.

"I see mist and clouds beginning to rise. They are dancing, billowing and ebbing. The energy is strong. The ball must really like you. It doesn't always respond this quickly.

"I see you in the crystal, walking into a mist. I see it enfolding you, embracing you . . . The mist is beginning to dissipate, and a rainbow is showing up around you in the ball. I am seeing you walking through a pine forest with sunlight penetrating through the branches sporadically.

"There are other forms in the distance, as you walk through this forest. I can't see them clearly yet, but they are reflections of the future. Perhaps they will clarify themselves as we get further into this.

"I am seeing you step out of the pine forest into a clearing. In the clearing is a wagon—what appears to be part of a gypsy caravan. A gypsy-like man is sitting next to a small campfire, playing a violin. As the music rises, the smoke from the fire dances with it . . . ."

Today, images and scenarios such as that described above are usually dealt with in one of two ways. People either place them in the category of the ridiculous, or at the center of their belief system, as part of the reality of their lives. The truth, as it so often is, can be found between these extremes.

Divination, oracles, seership, scrying, fortune telling—all of these words and phrases conjure images of mystery and the occult. Scenes such as that described above have been depicted in movies, on television and in books. Many embrace these possibilities, while others scoff. Even those who outwardly scoff at them experience a twinge of inner excitement at the idea of gaining access to hidden or forbidden knowledge.

This is a wonderful time to be living. It is a time filled with adventure and mystery. Much of what used to be considered the stuff of fiction or the fodder of metaphysical "mumbo jumbo" can now be proven. We live in a time in which the technology and knowledge available to us can validate much metaphysical and psychic theory. We are increasingly aware of human possibilities. We understand and prove daily that the human mind and consciousness is much more capable and powerful than had even been imagined in the past. This places the idea of divination closer to the realm of scientific validity.

Divination is defined by the *Random House Dictionary of the English Language* as "(1) the practice of attempting to foretell events or discover hidden knowledge by occult or supernatural means, (2) augury; prophecy and (3) perception by intuition; instinctive foresight."[1] Through the methods in this book, you will prove to yourself that all three of these definitions can become a reality in your life, along with other aspects of divination not included in this limited definition.

As to the first definition, through the use of crystal balls and crystal bowls this book will take the process of divination out of the realm of occult and supernatural and place it in the realm of natural knowledge, within the inherent ability of everyone. You will be able to prove to yourself just how easy and natural divination and seership can be. When this is realized, then even such things as augury and prophecy, as defined in the second definition, become probabilities. By practicing with the techniques provided in this book, your intuitive perception will be enhanced and your natural instinctive foresight will again reawaken and become stronger (definition 3).

Individuals around the world have practiced divination and seership, using a variety of techniques to gain knowledge of future or unknown events. They have been called seers, scryers (those who descry or far-see), oracles, necromancers, sorcerers, and by many other names throughout the ages, and people used to rely on these diviners, seers, and oracles for most aspects of their lives.

In ancient times, the training of seers was often confined to religious temples or aligned with religious beliefs of the society. Some believe that many methods of divination arose from the Wise Woman Tradition, which was familial. Grandmothers would pass it on to their daughters, who would then pass the teaching on to their daughters, and so on,

---

1 Stein, Jess, ed. *The Random House Dictionary of the English Language*. Random House, New York, 1970, p. 419.

**In old legends, the dragon would become a hawk.
The author often uses crystal balls with his hawk, Phoenix,
in storytelling sessions with school children,
to teach animal and natural wonders.**

generation after generation. The kind of divination technique varied with the family; some families were "weather wise," while others would talk to animals.

In actuality, divination can involve any method by which events are interpreted and/or explained. Divination is more than foretelling the future. It does involve prediction, but it can also involve divining some truth or interpreting omens and signs as part of its practice.

Divination often incorporates methods by which events are interpreted and explained. The most commonly recognized tools and methods in our modern society are runes, tarot, astrology, dreams, and I Ching. A wide variety of strange and unusual methods of divination have been employed, from the reading of entrails to the study of cloud formations. The list on page 8 provides just a brief look at some of the diversity.

DIVERSITY OF DIVINATION

Aeromancy	The casting of dirt or sand into the wind to determine answers by the direction the wind takes it.
Apantomancy	Observing objects that appear haphazardly.
Belomancy	Divination by the flight of arrows.
Bibliomancy	Consulting a passage or line in a book at random.
Catoptromancy	Divination through a lens or a magic mirror.
Ceromancy	Dropping melted wax into water and observing results.
Chiromancy	Divination by the lines of the hand.
Crystalomancy	Divination by clear globe, pool of water, mirror or transparent object.
Geloscopy	Interpretation of a person's laughter.
Gyromancy	Spinning and falling to ground, leading to oracles.
Hepatoscopy	Observation of a sheep's liver.
Myomancy	Divination by studying the entrails or the movements of rodents.
Oenisticy	Divination by studying the flight of birds.
Onomancy	Divination by rearranging the letters in a name.
Ooscopy	Using an egg to determine the sex of an unborn child.
Phrenology	Studying the bumps and contours of the head.
Physiognomy	The study of human facial features.
Pyromancy	Divination by smoke and fire.
Tasseography	The reading of tea leaves and their shapes.
Xylomancy	Observation of the position of twigs on the ground.

The history of humanity is filled with famous and infamous individuals practicing various forms of divination. Records of it appear frequently in myth and scripture. In Greece, oracles at Delphi, Dodona, and Delos were primary sites used by the Minoans for divination, prior to 1200 B.C.[2] A Greek method of divination using thimbles (cubomancy) would eventually be picked up and used by the Romans, specifically the Emperors Augustus and Tiberius.[3] The Emperor Julian the Apostate was believed to have practiced a form of divination which involved consulting the intestines of sacrificed children.[4]

Divination is even found in Biblical scriptures, both Old and New Testaments. In I Samuel 2, Saul prohibits divination by necromancy or divination of the dead. This particular type of divination took many forms in different societies. Sometimes it involved a fastidious ritual to communicate with the recently deceased corpse. At other times it involved techniques for invoking and communicating with the spirits of the dead, similar to what is practiced by modern spiritualists.

Today, divination still is practiced. People mediate with spirits (channel), perform psychic readings, practice astrology, and interpret dreams. Yet, with the variety of forms currently being practiced in society, it is still crystal gazing that is the epitome of symbols reflecting divination, seership, and the mysteries of the universe.

More than any other method, crystal gazing instills simultaneously a sense of wonder, a sense of excitement, and a sense of fear. It stirs primal memories and instinctive responses to the universe and all that affects us through it.

Variations of this form of divination are recorded throughout history. The use of a lens or magic mirror has been linked to such individuals as Apuleius, the Roman philosopher and novelist, St. Augustine, and even Roger Bacon. The crystal ball has been associated with figures such as Pythagoras, Aesculapius, and Anton Mesmer. Arthur Conan Doyle, William Butler Yeats, Sir Oliver Lodge, C. W. Leadbeater and William James are also notables who have experimented with it.

The time of crystal gazing has not passed. It is as effective now as it ever was, and, in fact, is still evolving—from it has grown the wonder of crystal bowls, and all of the healing and psychic applications of crystals in general.

---

2 Matthews, John, ed. *The World Atlas of Divination*. Little, Brown and Company, Boston, 1992, p. 69.

3 Baskin, Wade. *The Sorcerer's Handbook*. Citadel Press, Secaucus, NJ, 1974, p. 179.

4 Ibid., p. 178.

In the ancient Hermetic Tradition is a principle that embodies why divination in any form works. The Tradition's Principle of Correspondence states: "As above, so below; as below, so above. This principle embodies the truth that there is always a Correspondence between the laws and phenomena of the various planes of Being and Life."[5] In other words, there is a relationship between all planes of existence, physical and spiritual, and all that occurs on them. Whatever happens on one level, reflects itself on the other.

There are events and patterns that are seemingly beyond our awareness and understanding. This principle, with its universal applications, helps us to see what had seemed unknowable. Through it we can understand the hidden secrets of Nature. By studying the events on earth, we discover insights into heaven. The principle embraces the idea that apparently random events are in reality parts of a much greater design. By studying them, we awaken within ourselves indications and realizations of the direction the universe and our life are moving.

Divination helps us to move from the unknown to the known. When we learn to open our eyes to the unseen, we become seers. Through the exercises in this book, you will learn to take the ancient agent of the crystal ball, and its offspring, the crystal bowl, and begin a new direction for divining the future, healing the past, and re-creating your present.

Preparing for Divination and Seership

The human spirit is mythic in its proportions. The development of divination and seership helps us to discover that mythic part of ourselves that is capable of creation. It is what enables us to move from mere psychism to true divination.

Divination and seership always begins with the self. Seers need to be able to shed or set aside the outer self and look closely behind their own masks or the masks of others for whom they are *seeing*. Through the development of divination and seership, we learn to see ourselves and the world differently. We learn to see connections and patterns where previously we had not seen them. This goes back to that Principle of Correspondence discussed earlier. Everything is connected to everything else. Nothing is insignificant or of no consequence. The lesser will reflect patterns of the greater.

---

5 Three Initiates. *The Kybalion*. Yogi Publication Society, Chicago, 1940, p. 28.

In many ways it is like standing between two mirrors. There are multiple reflections in both mirrors, but all are linked to the one primary image. With seership and divination, we learn to see all the threads and pieces, past and/or future, leading to or out from a specific point in time or place.

Divination and seership do not have to be solely predictive. They have many other applications. They can be used for self-discovery, clarification, new perspectives, and even for accessing hidden knowledge. It is effective when we are confused or going through transitions. It helps us when initiating new projects and new paths, or when ending the old. It reveals possibilities and optional courses of action. It can be used to uncover the when, where, how, and why of situations.

Does this mean that what is divined *has* to come to pass? Does this mean that life events are predestined? Anytime people begin to explore divination, seership, and other aspects of the psychic realm, there is concern over the question of free will versus fate. If we divine the future, can we then change it? If we explore the past, will that change the present?

What is divined does not *have* to come to pass. There are many factors that can influence the ultimate outcome of events. We always have free will. We have the freedom to make choices, to take actions, to make decisions, or not to do so. By our action or inaction, there are consequences—good, bad or indifferent—that are more likely to occur. Our choices and actions (or lack of) set up certain probabilities that can be foreseen and predicted. Certain patterns, streams, or probabilities of events are set in motion.

Learning to divine involves recognizing links and patterns to a great degree. If you can see the pattern that has brought a person to a certain point in his or her life, then you can see where that pattern is likely to lead if it is not changed. Divination and seership help you to realize that there are few limitations and many choices within our lives. They help you to realize the more probable consequences, and thus you can take more beneficial actions. The following two exercises will help you to shift your consciousness to more easily see or divine patterns.

Exercise 1—
Beginning Seership

If we cannot see a pattern, we will be unable to change it or to fully take advantage of it. One way of developing the ability to see patterns is to begin by seeing everything and everyone that we encounter as symbolic. Although some may see this as being superstitious, the more we work with symbolism, the easier it is to filter and separate the inconsequential from the significant. As with all skill development, it does require practice.

To understand symbols is to understand ourselves—including our instinctive actions and abilities. Symbols help us to understand our beliefs, superstitions, fears, potentials, and patterns. Symbols are bridges that help us to cross from the rational to more intuitive levels of perception. They lead us to the unlimited regions of the subconscious mind.

Sometimes, as we go through life, we form our own realities and we become complacent. We can use symbols to shake us from complacency. Symbols span the world of thought and being, the mental and the physical. They provide hidden and veiled messages about the world around us. They bridge what was with what now is, and what is with what is possible. They provide the clues to the hidden realities around us. By working with them daily, we open all of the doorways to our intuitive self.

So how do we work with them to open to that part of us capable of seership? Studying the symbols you use in your everyday life is a starting point. What is the significance behind the symbols in your church? Examine your surroundings, decor, and furnishings. Step outside of yourself and ask, "What are they saying about me?" Look at your clothes, trinkets, jewelry, etc. What are they symbolizing about you and your attitudes? Why do you choose to live where you do, in the manner you do? What does this reflect about you?

The next step is to try to see patterns and relationships. Start simply. Examine four or five of your friends. List them on a piece of paper. What are the most outstanding qualities about each? What aggravates you the most about each? What quality or qualities do they have in common? What does this then say about you?

Take a look at your biological family and your work family. Are there patterns, attitudes, behaviors, forms of expression that all members seem to have or use periodically? When does this usually come out? How do others respond to it?

The following is an imaginative exercise that is fun and beneficial to do periodically—once or twice a year. It helps you to recognize and identify changing patterns in yourself and your life. It requires that you step outside your human personality. By doing so you are able to become more objective.

When I taught school, I would use exercises such as this to help students identify their values and their patterns of behavior in connection to them. It was beneficial to stimulate discussions. This exercise will help you define the qualities and abilities you value most. If we intend to become a seer and divine information for ourselves and others, we have to be able to see the relationships between actions and their effects. We have to see the value of various actions/inactions and their consequences. If we cannot see these, we are destined to repeat patterns that are often detrimental to us.

Using your imagination, fill in the blanks for each of the following. Go with your first thought. If two come to mind, write them both down. Have fun with this. By placing yourself in these conditions, you learn how to step outside of yourself and your personality to see from an objectively intuitive perspective. This every seer must learn to do.

If I were a stone, I would be _____

If I were a tree, I would be _____

If I were a bird, I would be _____

If I were an insect, I would be _____

If I were a machine, I would be _____

If I were a tool, I would be _____

If I were a fruit, I would be _____

If I were a flower, I would be _____

If I were a kind of weather, I would be _____

If I were a mythical creature, I would be _____

If I were a musical instrument, I would be _____

If I were a kind of profession, I would be _____

If I were a law, I would be _____

If I were an animal, I would be _____

If I were anything in the world, I would be _____

If I were a color, I would be _____

If I were a fragrance, I would be _____

If I were an emotion, I would be _____

If I were a state, I would be _____

If I were a vegetable, I would be _____

After making your choices, the next step is to try and determine patterns in your answers. In order to do this, you have to first look at the qualities and characteristics of the answer. For example, if you chose "PINE" for the kind of tree, study the pine tree. Read about the myth and lore of it. Study its characteristics, herbal and otherwise.

Do this with each answer in turn. Then begin to compare them. Are there similar qualities associated with the tree as there are with the animal? What does the profession you chose have in common with the tree or the bird?

Some of the similarities may be clear—others so very subtle you may have to work with them to make connections. With some you may not be able to find any links, and that's fine. Don't be discouraged. If you have three or more in which similar qualities and/or connections are showing up, then there is some kind of pattern beginning to form. The more similarities you find in your answers, the more important the pattern and its significance.

That quality or characteristic is one of significance to you. Take time and contemplate it. Where and when in your life has that quality or characteristic appeared? Where would you like to see it? Did it ever show up when you didn't want it to?

It is important to treat this exercise as fun. It is not designed to create any kind of psychological profile. Its intent is to stimulate your subconscious into seeing relationships and connections. It is designed to exercise your natural ability to see patterns and relationships to everything in your life.

In traditional metaphysics, we often hear that humans are microcosms. We are reflections of the Macrocosm, of the universe. We have all energies within us, and, because of this, everything around us impacts upon us, whether we realize it or not. As we look for connections, we grow in our consciousness of how all life impacts upon us and how we impact upon all life. We become seers-in-the-making.

Treat it like a game. Try to find the hidden pieces, the hidden links. As you begin to do this, you will find it easier to relate circumstances and see connections in other areas of your life. With practice you will begin to see more and more connections to everything and everyone around you. Everything will take on much greater significance. The subtleties of life will become more obvious, and you will find it easier to see the choices ahead for you and others, and their true value.

Exercise 2— Ariadne's Thread

Many societies had gods and goddesses linked to the divination process. The more commonly recognized figures of myth and lore were often involved with the practice of divination. Reading their stories and myths can widen your perception of the great diversity found within this practice.

Just as the gods and goddesses had their own way of divining, each of us must also learn to do so. Guidelines can be given, but you must take the guidelines and adapt them to yourself and your own unique circumstances. You must find your own way through the maze of life. You must learn to see in your own way.

Divining, whether with a crystal ball or a tarot deck, is like finding your way through a maze. The tools you use help you to see where the path ahead is leading, so that you don't become entrapped in the maze of life itself. They help you to see through the smoke and haze of everyday life, enabling you to work your way through the labyrinth of life's daily activities and problems from a perspective that is more creative and effective.

Mazes and labyrinths have been found all over the world. Gardens have been landscaped in this fashion. Buildings have been constructed with mazelike dimensions and structures. Stories and myths tell of the hero's journey through a maze of difficulties to an eventual reward. Such tales were often very symbolic.

The most common myth of a labyrinth or maze is in the Roman tale of Theseus. Theseus was a hero who at a very early age accomplished many great feats. His greatest feat was the slaying of the Minotaur, a beast with the body and limbs of a human and the head of a bull.

King Minos of Athens employed the architect Daedalos to create a vast labyrinth with intricate, winding passages from which no one who entered could ever find his/her way out. Adding to the difficulty was the fact that the Minotaur roamed throughout it. To control the Minotaur and keep him contained in the labyrinth, the king was compelled to send regular tributes of young men and maidens into the labyrinth to eventually be eaten by the Minotaur.

When Theseus heard of this, he offered himself as a victim, so that he could do battle with the Minotaur and hopefully free Athens of this evil, once and for all. Before entering into the labyrinth, he won the favor of Ariadne, the daughter of Minos. He obtained from her a thread that, by holding onto it throughout his wanderings in the labyrinth, enabled him to find his way out the same way he had gone in. Theseus met and defeated the Minotaur, and then used Ariadne's thread to guide himself out of the many intricate passages of the labyrinth.

Most of us have worked with some form of maze on paper. There are circle links, loops, knots, and a variety of geometric formations. Some common and familiar samples are found at the end of this chapter.

All mazes and labyrinths provide a focus for the mind. The shapes and their intricacies force the subconscious into new perceptions. Mazes challenge the subconscious to shift and stimulate intuitive and creative perceptions for their resolution. Thus they help us to consciously access our inner potentials and new levels of awareness. They help us to shift from mundane perceptions to more universal ones. Through them we learn to process information in new ways. The resolution of mazes requires the use of both right and left hemispheres of the brain. They stimulate balanced brain function and activity.

We actually have a double brain—two hemispheres. Each hemisphere of our brain processes information in different ways. The left hemisphere is more logical, more rational in its approach to assimilating and using information. It analyzes, counts, follows step-by-step procedures, and it is sequential in its learning.

The right hemisphere differs in the way it functions. Through it we see how things exist in space (spatial relationships), and how parts go together. It is the key to the imaginative faculties, and through it we dream, understand metaphors, and create new combinations of ideas.

When both hemispheres work together, we assimilate information more easily and retain it longer. We can more consciously and practically access and apply our intuitive faculty, and we more easily open to deeper insights. Through balanced activities of both brain hemispheres, we access deeper levels of our consciousness in a more controlled and focused manner.

The most effective resolution of mazes requires activity of both hemispheres. There is a logical approach to attacking and resolving any maze (left brain), but there is also a need to work with the imaginative faculty in seeing the spatial relationships of our steps (past and future) in connection to the overall maze and our present position in it (right brain). You have to know where you have been, how you got there, and where it is likely to lead. For this to occur, both hemispheres are necessary, and thus mazes and labyrinths assist us in using both sides of the brain.

Mazes teach us to utilize our imagination and focus its strength, drawing us into positive solutions and successes. They help us recognize what limits and repeats itself within our lives. This in turn facilitates the access and implementation of greater levels of energy and consciousness for a particular task or for our overall life.

It is amazing how often people compare life and all of its experiences to wandering about blindly in a maze! Yet few people realize how even simple mazes and labyrinths, such as those included in this chapter, can be wonderfully magical tools. The maneuvering of oneself through a task or a stressful period in one's life is like working a maze. The successful maneuvering in both cases requires a deep and balanced perspective. It is a mirroring that reflects the Principle of Correspondence discussed earlier.

Working with mazes and labyrinths will help you develop this mirrored perspective in regard to all aspects of life. It is a wonderful preparation technique for honing your divination abilities for future crystal ball work. It not only increases your overall effectiveness in life, but it also facilitates your ability to access and apply the energies of the crystal ball and crystal bowl for even more effective scrying.

Despite the fact that there are many types of mazes, the principle in solving all of them is the same. This applies to mazes found at the end of this chapter or to the mazes of life experiences found throughout your existence. In fact, though I will be describing typical mazes, such as those depicted later in this chapter, *everything* that applies to them applies to any maze or labyrinth you find anywhere in your life.

A typical maze diagram of any sort has a position in which to start and a point at which you will finish. Sometimes that starting point is in the middle, as we often don't realize we are in a maze until we are mired in all of its entanglements. The task with any typical maze is to get from start to finish without crossing lines and in one continuous line or movement. *Every maze has a solution to it, or it is not truly a maze!* None is impossible to solve, no matter how intricate it may seem. If you work patiently and carefully, you can arrive at a solution to any maze.

Using a Maze to Develop Seership and Insight

The process of using a maze for any of the above purposes, especially for developing seership and insight, is rather simple:

1. First you must begin to think of the maze as a tool. Mazes provide a focus for the mind, one that shifts the consciousness to a level that can more easily resolve and create. Visualize the maze as a physical, artistic reflection/representation of the problem you need resolved or the task ahead that you seek to accomplish. The maze will represent whatever you wish. For example, if you have found yourself entangled in a problem, visualize the maze as representing that problem. As you work your way through the maze, know that you are also working your way through the problem you are entangled in. This alone begins to release the energy that will provide the beginning of a solution.

   Meditate upon the maze and what you wish it to represent for you. Focus on the idea that, as you resolve the maze, your own individual purposes are crystallized and released for manifestation. Meditation on the purpose for the maze stimulates your subconscious so that it will provide the answers and directions you need to accomplish that particular purpose.

2. Be patient. Mazes (whether in life or on paper) are not always resolved on the first try. Sometimes they are, and this often provides insight into how easily the situation, represented by the maze, can and will be resolved with the right perspective.

   If you find yourself backtracking on the maze, the number of times you do so often provides insight into the time element in resolving or accomplishing what the maze represents for you. It may also reflect that first efforts in anything may not be successful, but it also reminds us that if we don't become discouraged, we will eventually reach our goal.

3. Always keep an eye on the finish point. Hold in the back of your mind, throughout the process, what this maze represents for you. This helps you to stay on track and it stimulates the subconscious for continuous new directions and insights.

   An old axiom says: "All energy follows thought." Where you put your thoughts or focus, that is where energy goes. If you are focusing on the best way to accomplish a particular goal in your life, see the finish line of the maze as that particular goal or as an important step that will lead to the ultimate goal you seek. Also, if you focus on the finish—the goal—you will be less likely to be distracted by the inconsequential.

As you resolve and work the maze with your goal in mind, it triggers responses from the subconscious mind. Often, by the time you resolve the maze, you will have already come up with new ideas and possibilities. Sometimes it takes a little longer, but new insight and perspective ALWAYS shows itself within 24 hours.

4. While working the maze, ALWAYS look ahead. Looking ahead to the next level of the maze does several important things for you. First, it helps you to recognize what repercussions are likely for the moves you have made to that point, i.e., dead ends, new openings, a need to change or reverse directions, etc. It sends a strong message to the subconscious to always be aware of what is directly ahead of you at any point in time.

This helps awaken the divination of time. You begin to recognize patterns. You begin to realize how a certain course is very soon going to be blocked or opened further down the road. In physics we are taught that every action has an equal, but opposite, reaction. Everything we do has a rippling effect, and the subconscious mind is always aware of this. By looking ahead more consciously, the subconscious is able to relay its perceptions more clearly.

It also helps prevent you from becoming too enmeshed in the present. Yes, we do have to stay grounded and focused in the present, but it is easy to become so mired in our problems that we either cannot, or refuse to, see other possibilities. Mazes are powerful tools to help us see new doors and possibilities in all situations, even those that seem hopeless, and they help stimulate opportunities to walk through those new doors or act upon those new possibilities. They help us to recognize a course of action, so that we do not become enmeshed and wallow in self-pity and inactivity.

5. Sometimes it is easier to work a maze backward. Mazes on paper or in life can become tricky, and it is easy at times to feel lost. If you are feeling lost in your efforts, work it in reverse. Put yourself in the position of already having reached your goal. Then trace your steps back from it to where you are now.

It is easy to feel frustrated and bogged down with where we are at any particular point in time. At such times it is important to get a clear perspective, or the frustration will only build. Jump ahead to the end, and work your way back. This will do several things for you. It shifts your focus from the mire or walls you now find blocking your movement, and it will help you to ease your sense of frustration and helplessness.

Mazes and labyrinths have great applications to divining and seership in many areas of life. They can be used to stimulate insight into healing, to problem-solve, and even to find new directions. They can be used to awaken creativity, to untangle life's difficulties, and even to pursue life's rewards more successfully. The following are just some of the ways mazes can be used as a magical and divination tool, particularly in preparation prior to divination with crystal balls.

For many people, the quest for a goal—whether it is manifesting a new job or notoriety—can be reflected and used in meditation, and as a preliminary ritual to release the energy that will open up doors.

Many people feel that their individual goals and dreams are like a carrot that is constantly dangling in front of them, teasing, and yet always just out of reach. Working mazes such as those found on the next two pages can initiate the process of putting the carrot within grasp. Even a childlike maze, such as in the first example, can be a powerful tool.

Mazes such as the one on the next page, where there is more than one starting point, can be used to help create a proper and more successful mindset when there is competition in achieving a particular goal.

Adapt it for your own purposes. Let each starting point represent a different, but specific, path or approach to achieving your goal. Determine and assign each starting point ahead of time.

When you attempt to solve the maze, which do you solve more easily and quickly? You now have the answer as to the best and most successful approach for you to take in regard to accomplishing this particular goal.

Sometimes what we seek seems easier to accomplish than it actually is. This is why divination can be a wonderful tool. With it we can foresee possible problems in any situation or circumstance. The following maze may look simple, but it is a fooler. With proper figuring in the beginning there will be an easy sweep at the end.

START

FINISH

The following two mazes reflect a type in which the starting and finishing points are internal. Sometimes we find ourselves in situations that have already entangled us without realizing. Working these types of mazes while focusing upon the particular situation will stimulate intuitive insight and possible resolutions.

The second example of this type of maze, shown below, is beneficial for times when we are so focused on what we hope to achieve that we find ourselves in entanglements. Sometimes we have to move away— to get some distance before we can see our way clearly to accomplishing our goals. In this second maze, you will have to work your way to the top and all the way down to the bottom before the end becomes apparent.

Circle link mazes are some of the most beneficial mazes with which to work from all aspects of psychic development, but especially in connection to using crystal balls and bowls. By their circular shapes alone, they have great connections.

The circle is one of the most ancient symbols which will be discussed frequently throughout the book, for it, in itself, is a powerful magical tool. It has no end and no beginning. It represents the dance of life. The circle is the archetypal symbol for wholeness, that which ties everything together. It is the symbol that joins the inner with the outer, and thus has even greater significance when using it in mazes for linking intuition with our outer purposes.

Circle link mazes are not only very symbolic, but they have a great many practical and mystical applications. They can help us to gain perspective in untangling problems, difficulties, and even relationships. They can be used as dynamic tools for shifts in consciousness and in health. They are particularly effective as a preparation tool before divining or scrying with a crystal ball.

I have seen a single circle link marked off on the ground and then watched individuals trace their way from the outside to the inside and back again. This simple act releases stress being held in the body by a particular problem that the individual focuses upon. It stimulates insight and new perspective, usually in the time it takes to reach the inner or the outer. It is a tremendous release tool, whose potentials in the healing field are just now beginning to be explored.

Circle link mazes can be difficult to solve, and they often test our powers of concentration. They remind us that everything is connected to everything else in thought, word, and/or deed. The following are examples of circle link mazes. There is not time within this text to cover their many metaphysical and psychic applications. They will be explored in greater detail in a forthcoming book, *How to Unfold Your Psychic Abilities*.

START

FINISH

START

FINISH

START

FINISH

Chapter Two

Clairvoyance for Psychic Gazing & Scrying

Gazing and scrying has a long and notable history. People around the world used to rely on seers, oracles, and scryers. The word "scry" derives from "descry" which means "to make out something unclear or distant by looking carefully; to discern."[6]

Technically, crystal gazing is a mode of divination, usually with the aid of a crystal, but it can be a generic reference to divination with any transparent or reflecting surface; be it a mirror, sphere, pool, or bowl of water.

Many legends and tales speak of its use. Its practice is found in Greece, Rome, and throughout Mesopotamia. The Druids of England utilized gazing, as did people in Scotland, France, Germany, and elsewhere throughout Europe. Egypt, Islam, India, Babylon, and Persia also had their crystal gazing practitioners.

Probably the most famous and widespread legend of its use is found in the "Legend of the Magical Tower." Variations of this particular tale have been found in India, Persia, Europe, Greece, and Rome. It is a tale also known as "The Mirror Castle." In this story, a magician builds a tower filled with many wonders. One of these was a mirror that shone out

---

6 Stein, Jess, ed. *The Random House Dictionary of the English Language*. Random House, New York, 1970, p. 390.

over the entire town. It had the ability to reflect the approach of an enemy while still at a great distance.

Aspects of crystal gazing have been found throughout the literary history of the world. It is found in such folktales as those of the Brothers Grimm. Chaucer refers to it in the "Squire's Tale" in his work, *Canterbury Tales*. Edmund Spencer speaks of it in *The Faerie Queen*. William Shakespeare refers to it in *Measure for Measure* and in *Macbeth*. Ben Johnson spoke of it in *The Alchemist*. It is found in *The Lay of the Last Minstrel* by Sir Walter Scott, and it is reflected in Lewis Carrol's *Through the Looking Glass*. Goethe, in his tale of *Faust*, introduces a magic mirror that enables Faust to see things in it.

Even historical figures have been linked with the mysteries of crystal gazing and scrying. In the thirteenth century, Roger Bacon—the man responsible for much of our modern methods of scientific investigation—was rumored to use polished beryl to scry. Henry Cornelius Agrippa, in the sixteenth century, was believed to have had magic mirrors in which future events would appear. Also in the sixteenth century, Nostradamus, while under the patronage of Catherine, was credited with using this to assist her in seeing the line of future kings of France.

In the late sixteenth and early seventeenth centuries, Dr. John Dee, with the assistance of Edward Kelly, used a stone of crystal to communicate with the angels. From this, Dee gave to the world an angelic alphabet and language called Enochian. This alphabet has been used by many occult societies, including The Golden Dawn.

The popularity of gazing and scrying with crystals does not stop there. In the eighteenth century, Giuseppe Balsamo (Count Alessandro Cagliostro) achieved great notoriety with scrying, but he was also known as a charlatan. He often used children in his scrying process, a reflection of a tradition used in more primitive societies. In such societies the sage did not always pretend to see spirit and scry. Instead the task was given to a young boy or girl of prepuberty age, for they would be a truer channel.

Today, the interest in crystal gazing has achieved new levels. No metaphysical or "new age" store is without its supply of crystal stones. Crystal spheres are available in many sizes and types, at prices that the average individual can afford. People are learning to use tools such as this to open to their own unique intuitive capabilities, finding that they do not have to depend upon a seer or psychic outside of themselves, if they learn the basics; and looking to those methods that ancient societies found to be the easiest and most effective.

Dragons and crystal balls have a long history in myth and lore. The dragon is often depicted guarding or carrying a crystal sphere or giant pearl which could fulfill wishes or multiply one's fortune.

Water Divination and Crystal Gazing

Divination through forms of psychic gazing was one of the most popular and prevalent methods in more ancient times, and it is becoming so again. While the crystal ball is the most commonly recognized form of gazing, there are many other forms in which psychic gazing can be utilized just as well. Diviners have used pools of black ink, mirrors, glass balls, tea leaves, and water.

Of these, water divination and scrying is one of the most common methods of gazing practiced around the world. Water has always been the element connected with the psychic and higher forms of sensitivity. Many methods of using water to divine have been, and still are, practiced. Some seers would use a particular pool of water. Others would employ the energies of a particular stream. Seers and oracles have used cauldrons or bowls of water to stimulate their psychic gazing. Still others have been known to use a rain puddle in order to divine.

Water divination is the method most closely related to crystal gazing. Many of the ancient seers believed crystals to be congealed water or ice. "It is reported that Pliny, the Elder (23–79 A.D.) subscribed to this belief, and that Seneca (4 B.C.?–65 A.D.) supported his opinion. This belief extended well into the Middle Ages."[7]

To understand why it was so common a tool used in scrying, you must remember that water is the creative element of life. Myths and tales around the planet speak of how all life came forth out of water. Water has always been mysterious. The great seas and oceans were older than anyone knew. They always changed, while they were always the same. The great waters shifted constantly, with no beginning and no end.

The magic and power in water had no bounds to the ancient seers. It had the ability to estrange you from your human aspects and the ability to bestow wisdom and spiritual sight. It could cure diseases and restore youth.

Water has always had a life of its own. It is a world in which many fantastic creatures and beings have been believed to exist, beings who are often more fact than fiction. Water sprites and other spirits often reveal themselves through water. There are spirits of pools and wells, and they can be as tiny as a droplet of water, or encompass an entire water source. The beings associated with this element stimulate our psychic natures just by contact with them or their water source. They awaken sensitivities and inspiration.

Traditionally, water has been the most traveled route into the faerie realm. It is the link to the astral dimension. Because of this, natural ponds, wells, and pools were always considered open doorways and windows, and thus very magical.[8]

Pools of water after a rain provide temporary windows into the faerie realm. Even rainwater captured in a dark bowl or cauldron becomes an open window to heightened perceptions for those who know how to use it, so it should not be surprising that water divination has had such widespread influence and popularity.

Begin by setting a bowl out in the rain, or by digging a small hole in the yard. Locating the hole near, but not directly under, a tree is an effective way of creating a window or doorway to the Faerie Realm. When it fills with water, you have created an intersection between the worlds.

---

7 Ferguson, Sibyl. *The Crystal Ball*. Samuel Weiser, Inc., York Beach, ME, 1983, p. 5.

8 Andrews, Ted. *Enchantment of the Faerie Realm*. Llewellyn Publications, St. Paul, MN, 1993, pp. 69–90.

Find a position near the puddle, or if you are using a bowl place it in front of you. Make sure you will be undisturbed, while still being able to look within it. Close your eyes and take a few moments to relax. You may wish to perform a brief meditation to balance and harmonize yourself with nature. With your left hand make several passes over the bowl or puddle, your watery window. This imparts sensitivity to the water and it is also a gesture of invitation to those spirits or beings associated with it.

Be patient and concentrate when gazing into the water. Do not stare intensely. Allow your gaze to be soft and half-focused, as if staring blankly, such as you do when daydreaming.

As with crystal gazing, the phenomena will vary. You may see a fogginess, like clouds or mist passing by. This is positive. It means that the window is opening—that your vision is being awakened. With time, colors, images, faces, and entire scenarios will appear. Each time you use a rain pool, bowl, or crystal for gazing, your results will increase.

It is good to practice both water divination and crystal gazing. The techniques and their phenomena are surprisingly similar. They also reinforce each other. Water divination will improve your effectiveness with crystal gazing, and crystal gazing will improve your effectiveness with water divination.

When teaching workshops and seminars on psychic development, I will often teach water divination and crystal gazing together. Their techniques are similar, and success is achieved easily through them. Water divination is particularly powerful and effective when crystal bowls are used. Their use will be explored in much more detail in Part Two of this book. Waters and crystals can even be used together in the divination process, with a crystal being placed in the water to give it extra power.

Both water divination and crystal gazing amplify innate psychic energies and focus them more easily for you, especially when used together. This should not be surprising when you understand that both crystals and water are great conductors of electrical energy, and the human body is a biochemical, electromagnetic energy system. Because of this, water and crystals focus the mind and facilitate altered states of consciousness. They stimulate and awaken your own inner clairvoyance more easily.

Clairvoyance and Crystal Gazing

Clairvoyance is a word that simply means "clear seeing." Although it is literally connected with the visual aspects of psychic phenomena, it is often generically used to relate to and encompass any kind of psychic experience. In the Middle Ages many of the strange and unusual psychic experiences were simply categorized under the name mirabilia.[9] For the purposes of this book, clairvoyance will refer to any of a variety of visionary experiences.

Many believe clairvoyance to be a gift, something unique to only a few, but this is not true. It is a natural ability in all of us. Each of us has the ability to develop and hone it. Yes, some people may find it easier to develop, just as some people find it easier to learn to read than others, but clairvoyance can still be learned by everyone.

As children, we are naturally more psychic and open to psychic phenomena. Unfortunately, we are often socialized out of recognizing and using it. We are told it is our imagination, or we are made to feel strange about ourselves because of our experiences. As a result, we close that part of ourselves down, to a great degree. It is still a faculty inherent within each of us, and all of our faculties can be developed and enhanced, no matter how blocked. In this book, we will provide exercises and methods for doing so, primarily through the use of the crystal ball and/or the crystal bowl.

Clairvoyant visions almost always show up in everyone during childhood. Children often know who is calling on the phone by the way the phone rings. To a child, the phone sounds different for different people. Dreams, whether night time or daydreams, are usually extraordinarily vivid, or seemingly nonexistent. Most people can remember significant experiences in childhood in which they knew something was going to happen, and it did. Most children see auras or, if asked, they will be able to tell you what color someone is. It is amazing how frequently people will remember and speak of childhood psychic experiences whenever I teach psychic development classes. Everyone has his or her own unique stories, and the first and strongest memories of their own psychic experiences to surface are from their childhood.

Usually these types of experiences are not understood for what they truly are, or they are ignored and discouraged. Most often, we are taught that they are figments of our imagination, planting the unfortunate

---

9 Cirlot, J. E. A *Dictionary of Symbols*. Philosophical Library, New York, 1971, p. 210.

impression within us that things of the imagination have no basis in reality. As a result, we shut off that part of us with the capability to see.

Everyone's visionary experiences will vary somewhat. Some people will see literally and others will see symbolically; others experience a combination of literal and symbolic images. Some experience no outer vision, but see images and visions in their minds. Some do not even experience images, but may simply have a feeling, impression, or inner knowing that such and such is about to occur. Some may hear a voice, as if being spoken to, and sometimes this voice is heard only in the mind. Some people experience fragrances while stimulating their intuition and natural clairvoyant abilities.

Our psychic abilities will manifest initially through the physical sense that is our more natural and stronger sense. If we are more visual, clairvoyance will more likely manifest. If we are more auditory, clairaudience (intuitive/psychic hearing) will more likely manifest. If we are more tactile, clairsentience (psychic feeling) will more likely manifest.

What often happens, though, in psychic development, is that those who see wish they could hear. Those who hear wish they could see. Those who feel wish they could see and hear. What few people realize is that if you focus on developing what is most natural for you, the other expressions will manifest as well. If you are visual, as you develop your clairvoyance, you will also start hearing and feeling and sensing psychically on other levels, as well.

Individuals with just general feelings and impressions have the most difficulty in trusting in their experiences. This is often because the right effort has not been applied to clarify and define these feeling. Most of the time, all it takes for success is asking the right questions.

Begin with a simple statement of what you feel or are impressed with. Don't judge or dismiss. Simply give your impression. Describe what you are feeling, no matter how obvious or trivial it may seem. Do this description in speech or on paper. Speaking or writing down your impression is essential to clarifying it and defining it on a more physically visual level. It takes that vague feeling out of the ethereal mental realm and grounds it. This initiates its clarification for you. In this definition process, be careful of the tendency to assume that it is all of the imagination. THE IMAGINATION WOULD NOT AFFECT YOU IF THERE WERE NO SIGNIFICANCE TO IT.

The human mind is capable of so much more than we often allow it. Estimates as to how much of our brains we actually use on a daily basis range from 10 percent to 20 percent, but even if it were closer to 50 percent, there is still a great deal going undeveloped and unused.

The human brain and the mind, although related, are not the same thing. It was believed for years that the brain was the organ through which the mind expresses itself most fully, but modern research is teaching us that our mind and our thoughts affect and express themselves through every cell in our body as well. There is obviously much about the activity of our mind and its capabilities that we still do not know.

We do know that the subconscious mind mediates all energy coming into and going out of the body. It controls over 90 percent of the body's functions, including the imaginative faculty. It is aware of much more than we consciously realize. It perceives and recognizes patterns and ripples in every aspect of our life. When we learn to consciously recognize what the subconscious mind already has perceived, then we are manifesting our innate clairvoyance.

Clairvoyance is a creative faculty of the mind. It is linked to that part of the mind that directs our image-making ability (imagination). A creative person is one who applies the imaginative faculty in new and unique expressions. Creative imagination—or imaginative cognition—is the key to opening the doors to true spiritual energies and our true clairvoyant abilities.

All clairvoyance is an aspect of creative imagination. Learning to consciously develop it awakens us to supersensible realities and experiences. What we often consider imagination is a reality in some form on levels beyond the normal sensory world. Through imagination and clairvoyance, we experience a new relationship to the world in color and form.

There is often great wonder about clairvoyant visions, especially those associated with crystal gazing. How are they produced? Are they like dreams? Did the eyes actually see them? Or was it the mind? Did they originate from the spirit world, or from something in the physical?

In developing any clairvoyance, we extend our physical sight to include psychic and spiritual sight. This includes the imagination, visions, dreams, auric sight, and more. Sometimes the images are actual, and sometimes they are symbolic. Sometimes they arise from the physical world, and sometimes from the spirit world. Clairvoyance may be either objective (external) or subjective (internal).

Objective clairvoyance is when you see what is not physical as objectively as you perceive anything in the physical world. You are seeing with the physical eyes. This applies to images, persons, and events (symbolic or real). You may see spirit beings or actual beings. You may see the unfolding of events—past, present, or future.

When using any gazing tool (pool, mirror, crystal bowl, crystal balls, etc.), the visions and images that appear and are seen in the reflective surface with the physical eyes are examples of objective clairvoyance. When using crystal balls, objective clairvoyance will manifest through images arising and being seen in the ball itself. These images may be literal or symbolic. With time and practice you will learn to recognize the difference.

Clairvoyance that is subjective or internal consists of images and impressions experienced in the mind, without the aid of the human eyes. These images and pictures may be of things physical or spiritual, past or present, remote or near. They may be actual or symbolic. Subjective clairvoyance may be nothing more than mental images received by you with some recognition of their meaning.

Dreams are an example of subjective clairvoyance that most people have experienced in some degree. Subjective clairvoyant experiences may seem imaginary, but it is important not to confuse something that is unreal with something that is imaginary!

There are two commonly accepted explanations for the clairvoyant phenomena that occurs with crystal gazing. The most obvious is that the phenomena is a manifestation of natural clairvoyant ability. The second does not deny clairvoyance as an explanation, but rather it provides a psychological construct for its explanation.

In this second explanation, it is believed that the images may have already been unconsciously observed. In other words, the images may be reproductions of things previously seen or perceived. The clairvoyance may simply be an external expression of what has been perceived internally. These images may have been unconsciously received from others, such as through impressions upon the auric field. (To further understand how this occurs, you may wish to consult my earlier work, *How to See and Read the Aura.*)

The subconscious mind then translates its earlier perceptions into images. These are then projected into the crystal or upon the reflected surface. The crystal or reflecting surface serves as a trigger and focus to bring forth the images. This doesn't negate the validity or worth of the images or visions. The true criteria for determining that is whether what is seen is useful or beneficial to those concerned.

Most psychic phenomena and true clairvoyant experiences are based upon certain basic principles. Understanding these will assist you in reawakening and developing your own clairvoyant ability in all areas, including scrying with crystal balls. These principles follow.

• **We construct our reality.**

That reality is influenced by our thoughts. All energy follows thought. Every thought or dream is an awareness of another reality which is coexisting with our own. We can choose to either focus our energy to bring it into probable reality, or we can continue along the path of limitation. Part of our creative process involves learning to recognize the creative possibilities within our limitations and, by doing so, move beyond them.

This often involves realizing that change is necessary in life. If we resist it, our reality becomes mired in problems. We do not see properly, and we continue to repeat patterns. When we learn to work with our imaginative faculties and recognize that change always provides opportunities to express our creativity, our ability to envision events and people from a more complete and truer perspective occurs. Then clairvoyance is integrated into every aspect of our life, and it is no longer something separate from us or our normal state of consciousness.

Believing in the psychic or clairvoyance of any sort, especially if we have had such experiences, encourages more of the same. This has been referred to as the "mirror factor" of life. The universe will reflect back to us what we believe, and we then confirm and experience more of what we believe. The stronger our beliefs, the greater and more frequent the feedback.

On the other hand, our society promotes a highly developed sense of doubt and skepticism. Many won't believe until they experience, so what does this do to the mirror effect? Are the mirrored experiences doubtful because of our own doubt?

Fortunately, we don't have to believe to experience. Everyone possesses the ability to awaken and consciously use their innate intuitive ability. The exercises in this book will provide the proof and help you in developing your beliefs. They provide the foundation for constructing a new universe upon a new belief system.

• **Everything in life is interconnected.**

Every part is connected to every other part. There is really no time or distance separating anything, except in our own perceptions. Every human is connected to every other human. Every event is linked to those of the past and to those in the future. Every aspect of nature is linked to every other expression of nature, including humans.

When we begin to truly recognize this, then our perceptions of people and life become more true and clear. We are able to recognize past patterns and those more likely to unfold. Everything and everyone takes on greater significance and meaning. Life rhythms can be used more effectively to our benefit.

• **Connections cannot be perceived through ordinary consciousness.**

Intuitive flashes are reminders of your ability to use and access your imaginative faculty. If you have ever had a hunch that something would happen and it did, it was a reminder of your ability to connect with all things at all times. You can learn to do this in a very conscious manner, so that you can access and apply extraordinary insight in regard to ordinary situations.

This requires that you learn to use altered states and access the subconscious mind at any time you desire, to any degree that you desire. You can help yourselves become more receptive to your intuitive connections to life through developing and utilizing specific techniques, and any of a variety of tools, including crystal balls and bowls. Ideally, we should be able to access our intuitive faculty at any time we desire, to any degree we desire.

• **All things are possible, but some are more probable.**

As you develop your intuition, you will find that it does not mean that what you have divined WILL come to pass. Free will is always a factor and is a part of everyone's life. This creates what I call "free variables" in life. As long as you are in the physical, there are going to be some events and situations that you are not going to be able to completely control or entirely know.

Not everything you perceive is set in stone, but what you perceive is often a reflection of probabilities. Your clairvoyant impressions, images, and visions reflect probable patterns likely to unfold. Your subconscious mind and its clairvoyant ability will help you to see certain events and the repercussions that are more probable than others. If we are able to see probable outcomes, we can then initiate actions or changes that will facilitate the more favorable outcome(s).

• **Focus and concentration are essential to develop.**

With all forms of psychic gazing, it is important to learn to detach from everyday concerns. Most people live their lives with a kind of tunnel vision. There is only security in the five physical senses. This is why so many psychics use tools such as card, runes, crystal balls, etc. They provide a focus that enables them to shift from their normal, tunnel-like vision and day-to-day distractions. If you truly wish to develop your own clairvoyant ability, you will need to be able to focus and concentrate without being distracted.

One of the most difficult faculties to develop is concentration and focus. Most of us have such busy lives that we are easily distracted, and the mind often seems scattered. By developing focused attention, you will become more successful in all aspects of life—not just the psychic.

Concentration is the art of holding the image that you have created or allowed to surface within the mind—without the mind wandering to other things. You should learn to hold an image to the exclusion of all others.

Close your eyes and practice holding an image in the mind for a pre-determined period of time every day. This will enhance all expressions of concentration and focus, but it will especially be helpful when focusing upon the crystal ball. Make your visualization exercise as life-like as possible. For example, visualize an orange. See its shape, color, and size. Feel the texture. What does it feel like when it is peeled? Notice the fragrance as the juice squirts out. In your mind recreate the image and full experience of this piece of fruit. Do this with other things as well.

Spending only five minutes a day, every day, will accelerate your overall development. You are training the mind. This will help you in working more effectively with psychic gazing, but it has other applications as well. For example, if you have had a particularly hectic and scattered day, or if you are feeling "out of touch," perform this exercise. It will restore a sense of calm and control. It helps you to regain your focus.

- **Your health will influence your abilities.**

There are other considerations as well in preparing to seriously develop your own scrying ability. Your health, body or mind, will affect the clarity of your visions and intuitional insights. This is common sense. If the pipes in your home are rusty and gunked up, the water flowing through them is very likely going to carry with it rust and gunk residue. No matter how spiritual a person may profess to be, if the body and mind is unhealthy or unbalanced, it is highly likely that what comes through from the intuition will also be unhealthy or unbalanced.

This doesn't mean that you have to become a vegetarian or do aerobics five times a week or such things. Moderation is the key to normal development and expression. A balanced diet and some regular fresh air and exercise will do wonders to enhance your abilities.

There are some foods that are often considered more beneficial for developing your intuitive faculties. These are sometimes referred to as "high vibrational" foods. These include vegetables, pineapples, papaya, lemons, oranges, and mangoes.

Meat, particularly red meat, is not a "high vibrational" food. It is one of the most difficult food substances for the human body to digest and it takes the longest. It can take from 6 to 40 hours to digest beef. This does not mean that you should give up meat. Just don't eat it every day, or switch to fish or white meat. Keep in mind that digestion uses more energy than any other process of the mind or body. If the body's energies are focused on digestion, it will be much more difficult to consciously access your intuitive abilities.

Reducing salt intake will also facilitate your awakening abilities. Just as salt will corrode wires, it can also inhibit our consciously linking with our intuitive faculties. Drugs, alcohol, tobacco, and such substances can also inhibit our development.

On the other hand, by increasing our daily water intake the process is facilitated. Water is a great conductor of electrical energy. It is cleansing to the body, and occasionally cleansing and detoxifying your body and its systems will speed your development. Fasting periodically is one of the most beneficial methods. It does no harm to the body or mind to fast for two to three days. Our body and its systems occasionally need the rest.

Exercises to Stimulate Gazing Abilities

If you are to open to true gazing visions, you must keep several things in mind. They will help you in awakening and unfolding your innate abilities, and keeping them in mind will assist you in getting the most out of the exercises and techniques given.

Patient persistence is necessary. Remember that everyone develops at his or her own speed. Without patience, you will not be able to access the subconscious mind. Impatience and frustration will hinder the awakening. Patient persistence is the key. As long as you persist, you will be rewarded.

The exercises that follow are designed to be used either in preparation for the actual crystal gazing techniques or in conjunction with them. Work with them every day for a month, for only 15–30 minutes, and at the end of that month's time you will get results. The quality and quantity of results may vary from individual to individual, but EVERYONE will achieve some noticeable results by persisting with the exercises everyday for one month.

Many find it helpful to use lunar influences. Working with lunar cycles can give your awakening vision a gentle nudge. Begin the exercises at the time of the new moon or its waxing phase. You will start to see some results by the time of the full moon.

Using the lunar cycles can be effective for a number of reasons. Take a good look at the full moon. Do you see how much it resembles a crystal sphere? The moon is also highly symbolic of the subconscious and the inner feminine energies. These feminine energies are the energies of creativity, intuition, and creative imagination. It is these we are trying to awaken and give conscious expression to through gazing. Dreams, visions, and the subconscious fall under the rulership of the moon in astrology. The moon reflects the sun, and in gazing we are looking for reflections.

Work on maintaining calmness and concentration. I spoke earlier of learning to hold an image or idea to the exclusion of everything else. Single-minded focus will only enhance your gazing abilities. Some of the other exercises in this chapter will assist in developing this. Simply attending to your crystal work every day for a month will lay the foundation to developing this ability. Try to perform your crystal gazing work at the same time every day, or as near to it as possible.

Use aids to your unfoldment. This includes general meditation, but also those things that can make meditation more effective. Candles and fragrances can be very beneficial to helping us attune to both the crystal ball and to our own subconscious mind. Some of the most effective aids are provided for you in the exercises that follow in this chapter.

Don't be afraid to experiment with these aids and with all the exercises in this book. This book is a guide book only. It will provide a starting point, but your work with gazing will be unique to you. Don't compare your results to others. Remember that your innate visionary abilities will unfold in the manner best for you. The crystal serves as a focus and venue for its awakening.

For some, the work with these exercises in gazing will simply enhance perceptions in all areas of life. For others, visions of the past may unfold more clearly. For some practitioners, visions of the future may be the primary effect. Still others may see spirits, and some may experience a doorway to the astral. Don't allow your preconceptions about what you may experience prevent you from recognizing your experiences for what they are. In time they will define themselves for you, which, like the sphere, circles us back to patient persistence once more.

Exercise 3—
Aids to Unfolding Your Inner Vision

There are many ways to enhance and facilitate the awakening of your own inner vision so that it can be applied to crystal gazing. Some of the most beneficial and the easiest to use are candles and fragrances.

Candles

Fire has always been considered something holy and mysterious. Fire is found in all aspects of life. The fire from the sun sustains life. The fires of our passion awaken creativity and inspiration. Fire destroys and it creates.

Candles have been used for many mystical and psychic purposes for as long as they have been around. The candle is a symbol for the activation of more fire and visionary light in our lives. When we light a candle, we are participating in an ancient rite of creation. We are creating light where there was none, bringing warmth and vision where it is needed.

**Candles, dressed and cleaned with oils, are an effective aid
in visionary exercises and crystal gazing,
assisting the subconscious mind to see beyond the moment.**

The practice of using candles to enhance meditation and facilitate accessing other levels of consciousness is well known to most psychics. The color of the candle and the colors vibrational force is activated, released, and amplified when lit. As the candle burns, its color is released into the surrounding area and affects those within that area.

The color of the candle that you use is determined by your purpose. Different colors affect us in different ways—physically, emotionally, mentally, and spiritually. For more detailed information on colors and their effects, you may wish to consult my earlier book, *How to Heal With Color*.

Candles should be dressed and cleaned before their use. This eliminates any negativity attached to the candle during its making. It also strengthens the color so that it works more effectively for you.

There are several candle-dressing oils on the market, or you can use plain olive oil. Rub the candle in the same direction, for visionary purposes. Rubbing it from bottom to top may symbolize the bringing of the candle's light out and into the atmosphere. From top to bottom may reflect the carrying of the light internally, to awaken your own innate visions. You must decide what it signifies, and once you decide, stick with it. You may even wish to carve the astrological symbol for the moon into the candle to enhance its effectiveness as it burns.

The following colors for candles provide a beginning point to using them with visionary exercises and crystal gazing. They do have other uses and applications than those listed; these are guidelines only. These colored candles will stimulate the subconscious mind to help you more effectively bring forth visions of the type you desire.

Colors	Areas of Visionary Insight Colors Help Promote
Red	Passion, love, issues of will, change
Orange	Emotions, creativity, truth, education
Yellow	Education, communication, clarity, pride
Green	Nature, creativity, relationships, health, money
Blue	Money, issues of abundance or lack, spiritual call
Silver	Intuitive development, mother and father insight
Brown	Finding the lost, common sense, discrimination
Gold	Spirituality, issues of prosperity
Violet/Purple	Dreamwork, increasing lunar effects, past lives

WHITE—This is a good, general, all-purpose color to use. It is very strengthening and is a color that awakens creativity. You can rarely go wrong by using a white candle for gazing.

BLACK—Black candles have gotten a bad rap over the years. People associate them with negativity. Black candles are protective, and they help to calm and ground us. Black stimulates the feminine, and, in meditation and gazing, a black candle will help us go within ourselves to find our inner light. It is a color I prefer to use with crystal gazing. Using a black and a white together when scrying with a crystal ball can also be very effective.

DARK BLUE (INDIGO)—This color activates the brow chakra or the third-eye area of the body. This is a point of inner vision and intuition. This color candle is even more effective to use when crystal gazing if you carve lunar symbols into it. The color has a sedative effect, and it can help you achieve deeper levels of consciousness.

Although any candle can be used to assist in meditation and crystal gazing, I have found these three to be the most effective for any gazing purpose. Other colors can be used to stimulate visions in regard to specific issues or problems areas.

Fragrances

Fragrance is one of the most effective means of altering consciousness. Every fragrance alters the vibrational frequency of the environment and the individual, according to its own unique qualities. Scents influence the olfactory nerves in varying degrees, and thus they influence our consciousness.

Essential oils, incenses, and perfumes are the most common forms, but historically fragrances have been used for many mundane and ritual purposes. Confucius said that while candles illumine men's hearts, incense perfumes bad smells. This is, of course, but one application. Other applications have ties to health and therapy, romance, and spiritual upliftment. Our focus will be on using fragrance to aid our crystal gazing perceptions.

There are a number of effective ways of using fragrances. Two of the most common and easiest for the average individual are through the use of incense or essential oils. Most of the early incenses were made from bark, dried herbs, and plants. Incense is an excellent aid to elevating the consciousness, especially in gazing activities. Incense facilitates meditation and opening of the mind. All you need do is allow the incense to burn in the room where you will be gazing.

Essential oils are made through a complex distilling process. They are very potent and intoxicating. Because of this, they are best used in a diluted form. Essential oils can be used in baths or in anointing prior to gazing activities. In baths, a single capful of oil per bath is all that is necessary. They can also be worn like a perfume, but you must be careful, as many essential oils are harsh and can burn the skin. It is best to dilute them, and always test a drop on the inside of the arm before using the oil on more sensitive areas of the body. Massaging the oil into the brow or third eye center will enhance your visionary abilities. One of the easiest ways of using oils in gazing is to anoint the ball itself, according to the purpose of your gazing.

Fragrances should be experimented with. This can be quite enjoyable because we each have our own likes and dislikes. We each will have certain fragrances that are more conducive to our own purposes. The following suggestions are guidelines only:

APPLE BLOSSOM—This fragrance is most effective with gazing when the visions are symbolic. It is one that is beneficial to use to help connect you with the deva or spirit of the crystal ball you are using.

EUCALYPTUS—This penetrating oil is good to use when anointing the brow chakra or third eye area to awaken visionary capabilities prior to the gazing. It will alleviate fears of the gazing process, calming the emotions.

FRANKINCENSE—This general, all-purpose fragrance is a good purifier of the human energy field and the environment. It can be used to cleanse and purify the area in which you will be gazing.

LAVENDER—Lavender has always been considered a magical herb, one which provides protection. It helps open up visionary states and moves us past emotional issues that may be hindering the full expression of our intuition. It is most effective when used as a bath prior to gazing.

LILAC—This fragrance is beneficial for those wishing to truly connect with the spirit of the crystal ball. It will help when gazing specifically for past lives and their impact upon the present health of an individual. It stimulates clairvoyance.

PENNYROYAL—This fragrance and its flower elixir counterpart should be used to wash the crystal after the completion of the gazing session. It cleans the crystal of the previous influences so that images in response to specific questions will arise true and clear.

If gazing for several individuals, using a pennyroyal dip for the ball is helpful. Simply have a bowl of water with a drop or two of pennyroyal oil in it. Gently splash the ball to remove the previous person's influences before you gaze for the next. You will need a soft cloth to dry the ball. An easier method is having at hand a wash cloth that has been soaked in the pennyroyal water, and then just wipe the ball between sessions.

SAGE—This cleansing fragrance allows for a greater flow of spiritual insight into the physical. It releases tensions that can block the intuitive faculty, while stimulating the intuition.

SANDALWOOD—Sandalwood fragrance awakens the feminine energies within us. It can be used with lavender oil for spirit gazing with the ball. It deepens altered states of consciousness, and it is good to use by itself when gazing for insight into health problems and issues.

WISTERIA—Wisteria awakens spiritual perceptions and inspirations. It can be used with crystal gazing for illumination on health matters. It is very cleansing and balancing so that there is greater clarity in your clairvoyance.

A study of fragrances and their various qualities will help you in determining specific uses for specific oils in your gazing activities. Traditionally, a number of fragrances have been associated with lunar influences, and these can be beneficial to used to enhance any crystal gazing activity. The following is a list of common herbs and fragrances associated with the moon:

Jasmine	Iris	Lily
Wild rose	Wintergreen	Anise
Camphor	Mugwort	Ash
Clary Sage	Orris Root	Chamomile

Exercise 4—
Communing with the Ancient Seers

Mythology and folklore is filled with individuals who were known as seers. Often they were the moon goddesses and gods, but they could also be individuals who used scrying tools. Because the moon was symbolic of the feminine forces in the universe in most cultures, goddess figures were often depicted as most representative of its influences.

Studying the various moon goddesses, especially in those cultures or traditions to which you are drawn, will help you to connect more fully with your own intuitive, feminine side for gazing. Read the stories and myths of the goddesses of the moon and divination from different societies. Meditate upon them. Imagine yourself being overshadowed by their influence.

If there is one that you find yourself most resonant with, read and study as much about this goddess/god of the moon and divination as possible. When working with these ancient beings of mythology, it is important to grasp a good foundation of the teachings and energies associated with the entire mythology, and not just an individual character's part in it.

Most of the ancient divine beings had symbols and images that reflected their influence. Use these in your meditation and gazing work. Draw them on a cloth upon which you set your crystal ball. Paint the symbols on your body. Use candles the color appropriate to that divine being. An old axiom states: "All energy follows thought." Where we put our thoughts, that is where energy goes. By focusing on the qualities, symbols, and colors of a particular divine being, we release their archetypal force into our lives.

On the next two pages are some of the major beings associated with the moon and divination, including their primary colors and symbols.

Visualize in meditation this being coming to you and presenting you with a gift that is representative of the being, and the power of divination that you seek through your crystal. Although this may seem a small thing to some, its effects are both subtle and powerful. It will greatly enhance your gazing activities.

Every culture has had deities and prominent figures tied to magic, prophecy, and the moon. From Inanna of Sumeria to Amaterasu of Japan, from the Spider Woman of the Kiowa to Kali of India—all societies recognized the mystery of the life currents within the universe. By studying and working with the deity forms that reflect those currents, we awaken and strengthen our own innate seership.

GREEK

Artemis	Goddess of the forest and the moon Color of amethyst Symbols of the bear and the dog
Apollo	God of prophecy and music Colors of yellow and gold Symbols of the lyre and archery bow
Hecate	Goddess of the moon Color of black with silver flecks Symbols of black hooded cloak/dark of the moon
Selene	Goddess of the moon Colors of silver and white Symbols of wings, diadem, and chariot
Pan	God of prophecy and healing Color of forest green Symbols of syrinx and pan flute

EGYPTIAN

Isis	Goddess of moon and magic Color of sky blue Symbols of throne, buckle, and wings
Nepthys	Goddess of intuition and tranquility Colors of pale green and silver grays Symbols of the chalice and basket
Anubis	God of guardianship and guidance Colors of black and silver Symbols of jackal and sarcophagus
Maat	Goddess of truth Colors of violet and lapis lazuli Symbols of the scales and the feather

CELTIC

Danu	Goddess of intuition, understanding and wisdom Color of green Symbols of water and newly planted seeds
Morrigan	Goddess of enchantment Color of green and black Symbols of crossed spears and the raven
Cerridwen	Goddess of magic and prophecy Color of green Symbol of the cauldron of wisdom
Morgan Le Fay	Queen of the fairies, healing and magic Color of green Symbol of the hand extending sword out of water

Celtic (cont'd)

Merlin	Celtic prophet Color of green Symbols of the harp and staff
Nuada	God of the moon Color of silver Symbol of the invincible sword

TEUTONIC

Odin	Father god of foresight, prophecy, and poetry Color of deep blue or indigo Symbols of ravens, wolves, spear, eight-legged steed
Frigga	All-knowing wife of Odin Color of deep green Symbols of golden spindle and sacred necklace
Heimdall	Watchman of Asgard Colors of the rainbow Symbols of the trumpet horn and the rainbow
Norns	The spinners of fate Colors vary Symbols of spinning wheel, the bee, and two swans

OTHER TRADITIONS

Bomu Rambi	West African Symbol of necklace with crescent shaped moon
Jezanna	West African Symbol of moon aglow with golden fire
Mawa	West African Symbolized as figure breathing forth life
Changing Woman	Navajo Symbols of bed of flowers and rainbow
Huitica	Columbian Symbols of spinning and weaving
Ix Chel	Mayan Symbol of the eagle woman
Kali	East Indian Symbols of the yoni or womb
Kwan Yin	Chinese Symbols of female surrounded by lotus and children
Ishtar	Sumerian Symbols of double-serpent scepter, the breast producing milk, and the lion

Exercise 5—
The Psychic Breath

Fresh air and proper breathing are essential to developing and strengthening your clairvoyance. It is especially important for all crystal gazing activities. It balances, relaxes, and facilitates focus. Using breathing techniques outside in the fresh air, particularly the early morning air, will amplify your natural clairvoyance.

Psychic breathing is usually some form of nostril breathing. Many people have a bad habit of mouth breathing, not realizing that nostril breathing is more natural and healthier. The nose provides specialized surfaces for the absorption of prana from the air. Prana can be likened to the vitalizing aspect that exists within air. Many Eastern breathing techniques require a conscious focus upon the tip of the nose and the entire nasal area during inhalation. This enhances prana absorption, raising the vitality of the entire energy system.

In yoga there is a moon breath (*ida*), a sun breath (*pingala*), and a balancing of the two (*susumna*). Your energy has polarity—positive and negative, male and female, sun and moon. Using balanced breathing as described below is beneficial to balance the hemisphere of the brain. This, in turn, facilitates a more conscious accessing of your intuitive faculties. It also enhances your ability to remember and assimilate information.

The basic technique is comprised of alternate breaths, breathing in through one nostril and then breathing out the other. The technique is enhanced by holding the appropriate nostril closed with the thumb and fingers.

1. Begin by making yourself comfortable in a seated position. Place your tongue against the roof of your mouth behind your front teeth. This creates a natural circuit in the body.

2. Using your thumb, close your right nostril, and then inhale through your left nostril for a slow count of four. This is the moon or ida breath inhalation.

3. Keeping your right nostril closed with your thumb, use the fingers of the same hand to close down over the left nostril. In this way the nose is pinched closed between the thumb and fingers. Hold the breath for a count of ten.

4. Release the thumb, opening your right nostril. Keep the left nostril closed with the fingers. Exhale slowly out through the right nostril for a count of four.

5. Now reverse the process by closing the left nostril and breathing in through the right (pingala breath) for a count of four. Close off both nostrils and hold for a count of ten, and then exhale slowly out through the left nostril, keeping the right nostril closed.

6. Repeat for five breaths through each nostril, alternating each side. Breathe in one nostril, hold, and then exhale out the other.

7. Reverse and repeat the procedure.

This exercise is a good energy pick-me-up. It is beneficial to do daily, but especially after crystal gazing or any psychic session. To enhance your intuitive visions for gazing, use only the moon or ida breath, prior to the actual gazing session.

As you draw air in through the left nostril, visualize your lungs and entire body being filled with silvery energy. Envision it circulating within the body and mind. As described above, inhale through the left and exhale out the right, but rather than alternate nostrils, inhale only through the left for five to ten breaths.

This one-sided breathing will strongly activate your lunar/feminine aspects, energizing and strengthening your clairvoyance, and it will greatly amplify the results of the gazing activity.

Chapter Three

Basic
Preparations
for Gazing

Before beginning your crystal gazing you will need a crystal ball. I recommend that in the beginning it be a minimum of one-and-one-half inches in diameter (approximately 3.8 cm.). Anything smaller can detract from your purpose, because it will be too small to allow easy recognition of images within it.

Prices for crystal balls vary, but they are more accessible to the general public than ever before. Do some comparative shopping. Attend rock, gem, and mineral shows, and you will find quality spheres at affordable prices. When you find a ball that catches your eye and that you feel comfortable with, don't dicker with the price. Ask the seller if there are any discounts—you will be surprised how many will offer them. If it is within your budget, then purchase it. Although it may mean a monetary investment, keep in mind that you are investing in a sacred object that you will probably use the rest of your life.

The sphere need not be perfectly circular to be an effective gazing tool. I know of several individuals who use egg-shaped crystals quite effectively for gazing. For most people, the draw to the traditional circular sphere is more often a psychological crutch than anything else. You will gaze best with what you feel most comfortable.

I also recommend that the first sphere with which you work be of quartz crystal, and not Austrian lead crystal. Although the Austrian crystal can be used, the process of making such a sphere an effective gazing and scrying tool is a little more complicated. Whether quartz crystal or Austrian crystal, it is most important that the sphere become a sacred object for you, and remember that it is really within yourself that you change the sphere from an ordinary object into a gazing crystal.

Quartz Crystal Balls

Quartz crystals, because of their composition and structure, have a natural form of electrical energy called piezoelectrical energy. "Piezo" comes from the Greek word *piezin* meaning "to squeeze." Any stress upon the crystal releases its particular frequency of electrical energy into the field surrounding it.

It takes very little to release a quartz crystal's energy. Even brain waves, generated by thought and focused in the direction of the crystal, will activate its release. Because of this it is quite simple to program quartz crystals to work in a directed manner for us. Since the human body is a biochemical, electromagnetic energy system, the natural electrical frequency of the quartz crystal ball will serve as a greater stimulus than an Austrian crystal ball. Thus quartz crystal balls lend themselves readily for use in gazing and scrying.

There are different types of quartz spheres available today, and all can be effective with gazing. The following descriptions may help you choose the one that best suits you.

Amethyst Crystal Balls

Amethyst is a crystalline stone that is excellent for shifting consciousness. It can help us bridge more easily into other levels of consciousness, especially the intuitive. Its violet color is a combination of red and blue, symbolizing the duality of the physical and the spiritual. Amethys crystal balls awaken the intuitive faculty, and are effective spheres to use in gazing for individuals who have fears about gazing and opening up. They are also quite effective to use in scrying for health issues, and for revealing the tides of change, along with insight into important dream activity.

Amethyst spheres will often reveal the presence of loved ones who have passed on. It can be one of the best spheres to use for communication with spirit guides. Its energy is such that it helps us to stay centered and calm in the midst of such connections.

**Crystal balls always capture the imagination.
Pictured above are part of the author's personal collection
of scrying spheres and crystals.**

Their only drawback is that amethyst spheres rarely are completely clear, and they can be expensive, especially when you get past the one-and-one-half inch diameter size (approximately 4 cm. or larger).

Malachite Crystal Balls

Malachite is a very old stone of a deep green color. It has a long history of being used for healing purposes. Malachite always has lines, circles, and designs within its rich green shades. The patterns of these lines reveal much about the particular uses and purposes of the stone.

Malachite spheres with circular patterns are effective to use in gazing to detect patterns within your own or someone else's life. Malachite can be a wonderful tool for revealing past-life connections and where present activities and patterns of behavior are leading in the future, and is useful in healing issues and relationships. It is a sphere that can be used effectively for and by those who have a strong connection to the earth, or who wish to establish such a link. It can reveal the best ways of attuning to those beings and creatures of the natural world. This includes totems, nature spirits, and devas. It can also provide insight into creativity and artistic expression.

Malachite can be expensive, and it is a soft stone, requiring care in its handling as it will scratch easily. It should also be cleaned after each gazing, but use a soft cloth for this purpose because of its delicacy.

Obsidian Crystal Balls

Obsidian spheres can be powerful tools for scrying. Obsidian is a powerful mirror of the soul, one of the most effective scrying stones for revealing what is truly reflected in the souls of others, or in yourself. It is a stone whose black or other dark colors help us to go within the hidden places of our own mind and bring out the inner light. The stones often have concentric circles that, when focused upon, can reveal the pattern of our spiritual path and the patterns we must overcome to attain mastery. They can reveal the darker aspects of an individual's nature, and bring light to what is hidden—good, bad, or indifferent.

Black contains the full light spectrum. It is the potential of the unknown, and so obsidian spheres can help awaken our vision of those potentials. The images and visions that are awakened within these spheres are often blunt, and as the old saying goes: "Sometimes the truth hurts."

**Obsidian balls and spheres are powerful scrying tools,
but are not usually recommended for beginners.**

When gazing with obsidian balls, it is beneficial to hold within your hands, or have somewhere upon you, a clear quartz crystal to help ground you. Obsidian balls are deceptively powerful and can be used for great penetration. They not only will reveal, but can also help manifest, darker aspects of an individual's nature. The information and the effects of the visions they stimulate often require serious processing. If gazing for others with obsidian balls, it is beneficial to have some formal counseling training, so that you are able to assist the person in the most beneficial manner with that processing. It is not a gazing tool for the beginner or the dabbler.

Rose Quartz Crystal Balls

Rose quartz balls are very loving and gentle tools to work with. They can be wonderful tools for spirit guide gazing and for past-life scrying. The stone's pink color reflects the gentleness with which it will reveal answers and open vision to provide direction.

It is a good sphere to use also in gazing for health issues, as well as any issue of the heart—especially for insight into love relationships of any kind. Rose Quartz is very effective when gazing for children, and they make an excellent first sphere for children to use in learning to gaze themselves.

The only drawback is that they are often milky, and some people find this distracting when gazing. They are also difficult to find above the two-inch diameter size (approximately 5 cm. or more) of good quality and price.

Clear Quartz Crystal Balls

Quartz crystal balls are the most common. They can be used for any type of scrying or gazing. Their electrical properties awaken spiritual insight and vision, and it is often easier to see the expression of those inner visions within the physical ball itself.

There often arises discussion as to whether a clear ball or one with formations and clouds is more effective for gazing. Clear quartz crystal balls are frequently much more expensive, but this doesn't mean they are better scrying tools. It has been my experience that a ball with natural formations, occlusions, clouds, and patterns in it can be easiest to use for beginners.

Although this is an individual thing, the ball with patterns and formations provides doorways and windows, and the formations will serve in many ways like Rorschach ink blot tests. (Named after the Swiss psychiatrist Hermann Rorschach, this test reveals underlying patterns through the use of a series of ink-blot designs to which the subject responds by telling what image or emotion the designs evoke. In crystal gazing, what you see in the patterns and formations of your ball reflects the message your subconscious is trying to get across to you about yourself or the one for whom you are gazing.

RORSCHACH INK BLOT TEST—
Ink blots can be made by dabbing ink onto paper and folding it in half. What you see when you look at these blots will tell you a great deal about your hidden self. Everything you see in them has significance. You can even use blots for psychic development. Just muse about them casually, and trust in your imagination!

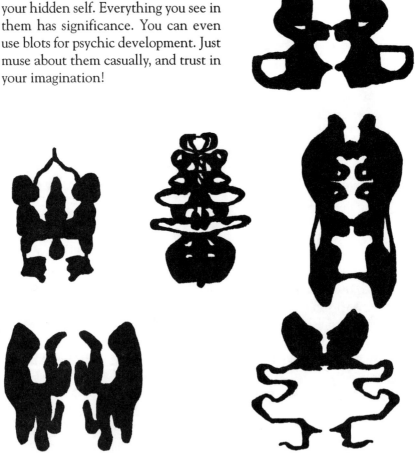

The subconscious mind is truly a wonder. It mediates 90 percent of our energies—physical, emotional, mental, and spiritual. Nothing gets by its perceptive abilities. We are not always—nor do we need to be—conscious of its many perceptions. When we sit down to gaze, we are asking the subconscious to give us a more conscious communication. The images we see and the emotions we feel as we gaze into the ball provide insight into what the subconscious has recognized as most important. As we focus upon our questions and our ball, the subconscious mind translates the appropriate answers to the conscious mind through recognizable images in the formations of the ball. What we see or imagine we see has significance! Each time we gaze into those patterns, occlusions and clouds, we will see something different. The subconscious mind works to help us see in the formations responses that apply to our question or to that of the person for whom we are gazing.

Smokey quartz is a variation of the clear quartz variety. The balls are a darker shade or color. This is a ball that helps keep us grounded and balanced as we perform our gazing. It can be a good sphere to use with people who have a tendency to be overemotional. It is also a good ball to use with people who have a tendency to be negative and to put up blocks consciously or unconsciously to psychic activity of any kind. It is a good sphere to use for clarity of dreams and for revealing an individual's spiritual path and the best way to follow it in the physical.

A drawback to smokey quartz is that it can be expensive. Buyers should be aware that a lot of the smokey quartz on the market is not true smokey quartz, but clear quartz, radiated to turn it a darker color. True smokey quartz is usually transparent, with varying shades of dark tones within it.

Ultimately, your choice of gazing crystals should not rest on their clarity, color, size, or type. The ball that you are drawn to is the one that will work best for you. Choose it lovingly, and make sure you are attracted to it by more than just idle curiosity. In more ancient times, the average individual did not have access to the variety of crystals that we do today, so they often had to settle and make do with what is at hand. As you can see from the photos (p. 57), I have balls of different sizes, types, and clarity. The one I prefer to use most often is a smaller quartz crystal sphere that has a variety of formations within it.

The sphere does not need to be perfect to work for you. As long as you are comfortable with it, it will work! Remember that the crystal is more than just a stone sphere. It is going to become a sacred object. It is your child.

Initially, you will not have to understand how the crystal balls works to experience it. The exercises in this book are set up so that you will experience their effectiveness. In the beginning try not to be overly judgmental or critical, as this can block out your more primordial intuitive senses. After you have experienced the crystal gazing, then there will be time to analyze the experiences.

With practice and perseverance, you WILL see. The vision may be actual and literal, as if you are immersed in the vision itself. You may see it in the sphere as if looking through a window or doorway, or see the images upon a movie screen. The seeing may also be internal, with images and impressions appearing, not in the sphere, but in the mind, as you focus on the sphere. It will vary from person to person.

Approach the visions with common sense. They may be literal or symbolic, but keep in mind that there is a difference between visions obtained through a crystal as opposed to the attainment of crystal vision. The first is achieved by concentration upon a sphere. The latter is achieved through focus and concentration on a single idea, image or thought. Your work at developing seership through a crystal ball will aid in crystallizing your own visionary focus beyond the use of the sphere.

Crystal Ball Care and Dedication

Once you have found your crystal sphere, it is important to care for it properly. Treat it as a sacred object, something special and unique to you. Treat it with respect, and don't allow others to treat it as a toy.

Once you take possession of your ball, NO ONE else should ever handle it except when you are gazing for them! Allowing curious individuals to handle it not only disrespects the ball and its spirit, but it also affects the clarity of your sensitivity to the visions of the ball. The handlers will leave their imprints upon it. This can confuse and muddle your ability to scry with it.

How this imprinting by others occurs is easy to understand. Anything that has an atomic structure, including the human body, has an electromagnetic quality to it. Every atom of every molecule of every substance—animate and inanimate—is comprised of electrons and protons that are in constant motion. These electrons and protons are electrical and magnetic energy vibrations.

These subtle electromagnetic vibrations can interact with other electromagnetic vibrations. Because of the strong electromagnetic aspects of the human energy system, we are constantly giving off (electrical) and absorbing (magnetic) energy. Anything that has an atomic structure can be imprinted. Crystal balls have a crystalline structure similar to that of the human body. Thus those individuals who have handled your ball have magnetized it with their own individual energies. They have left their own energy imprints upon it. (For more detailed explanations of how this imprinting occurs, you may wish to consult two of my earlier works: *How to See and Read the Aura* and *How to Develop and Use Psychometry*.)

Because of this it will be necessary to thoroughly clean your ball of ALL previous imprints or influences—physical and spiritual. It is best to assume that the crystal has been handled by a variety of people who have imprinted it with their energies—good, bad, and/or indifferent. You will want to eliminate all previous influences in order to make the ball more programmable to your purposes—more attuned to you, and you to it.

Allowing the ball to soak in a small bowl of sea salt for 24–48 hours should be the first priority. This will eliminate any energy imprints from those who may have handled it before you took possession. The sea salt draws from the crystal ball any negative energies and erases any imprints. To avoid scratching the surface of softer balls, such as those made of malachite, place the ball upon a soft cloth in a bowl of sea salt water. You may wish to add some pennyroyal flower elixir or oil to the sea salt. Pennyroyal is cleansing of negative vibrations from crystals. It will further enhance the purification process.

At the end of the 24–48 hour period, remove the ball and give the now contaminated salt or salt water back to the earth to be cleansed and purified. Then place the crystal ball in a safe spot outside for a minimum of 24–48 hours, leaving it outside day and night. This will allow the crystal ball to become charged up, bringing it back to its full strength and potential. You will see a physical difference. The ball will be more clear and vibrant.

This charging and re-energizing aspect is further enhanced if you set the ball outside through the time from the waxing moon to the full moon. This is the time of the month in which lunar influences are reaching their peak, and you will want your ball as strongly charged with these influences as possible. I recommend that this be done upon first getting your sacred ball, and that it also be done periodically throughout the year. Charging your ball during this phase of the moon, and while the sun is in one of the astrological signs of water (Cancer, Scorpio, and/or Pisces) will even further strengthen its effectiveness as a scrying tool. Performing this charging two to three days before, and the day of, each full moon can be a powerful monthly ritual.

Having purified and charged the crystal ball, bring it inside and clean it physically with a mild solution of warm water and a gentle soap. Adding some pennyroyal oil (a drop will do) or pennyroyal flower elixir to the water solution is beneficial. Having given it a physical bath, rinse, dry, and polish it with a soft cloth or chamois.

The crystal ball should at least be physically cleaned before and after each use. If you are gazing for several individuals in succession, have a cloth dampened with water and a drop or two of pennyroyal oil or flower essence with which to cleanse the ball of imprints between gazings. You will also need a clean cloth to dry the ball after wiping the imprints of the previous person off.

If you have performed a great deal of scrying with others, you will want to purify it at the end of all the sessions with the sea salt solution described above. Some balls may require this after each use. Some will need to be cleansed and recharged frequently, while others can retain their charge and purity for greater lengths of time. Every ball is different, and it will take time to understand yours and what it needs fully. To be safe, regular cleansing and chargings are recommended.

The crystal ball should be housed in a quiet room. Some individuals keep it in a box on their home altar, or they have a special table or stand for it. Wherever it is to be housed, the area should be kept clean and uncluttered. The ball should be in a place where it is not accessible to the curious, but is available to you.

When not in use, it should be covered with a dark silk cloth. This insulates it and prevents it from inadvertently being imprinted upon. Some people prefer to have an extra piece of black or dark-colored silk upon which to set the ball when it is used in scrying. This will help prevent undesirable reflections in the sphere when gazing.

The color of the cloth used for covering the crystal ball is not nearly as important as the type of cloth. While many people recommend darker colors as being more insulating, others use a variety of colors. Use the color cloth that you are drawn to. It is preferable that it be of silk, rather than cotton. Silk is more insulating and protective. It will hold in the crystal ball's energies, while shielding it from outside influences.

You are, in essence, creating a sacred space for your crystal ball and your work with it. It is a way of honoring the crystal, its spirit, and your future work with it. It creates a sacred space within the home and within the mind, a place between worlds, a place where the subtle and the tangible can intersect and play. It is an essential part of the ritual of scrying, and it awakens the power within the sphere and within yourself.

It is an act of creation. It is a prayer that honors the creative aspects within you and within all of life. Creating your sacred space for the crystal ball is an act of dedication. You may wish to offer a prayer or a song, or some form of thanks for the opportunity and the relationship that is about to open. When you do this you begin to consecrate your work with the crystal sphere. You begin to acknowledge and, therefore, consecrate the divine within you.

There is no need to rush into trying to attune to your crystal ball. The process of purifying, cleansing, charging, and creating a sacred space for it will have already initiated this attunement. The ground work is laid through these activities.

To build on this, though, you must take time to get familiar with your crystal ball—and not on just the initial occasion. Even if you have had a ball for years, take it out periodically to reexamine it and all the natural wonders within it. The more time you spend with it, the more effective it will be for you.

Remember that the human body is a biochemical, electromagnetic energy system. It is continually giving off and absorbing energy fields that it interacts with. This means that every object is imprinted by the owner or handler of that object in a manner unique to the individual. With crystal gazing we begin by imprinting the ball (programming) it with our own energies. We then use gazing techniques to read or interpret that imprint for greater insight into our lives or the lives of those for whom we are gazing.

There are parts of the body that have a higher degree of energy activity associated with them. We can use these, individually or in combination, to more strongly imprint and program the crystal ball for our gazing purposes. This is referred to as magnetizing the ball, and it is most easily accomplished through the use of our hands, our breath, and our eyes.

Exercise 6—
Magnetizing the Ball through Breath

As described at the end of the last chapter, breath is a way of increasing our own energy and altering it within the body. There are breaths that can stimulate and breaths that will calm. There are breathing techniques to stimulate sexuality, and there are breathing techniques to heal. In yoga there are a variety of breathing techniques for a multitude of functions. These techniques are called pranayama.

Breath is life, and through breath we can bring to life our own clairvoyance and the life of the crystal sphere. Proper breathing stimulates and facilitates the absorption of prana (life force). This, is turn, vitalizes the body and the mind, healing and even awakening of our own creative energies.

The tantric technique of crow-beak breathing is effective for cooling the body, healing, and even clairvoyance. In this technique, air is inhaled slowly through the curled-up tongue. Roll the sides of the tongue up and allow it to protrude slightly. Hold the breath for as long as possible and then slowly exhale through both nostrils. Performing this at dawn and dusk, while outside will further enhance its effectiveness.

"In many cultures breath had strong mystical connotations. In the East, 'savoring the exhaled breath of a friend' is still a gesture of deep friendship. The Eskimos do not use the kiss to show affection, but instead rub noses and exchange breaths. Many Tantric and Taoist mystical treatises point to the binding power of complementary breaths."[10]

This same mystical breathing can be applied to magnetizing and imprinting your crystal sphere. You can use consciously controlled and directed breath to establish resonance with your crystal sphere, its spirit and its unique energies. You can use breath as a means of effecting a great link, a powerful attraction and connection at a very primal level through breathing.

1. Take your crystal ball and cup it in both hands at about chest level.

2. Take a few deep breaths, close your eyes, and relax.

3. Imagine and feel a soft, slow pulsation of the crystal sphere—as if it too is breathing.

---

10 Douglas, Nik and Slinger, Penny. *Sexual Secrets*. Destiny Books, New York, 1979, p. 41.

4. As you take several minutes to perform deep breathing, envision all that you wish to be able to do with this crystal sphere, and all that you wish it to do for you.

   You may even want to make a mental or actual list.

5. For this exercise, you will use the alternate nostril breathing as described in the last chapter. Lower your head to an inch or two from the crystal's surface. If you are male, begin by inhaling through the right nostril. If you are female, begin by inhaling through the left nostril. Envision this as if you are inhaling the breath of the crystal. Then hold the breath, and exhale out the opposite nostril only. Envision this as if you are breathing into the crystal sphere, and it in turn is inhaling your breath. You are breathing life into it.

   See this as an exchange of vitalities that links the two of you together. Visualize this as a sacred exchange in which you receive the life force of the crystal, while bestowing upon it your own life force. It is a sacred pact which ties your essence and spirit to that of the crystal sphere, and all of its mystical, symbolic, and archetypal forces. This subtle breathing interplay creates a union for mutual exchanges, nourishment, and commitment.

6. Repeat this breath three times, and then reverse the nostrils; for the male, three breaths, inhaling through the left and exhaling out the right; for the female, three breaths, inhaling through the right and exhaling out the left.

7. This can be performed as a prelude to any psychic gazing, to firmly establish and harmonize yourself with the ball for greater vision.

   The crystal sphere can also be given quick charges periodically through breathing. Hold the sphere in the left hand, and begin performing deep rhythmic breathing. With each inhalation see and feel your body filling with vibrant energy. As you exhale, hold the right hand over the top of the ball. Visualize the energy, acquired through your inhalation, streaming through your body and out of your hand to charge the crystal ball. Some people like to wiggle or shake the fingertips above the ball as if shaking drops of prana into the crystal ball itself.

Don't be afraid to experiment with these and other breathing techniques. Find those that feel good for you and seem right for your crystal. Remember you are developing a relationship with it, and it will take a little time and exploration to find what is best for this new union.

Exercise 7—
Magnetizing the Ball through the Eyes

It has often been said that the eyes are the windows of the soul. They have great symbolic significance when it comes to psychic gazing of any kind. The eyes are our organs for physical sight, but they are also symbols of inner sight and clairvoyance.

The eyes have the ability to project and absorb energy, thoughts, and emotions. We can tell much about a person by looking into his or her eyes. Our eyes and the ways in which we use them send and receive a variety of messages. They are vehicles of communication. For example, most people know that good, steady eye contact projects self-confidence and self-esteem. On the other hand, averting or lowering the eyes often demonstrates a lack of confidence and a lack of self-esteem. Shifting eyes may reflect untruthfulness, impatience, or nervousness. Our eyes do project.

This has been recognized universally. Why else would our languages be so full of idioms associated with the eyes and what they project? "If looks could kill . . .", "the look of love . . .", "to look down one's nose"—all express how one feels. "To have eyes for someone" or "to make eyes at" is to send a message of desire. "To keep an eye out" for someone is to stay attuned to them for protective purposes. "To look someone in the eyes" is a way to determine truthfulness and honesty. All these and many other similar idioms reveal how humans use the eyes to project and to receive.

What are These Men's Eyes Projecting?

"My wife will be home soon."   "I absolutely love your music!"

True or False? In the first picture, the man is being dishonest. Rubbing closed eyes is a sign of dishonesty. The second gentleman is also being dishonest. He is shutting out the music with his eyes.

When we bring our eyes and our attention to the crystal ball, we align ourselves with it. We project our energies and our intent upon it. Our breath, our eyes, and our touch serve to bring the body's energies and the ball's energies into resonance. The crystal ball will take on what we project, so we can work more harmoniously with it and its energies.

It is also because of this energy projection that we must be careful of our thoughts while looking upon and handling the crystal sphere. Our eyes will project our thoughts, and this will affect the magnetizing and programming of the crystal ball as a psychic gazing tool.

To further magnetize the ball with the eyes, spend time looking upon it. Don't force a concentrated stare; just fix the eyes upon the crystal in a soft, gentle gaze. A fierce stare will only give you a headache. Simply enjoy examining your crystal sphere. Every time you bring your eyes to look upon it, you will further enhance your connection to it, and it will, in turn, enhance your own unfolding clairvoyance.

Sit with it under a light, or outdoors. Study it. Roll it between your hands. Hold it up to the light. Are there rainbows reflected within it? Study and note the various planes, patterns, and occlusions it contains. The more familiar you are with it, the more fascinating it becomes, because you will continually see new things within it. The crystal spheres always change, and every change you see in it reflects a newness coming to life within you as well. Remember that the crystal ball is like a mirror. Enjoy the wonder of what it reflects.

As you look upon the ball and examine it, keep your mind on what you wish the ball to do for you. Imagine yourself being able to see everything you desire to see within it. Visualize yourself scrying the past, present, and future with great clarity and accuracy. See yourself seeing more fully and clearly in regard to all things and all people, at all times, and in all areas of your life—with the ball, and without. Know that with each glance, you awaken the crystal's ability to reveal, and it in turn will further awaken your own visionary ability.

Exercise 8—
Magnetizing the Ball With the Hands

Regular use and attention to the crystal sphere is necessary for developing and strengthening its magnetic fields and for enhancing its effectiveness. It is essential to establishing and maintaining your resonance with it. Periodically take out your crystal and just hold the sphere in both hands. Get a feel for its weight. Cup it gently and lovingly. Allow it to rest in the hollows of your palms as if the world were being cupped within divine hands. Each time you do this you strengthen your relationship with it.

Take a few deep breaths, close your eyes and calm the mind. Gently rub, stroke, and caress the sphere. This serves several functions. First, it helps you connect with the crystal ball more fully and easily; and second, it activates the natural energy field of the crystal. You are beginning the process of programming the subtle electromagnetic fields of the sphere to serve as a scrying mirror or psychic reflector.

Your hands are points of great energy activity. They are most active for sensory expression and impression. In other words, we can use the hands to direct and send energy out with a stronger focus, or we can use them to sense and absorb energies more strongly.

The ability to project and absorb energy through the hands has been taught everywhere upon the planet. Most often such teachings are found in relation to healing techniques. It has been called "The King's Touch," "therapeutic touch," the "laying on of hands," and by many other names throughout history. There are many ways of demonstrating and proving this ability of the hands, but it is not within the scope of this book to do so. If you are interested in exploring energy projection and healing, I then refer you to two of my earlier works which do provide exercises in this: *How to Develop and Use Psychometry* and *The Healer's Manual*.

By performing hand passes over the crystal ball, we charge the ball with our own energies. The energy given off by our hands is absorbed by the crystal ball. This in turn activates the ball's own energy field. Its magnetism will increase so that it can more easily reflect back the energies of its handler.

Hand passes can be performed by both hands, or either one individually. Some people recommend that there be greater emphasis on left-hand passes because the left side of the body has more magnetic polarity and will thus activate the magnetism of the ball more effectively. It has been my experience that this is much less important than the thoughts you hold during the hand passes.

If you believe the left hand is more effective, use it. If not, don't. There really are no absolutes—other than what works for you as an individual, and even that will change.

1. Begin by making yourself comfortable in a seated position.

2. Place the crystal ball gently upon your lap.

3. Close your eyes briefly, take a few deep breaths, and just relax. Rub the hands briskly together for about 30 seconds. This stimulates the chakras or energy centers in the palms of the hands, increasing their ability to project and sense energy.

4. Place both hands next to each other, touching, with palms down. As you begin the stroke, the hands separate.

5. Slowly and gently touching the surface of the ball at the top, stroke the ball, following its natural curve, until the hands touch again, this time underneath the ball. Now the palms are facing up, cupping the ball.

6. Bring the hands back to the top once more and again stroke the ball, down and around. Stroke the ball, doing the sides, the front and back, and so on—covering every surface.

7. Time your breathing with the stroking. As you exhale, stroke the ball downward. Visualize energy pouring through you, out your hands, and into the ball with each exhalation.

8. Gradually move the hands away about one–two inches from the surface of the ball and continue your breathing and stroking pattern. As you do this you will begin to feel the energy emanating from the ball. It may feel like a soft pressure, a tingling, a warmth, a coolness, a rubberiness, a pulsation or even a thickness around it. Every ball has its own energy field, and you will respond uniquely to each one.

9. Take a few minutes to define what your hands are feeling. Do not worry about whether you are imagining it or not. Do not worry that it may feel different from what others experience. In time your hands will become so sensitive to the subtle energies surrounding the ball that with only a few passes of the hands you will awaken its energy and be able to tell how strong it is.

10. It is always beneficial during the hand passes and breathing to keep your eyes softly focused upon the ball. Imagine and visualize the ball becoming stronger and more clear in imparting visions and stimulating your own clairvoyance.

Exercise 9—
Purifying and Charging through Vision

As you work with your crystal sphere, you will find simple and effective ways of purifying and magnetizing the ball for scrying purposes. Whatever techniques you use will be enhanced by your own focused imagination.

The imagination is a faculty of the mind. It is the image-producing faculty. What is imagined should not be confused with what is unreal. The two are *not* synonymous. The following exercise is one which employs the use of breath, the eyes, and the hands, in conjunction with the power of the imagination, to amplify the magnetizing of your crystal sphere.

1. Begin by relaxing in a seated position, with your crystal ball resting on either a stand or a table in front of you. Take several slow, deep breaths and center yourself.

2. Take the thumbs and the forefingers of each hand and touch them together (thumb to thumb and forefinger to forefinger). You are creating a circle, a sacred space in miniature. It is a symbol of infinity. Hold this circle over the top of the ball.

3. Begin rhythmic breathing. Inhale for a slow count of four, hold for a count of four, and exhale for a count of four. With each inhalation, imagine and feel yourself drawing a great abundance of energy into your body. As you hold your breath, this vibrant energy touches and overflows every cell in your body. As you exhale, breathe into the direction of that circle. Visualize it accumulating as a powerful light force of pure energy.

4. Continuing your breathing, slowly move this circle of hands down over the ball, allowing the thumb and fingers to pass over the ball entirely. For larger crystal spheres, you may have to separate the fingers a little to pass over it. This will not hurt as long as you maintain the fingers and thumbs in the shape and position of the circle. As the ball passes through the encircled hands, visualize the energy within that circle being absorbed into the ball, empowering and purifying it.

5. At the bottom of the crystal, separate the hands, breaking the circle, leaving the ball encased with that energy. Bring the hands back to the top and create the circle once more, filling it with energy again. Then repeat the procedure. You may do this several times. It provides a quick charge to the crystal sphere, and it can be a great prelude to your gazing.

Exercise 10—
Meeting the Crystal Angel

Meditation is one of the best ways of attuning to your crystal sphere. The meditation does not need to be on using it or scrying with it. Just having it around you while meditating in general will help establish a firmer resonance.

Creative imagination is the key to truly opening your intuitive faculty through crystal gazing. One of the greatest capacities of the mind is imaging. It has the ability to conjure images and perceptions of the subconscious. These images can reflect information from the past, present, or future. All images are connected to some archetypal force in the universe. Through meditation and the use of creative imagination, we can connect with those archetypal energies.

One of the most common and ancient beliefs throughout the world is that every aspect of nature has its spirit. Folklore research reveals that people all over the world believe in rare creatures, and humans have always tried to classify the numerous kinds of beings found within the natural world. The myriad forces and expressions of nature were always personified. Every flower had a fairy; every tree had its deva; every crystal had its angel.

Whether we call them nature spirits, fairies and elves, angels, devas, or any of a variety of names, does not really matter. It is enough to realize that there is some archetypal force that is manifesting and expressing itself through every aspect of nature. We exist in a living universe. There is life and energy in everything around us.

A variety of crystal meditations can be found in the multitude of books on crystals that have become so popular in the last decade. Any of these are suitable to do on a regular basis to further enhance your attunement to your crystal ball. The following meditation is also very beneficial. Through it you can meet the spirit of the crystal itself.

This meditation will help you to attune to the archetypal force that manifests through your crystal ball. It will also help you establish a stronger relationship with it—physically, emotionally, mentally, and spiritually. It will enhance your creative imagination and your scrying ability.

1. Choose a time for this meditation when you will not be disturbed. Make sure the phone is off the hook, and make any preparations necessary to prevent being disturbed or interrupted. All meditation cre-

ates a hyperesthetic state, in which you feel and experience the physical senses more intensely. If you are meditating and the phone rings, it will be very jarring to your nervous system.

2. You may wish to perform a progressive relaxation at the beginning. Take several deep breaths, close your eyes, and send warm, soothing energies to every part of your body. Take your time doing this. The more relaxed you are the more effective the meditation.

3. You may wish to play some soothing music throughout this exercise. You may also find that using a crystal bowl (as described in the second half of this book) is beneficial to do at the beginning of this meditation.

4. Take time to be familiar with your crystal ball. Have it resting either on your lap or on a steady surface in front of you throughout this exercise. You will need to be able to visualize the ball with your eyes closed.

5. Close your eyes and breathe deeply. Allow yourself to relax. Gather all of your energies around you, as if someone has wrapped you in an old comfortable quilt.

6. Gently stroke the ball, activating its energies, and experience the scene.

The Meeting

Within the darkness of your own mind, a scene begins to unfold. Faintly you hear the soft sound of water—a gentle stream that must be near by. As the scene becomes distinct, you find that you are sitting in a circular garden. It is dusk, and the full moon is beginning to rise in the sky.

You see that you are sitting upon soft grass. About ten yards in front of you is a small stream that runs through this garden. You can see the rippling reflection of the moon upon its surface. In front of you is your crystal ball.

As you look upon it, the ball begins to take on a luminous appearance. It seems as if the moon itself is illuminating and awakening it. You reach out gently with your hand and try to feel the soft moonlight reflected around the crystal ball. As you do, the ball begins to hum.

It is a soft sound, familiar and pleasing. The light of the moon reflecting off its surface grows brighter, making the ball seem larger. You watch, amazed at the play of moonlight upon it, and then you realize that the crystal is becoming larger. It is growing! It is as if the moonlight has awakened it.

You watch as the sphere expands—growing, stretching—in just a few moments time, it has become the size of a small house. You stand, amazed.

As you stand before the crystal sphere, you can see the planes and occlusions distinctly through the surface. The moonlight seems to have illuminated them, like soft street lights just coming on in the early evening. Every plane stands out like a pathway through a new world.

It is then that you notice a circular, cave-like opening, and somehow you know that it is an invitation to you. You breathe deeply and step through to the inner world of the crystal.

You find yourself suffused in light and color. The hum you heard from the outside now sounds like a soft song, unusual and yet somehow familiar. The colors and lights shift subtly, as if in response to the song of the crystal. It is as if the crystal is singing to you in greeting.

You see before you a sea of color—of every shade of the rainbow, and of great vibrancy. The planes that, from the outside, looked like miniature streets now seem even moreso, and you are sure that you could follow them to destinations of the past, the present, or the future.

Never before had you thought that color and sound had a life of its own, but within this crystal there is no doubt, and the colors and the crystal song grow stronger in response to this thought. As you look about, you feel as if you are looking at the whole universe for the first time—and it is singing to you.

It is then that you begin to feel as if you are not truly alone in this sphere. Slowly you turn, and standing behind you is a figure of crystalline light. The reflection of this being is so soft and bright that the features, although not clear, are quite beautiful. The eyes are soft as a mother's first look upon her newborn child. The moonlight coming through the crystal seems to center upon this being, casting rainbow-hued shadows about, like a prism in sunlight.

"Everything in life casts its reflections, like moonlight upon the water. If you learn to gaze within those reflections you will see shadows of all times, all people and all places."

As the moonlight fills this sphere, reflecting off the planes and formations, you catch glimpses and images of new life and adventures revealing themselves to you.

A crystal angel steps forward and raises a hand into the soft moonlight coming through the sphere. As the hand withdraws, you see within its palm a small crystal sphere—a miniature of that in which you stand. As you look upon it, you see your own face within it.

"This is my promise; to work with you, to help you see how all life reflects itself within your own. This crystal sphere will help remind you to see the night reflected within your days, and the days reflected within your nights. It will reveal new dimensions to your heart and soul."

The angel places within your hands the crystal sphere. The moonlight brightens around this magnificent being and encircles you. Shivers of joy and promise fill your body. You close your eyes and offer a silent prayer of thanks.

When you open your eyes, you find yourself sitting outside in the garden with your crystal ball on the ground before you. The moonlight casts a mystical glow around you and the ball, and in that moment you know that this is not just a crystal ball. It is life. It is the universe itself.

You breathe deeply as the scene around you slowly dissipates. You allow your awareness and consciousness to return to the room in which you began this mediation. You take your crystal ball in your hand, and you can feel it pulsing with new life; and for a moment you are sure that you hear it singing.

Chapter Four

Crystal Ball Gazing

The crystal ball is an ancient symbol of the occult or hidden. It is a mirror that reflects aspects of life. It has the ability of whispering special secrets to its friends. For it to be most effective for you, you must eliminate fears and preconceptions, and open yourself to new possibilities. You must make a commitment to it, and thus to yourself.

Remember that the ball is a symbol of the purest condition of your self. It is a microcosm, a miniature reflection of you and your most innate essence. Because of this, your consecration and your dedication of the ball and its use to a higher purpose is also a way of consecrating and rededicating yourself to your own higher purposes. By working with the crystal ball, you perform a kind of sympathetic magic that awakens your own inner abilities.

When we focus our eyes—our attention—upon someone or something, we direct energy. We establish psychic links, if only temporarily. "In sight, in mind," although a paraphrase of "out of sight, out of mind," has applications to psychic gazing. When we focus the eyes, we focus our thoughts, and we direct the energy of our thoughts along the line of our eyes.

When we begin gazing with the ball, our focus upon it will align us with its imprints. It brings to the mind and consciousness what we need to see. If we are gazing for others, we allow them to handle the ball briefly (as will be described fully later in this chapter). Because it is our ball, our focus upon it stimulates and releases images connected to that person. When we clean the ball after gazing for someone, all that remains is our own imprints, that with each use become more deeply imbedded into the energy matrix of the crystal. If we are gazing for ourselves, our personal connection to it is strengthened, and our focus upon it stimulates and releases images connected to our own questions.

Crystal visions can be subtle. They may be stimulated and viewed entirely within the ball or within the mind, and sometimes this will vary from one occasion to another.

Crystal visions are multidimensional: these images and visions may be literal, reflecting events and people as they actually are, have been, or will be; they may be symbolic, or they may even be a combination of the literal and symbolic. Initially, there is no way of truly knowing, so there will be some trial and error in the interpretive process. Keeping a crystal-gazing journal will help you with this. Exercise 11 will help you in creating and using a crystal-gazing journal.

With practice and perseverance you will see. This seeing may be within the ball itself, or it may all occur within the mind. One is neither better nor worse than the other. The visioning may even vary from occasion to occasion. An internal vision (within the mind) is most common in the beginning stages, but it often indicates the beginning of a sacred marriage between the seer and the seen.

How to Perform Crystal Gazing

By now you should be familiar with your ball and some of the basics of psychic perception—especially through the use of reflected images. Having performed all of the preparatory work, it is time to begin your crystal gazing.

The ball should be placed upon a stand or a table surface in a quiet room that will enable you to gaze upon it comfortably while you are seated. The stand or table should be covered with a black or dark cloth in order to prevent too many reflections from the room.

There are often questions about how much light to use in the room when gazing. Some people find bright light creates too many reflections, which they find distracting. Others find that the reflections enable them to see visions more easily. There will be some trial and error initially, but once you awaken fully your visionary ability with the ball, you will find that the degree of lighting will not matter.

Sacred Marriage of the Seer and the Seen

Darkening the room for the gazing can have both symbolic and actual significance. Symbolically, it can reflect the dimming of the outer vision, so the inner vision can come to life more fully. For many people muted lighting is more relaxing, and the more relaxed we are the easier it is to tap our intuitive faculties.

I recommend initially that you arrange the ball and the lighting so there is little or no reflected light, and use dim lighting in the area, especially overhead. In this way, there is less likelihood of doubt surfacing as to the legitimacy of the visions—as to whether they are truly arising from the ball itself or from outside influences.

You may wish to have a candle illuminating the crystal ball from behind, which can be beneficial. Many crystal ball stands have small lights built into them to illuminate the ball from the underside. Although this is not necessary, these arrangements allow the patterns within the ball to stand out more clearly.

Make yourself comfortable in a seated position, and remove the silk covering from the ball. (Remember that your crystal ball should always be covered when not in use. This has symbolic, as well as actual, significance.) Perform a progressive relaxation. Take several deep breaths and close your eyes. Send warm soothing thoughts and energy to every part of your body. Take your time with this. The more relaxed you are, the more effective the psychic gazing.

Open your eyes and take the ball in your hands. Gently stroke it, or you may wish to simply make hand passes over the surface of the ball, as described earlier. One is neither more effective than the other. Later, if you gaze for others, it will be okay to allow them to touch and handle the ball as well. You will be cleaning it between each gazing, so there won't be any interference. Allowing yourself or those for whom you are gazing to handle it will not interfere with the ball's visions. It will, in fact, enhance it. The primary reason given for not handling the ball itself in the past was to prevent fingerprints and smudges upon it.

Now visualize and imagine the ball coming to life for you as you make your hand passes or stroke it. Envision this act as if you are turning on its power (and your own). After doing this for several minutes, place the ball back on its stand.

Find a spot or pattern on the crystal ball that fascinates you and focus upon it. Look into and beyond that spot, not at the spot or its surface specifically. It is similar to looking beyond your reflection in the mirror, to see what is occurring behind the reflected image. See the ball itself or that spot on it as a window or doorway through which you are looking and observing events beyond it. If your ball is cloudy or milky, focus upon a clear spot or opening within its milkiness. Imagine this opening as a tube or spyglass through which you can see things more clearly and focused. Envision it as a hallway that you can peer down to see people, activities, and events at its other end. Use the imagery that seems to work best for you, and don't be afraid to adapt it over time.

Your gaze should be comfortable and relaxed. YOU SHOULD NOT BE STARING INTENSELY. Fix your eyes upon the ball as if looking beyond its outer surface. Use a gaze similar to that which you use when daydreaming—a blank, staring-off-into-space focus.

Maintain this gaze, and just keep your mind open. Don't try to get specific information. Don't worry if the mind wanders during the gazing. These digressions will often be significant and reflect areas of your life upon which the ball is trying to shed some light. It is more important at this point in your scrying development to allow the visions to arise along lines that are natural, and not consciously directed. Later, as you become more capable, you may wish to focus upon specific questions or concerns during your relaxation and stroking of the crystal ball, prior to the actual gazing.

Keep your gazing sessions between five and ten minutes in the beginning. For many who are just opening up psychically, scrying can be taxing to physical, emotional, mental, and spiritual energies. Gazing too long and too frequently will make your nervous system hypersensitive. As with anything, it takes time and training to develop psychic stamina. As your concentration and results improve, then extend your gazing time.

For beginners, it is also best to perform only one psychic gazing per day. Even for those who are more advanced, I recommend scrying only once per day for yourself. This prevents over-reliance on your ball, and it will also help prevent you from becoming superstitious about the results.

As you gaze, pay attention to anything you experience. Do your ears buzz or ring? Do you see a shifting in the ball? Are you impressed with ideas or images in the mind? Do you feel pressure, tickling, or other physical sensations upon your body? Don't try to define and understand them at this point; just acknowledge them and continue gazing. There will be time later to put them into perspective and analyze them. Don't be worried if you find your mind drifting into daydream scenarios or such. This is actually a good sign; it reflects that you have accessed the subconscious through the gazing. That scenario will have significance and meaning when later examined.

Everything that you experience in your gazing session, whether imagined or real, should be logged in some kind of journal. The recording of the experiences will do several things for you. First, it will send a message to the subconscious that you are ready to use any intuitive insights that it brings forward. Second, it will help you to understand your visions. Often people experience visions that seem incomprehensible until they speak of them or record them. Then the light goes on. This is a way of grounding the energy of the vision into the physical, which initiates understanding. The process of creating and using a scrying journal will be covered later in this chapter.

Images and visions in the crystal ball usually begin in the same way for most people. The first indiscriminate visual sensation that most people become aware of is an opaque clouding of the crystal ball. This may be an increase in milkiness, a shifting, mistlike appearance, or as clouds or fog forming within the ball. The crystal ball may look duller, and even pinpoints of light may seem to shine through the clouds that are forming. The opposite appearance may occur as well. There may even be an increase in clarity—with the ball seeming to have tiny sparkles or stars appearing within it.

Remember that every ball is different, and the way it reveals its activity will be different as well. ANY CHANGE THAT YOU NOTICE IN THE BALL REFLECTS THAT IT IS BEGINNING TO WORK. It doesn't matter whether the change is imagined or real, because sometimes the images appear within the ball, and sometimes they appear within the mind as you gaze upon the ball.

As the mists or clouds begin to form, make mental notes as to what their formations look like to you. You will see in their shapes the image that is most important for you. Everyone has lain out in the grass on a summer day, looked up at the clouds and tried to determine what those clouds look like, and it is this same process that we use with the appearance of the clouds in the ball. It is the same process we discussed in regard to the Rorschach test earlier (Chapter Two).

If the clouds begin to part or openings appear within the mist and clouds, focus upon that place as if it is a vision tunnel through the clouds. In time, as you do this, you will notice that the clouds begin to fade or dissipate. Sometimes it appears as if the opening is getting larger. THIS IS A PRELUDE TO THE CLOUDS BEING REPLACED BY ACTUAL IMAGES.

This opening is often accompanied by colors within the clouds, or throughout the ball. These colors have significance and meaning. A study of colorology will help you in understanding the messages from the ball. My earlier work, *How to See and Read the Aura*, will provide a good starting point.

Note everything that you experience. EVERYTHING HAS SIG-NIFICANCE! There will be time later to examine and apply common sense to the experiences. For now, it is most important to just acknowledge them.

Some people have whole scenarios reveal themselves in the ball, as if the person were watching a movie. For others, it may only be a single image, which may be either symbolic or literal. Always go with your first impression. Don't try to make the image fit what you wish it to. This does not honor your own intuitive faculty, nor does it honor the essence and spirit of the ball.

If you only get a single image, use free association. What does that image mean to you personally. The ball is yours, and it is attuned to your subconscious. Therefore, the images generated by it WILL be ones that you can interpret if you apply a little effort, and you will have time for doing so later.

Continue gazing and noting what you experience or imagine throughout the gazing. When the images and impressions begin to fade, it is time to close back down and ground yourself. Often the ending of images is preceded by a re-clouding or re-misting of the crystal ball. This phenomena is usually an indication that it is time to cease the gazing activity.

At this point, close your eyes and perform some deep breathing. Clear your mind. You may wish to perform some more hand passes over the ball or stroke it again, as you did in the beginning. This erases and cleanses the ball of this session's reflections and imprints. You may also wish to physically clean and shine it again. Then cover it with the silk cloth and put it away where it can rest until its next use. You may even wish to offer a prayer or affirmation of thanks as a definite closing down of the gazing activity. Then record your experiences in the journal, as described later. These recordings will help you determine the significance and validity of your scrying experiences.

Understanding the Phenomena in the Ball

Interpreting the phenomena that appears within the ball is individual, experimental, and developmental. It is individual in that everyone connects and works with the ball, and the ball with him or her, in a unique manner. Therefore the meanings given on the following pages are generic, and they may not hold true for you.

There is a much greater likelihood of their application to you if you familiarize yourself with them ahead of time. By doing so, you program your own internal computer—the subconscious mind. You are telling it (and the crystal ball and its spirit) what kind of feedback you wish. You are establishing a beginning vocabulary for higher communication between the subconscious and the crystal ball.

This interpretation is also experimental, because each ball is unique, and you must establish a relationship with it. What works for one ball may not work with another. What applies and works for one individual does not apply and work for all. The information in this book is a guideline; it should be used as a foundation only. To become powerful in gazing and scrying, you must take the information, adapt it, and apply your own creative imagination to working with it. That is what gives it power. That is what imbues it with magic.

Your interpretation will also be developmental. It will grow and change as you grow and change in your work with the crystal ball. Visions and images may become more crystalline, or they may become simpler in form but more abstract in meaning. One side of the ball may become literal, while the other may become symbolic. Regardless, the images and visions you see will always be those you are capable of interpreting. The interpretations won't always be easy; they may require effort. Correct interpretations, though, will always be within your capability. Since you are seeing, YOU must interpret!

The Phenomena and Their Meanings

General

- Cloudiness or mistiness indicates the appearance of images soon within the ball.

- Haziness or dullness hints of things which will likely appear soon within the ball, as well.

- New sparkle or light within the crystal may appear just prior the images.

- Sometimes the crystal becomes dark just before the images and visions begin.

- As you gaze, the brightness and darkness of the ball will shift, again reflecting that images and visions will appear soon.

- Changes in physical temperature will reveal much. Warmer temperatures reflect things of the spirit, while cooler reflect mundane things.

- Visions and images are not necessarily direct and literal reflections of actual events. They may be partial and figurative.

Clouds
- Clouding and images in the background reflect more remote events (the remote past or the remote future).

- Clouding and images to the forefront reflect events of the present or immediate future.

- Ascending clouds and mists are usually affirmations and "yes" responses. They may also reflect events on the horizon or those that are approaching. They hint at revelations.

- Descending clouds or mists reflect negative or "no" responses. They may also indicate events and things that are passing on or moving away. They may also hint at concealment.

- Clouds on or moving to the right may reflect masculine energies, assertiveness, something or someone new coming into your life. (This can be a spirit person or a physical person—a spiritual event or a mundane event. Only the rest of the images will help you to more specifically define it.)

- Clouds on the left or moving to the left reflect feminine energies, receptiveness, creativity, or something or someone moving away from your life.

- Clouds moving to or appearing in the front reflect situations surfacing in the present or very near future.

- Clouds moving to or appearing in the back of the ball reflect situations leaving, or events from the past affecting you, including past lives.

Timing
- Timing in regard to scrying with the crystal ball is not always or easily determined, especially since the images may be literal, symbolic, or a combination. It is often reflected by the movement of clouds in the ball, although this is not the only criteria for determining such. With practice you will develop a sense of timing, as well as a sense for those

events that are literal and those that are symbolic. Although it seems cliche, you will develop a "feel" for these with practice.

- Images and events that appear smaller or to the back of the crystal ball when gazing lengthwise are often connected to the distant future or past. Those that are larger and closer to the front of the ball have ties to the present or immediate future.

Colors

Often the clouds will appear in a variety of colors, frequently more than one color arising at a time. The various images will also often have colors associated with them during the crystal gazing. Colors are expressions of energy, and understanding them will shed much light on the communications from your crystal sphere.

- White = Spirit, increase, birth and creation

- Black = Protection, spirit, feminine, birth, past lives

- Red = Passion, sex, courage, aggravation, anger

- Orange = Courage, creativity, joy, wisdom, truth and dishonesty

- Yellow = Knowledge, new sunshine, optimism, health

- Green = Growth, money, relationships, emotions, nature, love

- Blue = Expansion, intuition, artistic inspiration, peace, judgments and legalities

- Violet = Spirit contact, purification, balance, humility, dream activity

- Pink = Compassion, new love, immaturity, truth

- Gold = Wealth, prosperity, enthusiasm, coming into one's power

- Aqua = Health, creativity, cooling

- Silver = Intuition, Mother energies, tides of change, causation

- Brown = Grounding, common sense, discrimination, finding the lost, new growth

- Gray = Initiation, hidden revealed, creative imagination

Understanding Crystal Visions

An actual vision is one in which you find yourself immersed within the vision. It is as real at the time as the dreams you have at night. You are a part of them and the events. You feel and experience everything personally.

Crystal visions usually have a more objective perspective to them. You are observing, from the outside, the events reflected within the crystal ball or within the mind. Although a true immersion into the visionary experience can occur, it is more often the exception in crystal gazing.

There are advanced techniques in crystal ball work in which we can use the work as an actual doorway to astral travel, and open ourselves to the conscious experience of other dimensions. This takes much more focus and preparation to accomplish, and some introductory exercises for this are found in the next chapter. This should not be experimented with until you have developed a high degree of control and accuracy in your own development through crystal gazing.

Many crystal-gazing images and visions are symbolic; the images and symbols that do arise will only be those that you have the ability to interpret. This is because symbology is the only language of the unconscious mind. It is the only way the unconscious has to communicate with the more conscious aspects of ourselves, and so it uses images to which it knows you can relate on some level.

You may have to put some effort into the interpretation, but you will be able to interpret the images. In many ways, symbolic crystal visions are similar to dream imagery and visions. They will have inner and outer meanings, and will often reflect a variety of possibilities. They will always represent more than what is at first apparent, and so we should always start with the obvious and move to the not-so-obvious in our interpretations. We must learn to employ analysis, intuition, and empathy in the interpretation process.

Most symbols in crystal visions will have both obvious and abstract qualities. At the very least, they WILL mean what we think they mean—and more. They are chameleon-like, assuming the form that encompasses the moods and attitudes and energies of the individual and his or her life.

Always begin the interpretation process with first impressions, and then move on. Don't stop with the obvious. What you see in the crystal ball will always represent more than what is apparent. Free associate with the images. What is the first thing you normally think of in connection to this image or symbol?

Is there a particular emotion that arises during your gazing? Note this emotion. Are you frightened? Frustrated? Excited? Happy? Sad? The emotion would not be arising if it weren't significant. Remember that crystal balls amplify and reflect. When gazing, the crystal ball will often exaggerate emotions, qualities, or situations to get the message across. It is a way for the psyche to give us a nudge. These are strong calls to attention.

Look for similarities in the vision symbols and images. Often the message is given in several different forms to make sure that it is received.

However the vision comes, approach it with common sense. The crystal ball should be, first and foremost, an aid to personal development. It should be seen as a tool to quicken us to new potentials and new creativity. It will help you to develop focus and concentration, and although it can be a wonderful developmental tool for your own use, it doesn't necessarily qualify you to counsel with others.

Special Reminders and Hints for Successful Gazing

- Practice consistently. To develop and learn anything requires time and practice.

- Perform your gazing practices in quiet, undisturbed areas. This will aid your concentration and focus. If there are others present, they should remain still once you start, for movement can cast interfering reflections.

- Don't gaze after eating. Digestion demands more of the body's energy than any other activity. Either perform your gazing before eating, or wait several hours afterward.

- Practice your gazing only for 5–10 minutes at a time, and after you have performed some form of relaxation or meditation exercise. The more relaxed and balanced you are, the easier it is for your inner vision to awaken and manifest.

- Create your own opening and closing ritual, so that you learn to turn your vision on and off at will. An opening ritual may be as simple as a gesture that you only use when crystal gazing, or it may be a particular meditation or affirmation. Use what you are comfortable with. The same goes for the closing ritual. It may be a gesture, prayer, affirmation, or anything that can serve to close down and ground yourself.

A very effective tool for this is the use of the crystal bowls discussed in the second half of this book. Play the crystal bowl at the beginning and at the end. The bowls stimulate the psychic faculty, while balancing us as well. Its sound also stimulates the crystal ball into activity, while cleansing it at the same time.

- Keep the area in which you store your crystal ball clean. From just a symbolic aspect, it is a way of affirming that your own intuition and vision clean and clear at all times.

- Clean and energize your crystal ball regularly. Use moonlight to charge it for higher vision, and sunlight for clarity. Physically clean the ball after each use, especially if you are gazing for others.

- Don't allow your ball to be handled except by those for whom you gaze. Others will be curious, but remember that this is your sacred object. Treat it as such.

- Roll the ball over your solar plexus and your brow/third eye area. This stimulates these chakras or energy centers. The third eye or brow area is linked to our higher intuitive faculty of clairvoyance (clear vision), and the solar plexus to our psychic faculty of clairsentience (clear feeling). This not only stimulates our own psychism but helps us connect it to the crystal ball.

- Use outside aids that will naturally stimulate your own intuitive faculties, especially in crystal ball gazing. Some of the most common and easiest to use fall into one of three categories, as described in the following three groups.

Astrological Aids
- Times of lunar increase, when the moon is waxing, are more effective for scrying with the crystal ball. This is especially so around the full moon (the day before, the day of, and the day after).

- Times in which the sun is in a water sign are also very effective for crystal ball gazing, i.e., the signs of Cancer, Scorpio, and Pisces.

- Some practitioners of crystal gazing work with planets and signs that govern the eyes, such as the sign of Libra.

Herbal Aids
Certain herbs have been associated with psychism. Using them in teas, or burning them as an incense are two of the most common forms of use. The following herbs are beneficial to use in either form with crystal gazing:

- Celandine (lesser) = This herb makes a good wash, bath, or drink in conjunction with crystal gazing. It is a psychic herb that restores a sense of delight in working with crystal balls.

- Mugwort = Long reputed as a visionary herb, whether used in teas, flower elixirs, or as incense. It stimulates awareness of visions and images in the ball, and it initiates clarity in the gazing experience.

- Sage = As a tea or as an incense awakens spiritual illumination in crystal gazing. It helps to integrate and synthesize the images, symbols, and visionary experiences with the crystal ball.

- Thyme = This herb is very effective to use in a tea or as an incense when gazing for past-life information and its effects upon the present.

- Vervain = Along with mugwort, this is one of the best herbs for crystal gazing. It is a visionary herb, and it is especially effective when scrying for spiritual quests.

Flower Elixir Aids

Flower elixirs are made from the flowers of various plants, flowers, and trees. They contain the etheric energy pattern of the flower. Each flower has its own unique characteristic. (For more information on these, consult my earlier book, *The Healer's Manual: A Beginner's Guide to Vibrational Therapies*.)

- Chaparral = This elixir stimulates deeper visionary states when gazing. It also helps us in understanding the symbols and archetypes found during the gazing experience.

- Forget-Me-Not = This elixir stimulates visions and can assist us in contacting spirit guides during crystal gazing.

- Live Forever = This elixir also helps us to see and understand messages from our spirit guides during gazing experiences. It can help us to coordinate our crystal-gazing visions into our waking, daily consciousness.

- Pennyroyal = This elixir is cleansing to the aura and to the crystal ball experience. It can be used to wash the ball after use, and it helps us to remain protected from negative experiences in its use.

- St. John's Wort = This elixir will stimulate past life experience with crystal gazing. It can be used to develop astral projection through the use of the ball as a doorway. It strengthens our inner vision and light.

Crystal Gazing for Others

It is most important to remember that development of crystal gazing ability does not qualify you to perform psychic readings or consultations professionally. If this is one of your personal goals, it can be a wonderful first step, but it is only one step. Although everyone is psychic, and anyone can develop and provide psychic/intuitive information, IT DOES NOT QUALIFY ANYONE TO BE A COUNSELOR OR AN ADVISOR TO OTHERS!

Equally important to the psychic message and information is its interpretation and application to the individual involved. How is that message being communicated? Is it empowering and helpful? Is it delusionary? Does it imply a lack of free will? Does it help the individual resolve issues in productive ways? If it is negative, are you capable of helping the individual to see the creative possibilities within it? These are just a few obvious considerations.

More than a few people have read some books or taken some development seminars and assumed that it qualified them to use their psychic abilities professionally and publicly. There are those who are simply looking for a reason to hang out their psychic shingle. For many of them, it is a way of saying to themselves and to their acquaintances, "Look at me; I'm special!" For others it is a way of adding glamour to what they perceive as dull and unproductive lives. Some even use it to assert their own "spirituality" to the world. Unfortunately, this is often to the detriment of others.

Many "fast-food psychics" believe that stepping out onto a professional path will move them further along the spiritual path of life. This is a major misconception. Psychic ability has no more to do with making or proving a person spiritual than any other natural ability would. Do we assume that someone who is muscular is more spiritual? Of course not, so when people make similar assumptions based upon psychic ability, they are revealing their ignorance. What is psychic is not always spiritual. What is occult or metaphysical is not always beneficial, and what is appealing is not always appropriate and useful.

If you truly wish to use your gazing ability for others, then do so responsibly. To be successful and effective at anything requires great time, energy, effort and continual preparation. It requires a genuine search for knowledge, and it demands a much greater depth of study.

You should have the ability to draw correspondences and see relationships. You must be able to discern and discriminate the truth from half-truths, illusions from reality. You must be able to take psychic information and apply it creatively and productively for yourself, as well as others. In general, the more educated you are, the more effective you will be as a psychic counselor. The greater and more in-depth your schooling, on any level, the greater your potential for being a physically, emotionally, mentally, psychically, and spiritually creative person. Training and development must be continual.

If you intend to use your psychic gazing ability for others, you must be able to process and apply information in new ways. You must be able to intuitively see possibilities for transforming ordinary data and experiences into new creations. You must be able to help yourself and others to see the creative possibilities within life situations and limitations, no matter how trying they may be.

To demonstrate the psychic without proper awareness of how to apply that knowledge beneficially makes you irresponsible and dangerous. If you intend to use your crystal-gazing ability responsibly for others, then the following three recommendations and suggestions are the least that you should consider.

First, take some courses in psychology and counseling at a local college. If you cannot afford to attend the classes as an actual student, audit them. You will still get the training and information; you just will not receive the accreditation. Second, take classes in public speaking, and interviewing techniques. Study and work on your communication skills—one-on-one and group situations alike.

This third suggestion can be one of the most beneficial. It is to serve as a volunteer. Volunteer for local help-lines, providing assistance and information referrals over the phone. This will help you develop awareness of the local health and social agencies that you can use for resources. It also provides wonderful experience in developing flexibility in communicating to a wider variety of individuals. It will even give you experience in crisis communication, and if you intend to be a professional psychic counselor, there WILL BE crises. Most people who will come to you will need more than just psychic information. They may need referrals to appropriate social agencies and/or professional, therapeutic counseling.

If after all of this and even further preparations on your own you have decided to explore crystal gazing professionally, there is still much to consider. The following basic considerations will help ensure your successful consultations with others:

Expect to Succeed

Most important to your success is your attitude. Expect to succeed. Keep in mind that you are learning something new. You will make mistakes, but you will also hone your skills. Remember that you have something to offer others. Visualize yourself as a catalyst for positive and creative change in the lives of others.

Make Your Preparations

Before gazing for anyone, including yourself, make your preparations. Put your mind in order. Clear out the rubbish of the day. Take time to relax before the person arrives. The more relaxed you are, the more effective you will be.

Don't eat within an hour of the scheduled time for your crystal gazing session, or for at least six hours if you are eating heavily. Make sure you will be undisturbed once the session begins.

Keep the consultation room preparations simple. Many people have misconceptions about anything of the psychic realm. Some see it still as the "devil's work" that is shrouded in mystery. This perception is often promoted by readers who provide their consultations in poorly lit rooms with pungent incense. If your client is uncomfortable and not relaxed, you are less likely to have a successful session. Let the atmosphere of your place of counseling reflect comfortableness. This sets a tone of professionalism and concern which will put the client more at ease.

If you require lowered lights for your crystal gazing, lower them after the client has arrived and after you have explained that it prevents inappropriate reflections from interfering. In this way your client will not be worried about being spooked by what is to occur.

Make your expectations clear. Let your clients know what they can and cannot expect from your consultation. Offer your credentials, and be prepared to offer references.

Let the clients know the costs and time involved. Be consistent with fees. If you are charging a regular fee, make sure you are worth it. Keep the fees reasonable. Exorbitant fees do not reflect the quality of the consultation.

Let the clients know ahead of time if they can record. Inform them of everything they will need to experience an enjoyable session. Explain what the session will entail.

Perform Your Crystal Gazing

Always begin by reviewing for the client how your session will operate. You and the client should take positions on opposite sides of the crystal ball. Uncover the ball, and request that the client pick it up and handle it. Let your client know that this is what will help you to scry with it for him or her. You may wish to tell the client to concentrate on any particular problems or issues upon which he or she would like to focus.

After several minutes, have the client return the ball to the stand. Take a brief moment and make a silent intention or prayer for the visions that you WILL receive. Now begin your gazing just as you would for yourself. If you feel the need, you may wish to turn the ball and look at it from different angles. It is perfectly all right.

Begin by describing out loud for the client what you see and feel while you are gazing. This describing becomes an audible signal to the subconscious mind to further enhance and clarify the vision. It also helps ease nervousness. In addition, it helps to bring out the visions and their understanding to the conscious mind.

Describe what you are seeing and feeling, even if obvious and general. What stands out most strongly for you? Be brief, but start generally, moving to finer points as you go along. Don't try to interpret everything as you go. Describe the images you are seeing first, and there will be time later to clarify and define them. For example, the session might start with: "I see the faint image of a man, standing alone . . . ." Initially, don't try to define who the man is and why he is alone. It is more important to capture the image and describe it first.

Having described one image fully, or one entire scenario, begin your interpretation. Remember, at the very least it means something similar to what you think it does. You would not have seen this image if you could not interpret it. Free associate with it. Of what does it remind you? What does it reflect for you?

Don't ask a lot of questions of the client. This is very disconcerting, and it undermines the client's confidence in you. He or she came to you for the psychic reading. Don't say such things as: "I see a man standing alone. Can you relate to this? Do you understand what this means?" It is not the client's job to interpret for you what you have seen. And if you are asking these kinds of questions of your client, you are not ready to be gazing for other people! It's your vision. YOU MUST INTERPRET!

The worst you are going to be is wrong, and if you are concerned about missing or being off in your interpretation, then you should not be trying to gaze or use your psychic abilities for others. Everybody is wrong sometimes. You need only be right about 20 percent of the time to be better than the laws of chance.

Never assume the client understands what you are saying. Nothing is more frustrating to the client. No matter how obvious something seems to you, it may not be so to the client. Ask the client. If there is hesitation or any indication of incomprehension, re-explain yourself. Sometimes you may have to say the same thing in three or four ways to get the message across and have it be understood. Keep all explanations simple and basic. Break them down and give examples to which the client can relate.

Make sure that you leave time to see if the client has any other specific concerns or questions that were not answered previously in the session through your gazing. Always try to see more for the client than only the issues with which he or she arrived. Giving them a little more than expected is a wonderful way to keep clients satisfied, but coming back.

Thank the client for the opportunity to serve them. Shake his or her hand. Some readers prefer to hug at the end, but any physical gesture is a way of disconnecting and breaking the psychic link at this point. Then cover the ball up.

Do not immediately start cleaning the ball or wiping it off. Your client may take offense, seeing your actions as if the ball had been contaminated. When the client has left, then cleanse the ball and quickly repolish in preparation for the next individual.

Practice using a sandwich technique in your gazing for others. Start with the obvious and the positive. This reinforces self-esteem and puts the client more at ease. Then move to the more troublesome images or issues reflected in the ball. Keep it a discussion. Present what you see and feel, and present options, choices, and possible ensuing events. Allow the client to provide his or her own input.

ALWAYS CONCLUDE ON A POSITIVE NOTE! No matter how difficult things may seem to be, as reflected by the ball, the client must know there are positive opportunities and options available. This doesn't mean that you avoid the negative, but by beginning with appreciation and then making suggestions the client can understand and with which they can work, you contribute to the client's growth and enlightenment. You empower the client and yourself.

Be Professional and Businesslike

Treat everyone with respect and consideration. No two people will ever be alike, but you should employ the same format and behavior with all, to the best of your ability. One area that reveals your respect for the client is punctuality. If the consultation is to be a half hour, make sure it is that. Stay as close to the scheduled time as possible. If you run long with a client, it is unfair to make others wait. Yes, sometimes it does happen, but you can schedule appointments to eliminate this as much as possible.

Let your clients know that you hold to your time frame as closely as possible. If they are late, it is not fair to put the next client behind schedule. If your clients know this, they will rarely ever be late.

Respect the individuality of the client. Don't embarrass them or preach at them. Direct them. Provide guidance and suggestion. Allow them to ask questions. It is not your role to lead the life for or make decisions for your client. Present the information in encouraging ways.

Being a professional, you should not be late for appointments, nor should you ever be rude, impatient, or disapproving. Develop objective detachment. Remove your personal opinions and personal judgments. It's not easy to forget yourself when counseling, but it is what will make you more effective.

After you have worked professionally for a length of time, you will have individuals coming to you, looking for simple solutions to situations that cannot be resolved quickly or easily, and psychic information is the last thing they may need. As a responsible professional, it is your task to recognize this. Individuals who come to you with intense personal problems rarely need or require psychic information. They do need therapy and counseling.

It is your task to refer such individuals to outside sources more qualified to assist them. Use your crystal gazing, if you must, to find the best way of directing them to the proper agency or health practitioner. If the individual insists on a psychic session, use your abilities to present options that encourage proper therapy. Guiding resolution through appropriate choices and courses of action is the most beneficial and professional thing you can do in any situation.

Remember that you are an outsider looking into another's life, but you are an outsider who can very strongly affect another's life. Be objective and warm, and the counseling becomes easier and more productive for you and your clients.

The Good Psychic

- The good psychic counselor is able to attune to the person and/or situation.

- The good psychic counselor is one who will, at the same time of tuning in, be able to perceive how the individual will respond to the psychic information. This information can then be expressed in a non-threatening, productive, and more receptive manner.

- The good psychic counselor will always express the information in a manner that will be understood by the individual.

- The good psychic counselor will provide insight, new possibilities, and beneficial options or courses of action in regard to the situation.

- The good psychic counselor will do all of this without intruding upon the free will of the client.

Exercise 11—
The Crystal Gazing Journal

Keeping a journal of your crystal gazing is one of the best ways to develop and confirm your own scrying abilities. It is an essential part of the development process. By maintaining a scrying and gazing journal, you are telling the subconscious mind that you are committed to expanding your visionary capabilities.

Recording your gazing sessions is also a means of grounding the scrying experience so that you can more easily understand and actualize the visions. Visions are often ethereal, and their significance can elude us. By recording them, we take them out of the ethereal realm and crystalize them into the physical. Recording them and looking at them in black and white will elicit many new significances. Remember that crystal visions are often multi-dimensional, with multiple meanings.

When you record your visions, you are also offering thanks to your higher self. It is a positive acknowledgement of your own gift. Every vision is a gift! If you intend to make crystal gazing an important part of your life, the recording of the vision is part of the gracious reception of the vision. It honors you and that part of you that has the visionary ability.

Recording your crystal visions and your responses to them serves many benefits. The recordings can be used in creative endeavors, and for future inspiration. They help us to consciously bridge levels of the mind, and it also helps us to ground the vision and its energies into greater recognition, helping us to see the quality of our visions. Recording is also a way of absorbing the archetypal energies reflected by the action.

By keeping a crystal gazing journal, our power to communicate (in writing and in word) improves, because our conscious mind is being aligned with our abstract mind. Most importantly, we develop the ability to interpret, create, and ultimately manipulate images and symbols, so that the archetypal energies reflected within the gazing can affect our lives more easily.

There are many ways of setting up and using a crystal gazing journal. Use your own creativity in the process. The more care you take in your journaling work, the stronger the lines of communication with the visionary state. The following are some basic guidelines that you may wish to incorporate:

Dedicate Your Journal

In the front of your journal, write some kind of dedication. Dedicate the journal and your crystal gazing to helping you understand your life and expand your consciousness. You may even wish to include a spiritual verse for inspiration and understanding.

Record the Time and Date of the Crystal Gazing

Have a place in your journal to record the time and date of the crystal gazing session. You may also wish to include the phase of the moon at the time of the gazing. You will probably find that the clarity of the visions you have during the gazing may very likely be affected by lunar influences. This record will help you to determine the most auspicious times.

Record Everything that You Experienced

List the major images and events that appear through the crystal gazing. Everything that you saw, felt, or imagined during the session has significance and should be treated as such. When you review and analyze the information later, you will be able to discern which had validity and which did not.

Create a crystal gazing report. Give your crystal gazing session a title. Don't make it fancy. Let it just state simply what the vision was about. What is the major issue or theme image running through the session? State this theme simply, in a single sentence.

What emotions, if any, surfaced during the session? What were you feeling while performing this gazing? What question(s) did the crystal gazing leave unanswered? If you can figure out what was not resolved or revealed through the gazing, it can sometimes provide insight into what is unresolved and unrevealed in your day-to-day life.

Question Yourself While Recording the Vision

1. Does this relate to something that has happened to you recently?

2. Does it seem to reflect more of what is yet to happen?

3. Does it relate to immediate problems, issues or concerns? Jot down anything that comes to mind in regard to the crystal vision. Visions often reflect what is going on in your life on many levels simultaneously. If any aspect of your life pops into your mind while recording the vision, the possibility is GREAT that it relates to the gazing session in some manner.

Relate Yourself to the Visions

Do not merely interpret the crystal visions. Try to relate it to your life. Remember that it may be symbolic or literal. Trust your first impressions, but don't stop with the obvious. The events, images, and symbols within the crystal vision represent aspects and energies of your life. They will often appear in the gazing in a manner that will help you to see them from a new perspective.

Personally relate yourself and your life to them. What does this image, person, or scenario represent for you? Begin with what the image has always meant to you personally. Later you can build upon it to uncover the more subtle significances. Always begin with the familiar and move to the unfamiliar.

Free associate with the images. This is a process made popular through psychological evaluations. In it, a word is given, and the individual responds with the first thing that comes to mind. Do this with the images, people, and major scenes from the crystal gazing. Don't worry about being off target. It would not come to mind if it wasn't significant on some level.

Perform a Periodic Review

Leave a space in your journal to review your progress. Then periodically go back and look over your crystal visions, comparing them to what has unfolded in your life since the previous session. Are there correlations? Did the crystal gazing reflect any major issues and events that you have encountered since your session? This is an excellent way of tracking your increased ability to understand the crystal visions and to determine what the visions are saying about your life.

Chapter Five

Crystal Ball Rituals

Mention the word ritual to a dozen people, and you will receive a dozen different reactions. Even if you mention it to a dozen metaphysicians, psychics, and spiritual persons, you will still receive different and confusing responses. Much has been written about ritual, but often it is ludicrous or absurd derivations of true ritual techniques. The opinions that people hold toward ritual are often based on entertainment performances, and have nothing to do with reality. Most of these are hype, and reveal little understanding of ritual's true potential for aligning our personal energies with those that are much greater and grander.

It was once assumed that rituals only concerned themselves with angels and demons, but what we must realize is that we use ritual every day of our life. How many of us follow a set routine or ritual every morning? Do we get up, shower, drink our coffee, read the paper, and then go to work? This is a ritual. We have personal rituals, military rituals, religious rituals, social rituals—rituals associated with every aspect of human behavior.

A ritual can be anything done with strong intention and/or emphasis. Ritual is a technique that helps us experience the inner worlds more fully. It is the use of an outer activity to experience inner realities. It opens the doors of passage to inner realms that operate beyond normal, physical consciousness.

The time of temple rituals with robes, lights, and sonorous music is passing away, but perhaps there will always remain a few who will keep the beauty and art of the ancient ritual traditions alive. Modern forms of ritual are more mental, and the temple need only be built in the mind.

All actions are empowered by the amount of significance we attach to them, and thus all rituals are only as powerful as they are significant. Through proper ritual, we learn to utilize and synthesize body, mind, and spirit. Ritual helps us to imprint upon deeper levels of our consciousness the command to integrate and activate energies—according to the purpose of the individual ritual itself. This helps us to cross thresholds in bridging to our innate potentials.

We can create our own powerful rituals built around using the crystal ball and the crystal bowls. The crystal sphere and the crystal bowl serve as instruments that help us to bridge more fully and more consciously to new levels of awareness. Through the ritual use of these tools we become more aware and more capable of using all aspects of ourself. We tap our inner resources more fully.

For any ritual to be effective, there are preliminary considerations. Know what your purpose is for the ritual. Know why you are creating it and involving yourself within it. Make sure that you will know what you need. Imbue and understand the significance of every aspect of it, remembering that the more significance you attribute to all aspects, the more powerful the effects will be.

Preparation is the key to any effective ritual, including those rituals using the crystal ball and the crystal bowls. This includes preparing yourself and your surroundings. The sample exercises in this chapter provide guidelines for basic crystal ball rituals that you can prepare, build upon and use effectively for yourself.

The first two are divination rituals of two distinct varieties. They will help you to see some of the possibilities for ritual scrying. The first employs the Qabala tradition for more powerful divinations with the crystal ball. Although it provides all that you need to have a successful divination session, the more you know of the Qabala and the Tree of Life, the more powerfully it will work for you. For further background on the Qabala, you may wish to consult two of my earlier books: *Simplified Magic: A Beginner's Guide to the New Age Qabala* and/or *Imagick: Qabalistic Pathworking for Imaginative Magicians*.

The second divination ritual employs the use of angelic and spirit influences to enhance the divination process. In recent times, there has been a rebirth of interest in angelic and spirit beings. Throughout the ages, people have used ritual to invoke their aid for guidance and protection. This ritual provides guidelines by which you can do so as well, to enhance your crystal ball gazing.

The crystal ball is not only a powerful divination tool, but it can also be a powerful instrument of health. The third type of crystal ball ritual in this chapter provides guidelines for using your crystal sphere for healing purposes. Preparations and procedures for effective healing rituals are outlined, along with variations with which you may wish to experiment.

Exercise 12—
Divination and the Tree of Life

Different traditions have had their own divination methods. One of the most ancient traditions is that of the mystical Qabala. It is a very ancient form of mysticism, with many philosophical and pragmatic dimensions. On one level, the Qabala teaches how the universe was formed through ten stages of development. On a more practical level, it teaches how to access different levels of the subconscious mind, so that we can more effectively tap our personal potentials and the energies of the universe.

The Tree of Life is the primary symbol and image for working with the system of the Qabala. It is a diagram with ten levels, containing ten spheres or Sephiroth, connected by 22 lines or paths. Each level represents specific and identifiable universal energies, and also a specific level of the subconscious mind through which we can more easily access those more universal energies (see illustration on p. 105).

For example, one level on the Tree of Life, Netzach, reflects the energies of pure emotions, love and relationships in the universe and within our life. Netzach also represents a specific level of our own subconscious mind which mediates and has accessible insight into all issues of emotion, love and relationships. By learning to access that level of the subconscious mind, we gain more direct understanding and perspective of emotions, love, and relationships affecting our life.

The use of crystal balls with the Qabala provide one of the most effective means for tapping the energies of our Higher Self.

Through them we can learn to consciously connect our essence with any other essence in a productive manner—especially for divination purposes.

Correspondences for the Tree of Life

MALKUTH

Divine Name: Adonai Ha-Aretz (*ah-doh-nye hah-ah-retz*)
Archangel: Sandalphon (Prince of Prayers)
Angels: Ashim (Blessed Souls)
Color: Black, Olive, Russet, and Citrine
Crystal Ball: Clear Quartz or Smokey Quartz
Divination Information: Affairs of the home; nature beings and spirit guides; uncovering hidden; health; how to overcome inertia.

YESOD

Divine Name: Shaddai El Chai (*shah-dye-ehl-keye*)
Archangel: Gabriel (Angel of Truth)
Angels: Cherubim (Angels of Light and Glory)
Color: Violet
Crystal Ball: Amethyst
Divination Information: General psychic information; emotional health; tides of change; dreamwork and insight; nature's omens; insight into divine plans.

HOD

Divine Name: Elohim Tzabaoth (*ehl-loh-heem tzah-bah-oath*)
Archangel: Michael (Prince of Splendor and Great Protector)
Angels: Beni Elohim (Sons of God)
Color: Orange
Crystal Ball: Citrine
Divination Information: Truth and dishonesty; communication; business wheeling and dealing; education; scientific knowledge and endeavors.

NETZACH

Divine Name: Jehovah Tzabaoth (*jah-hoh-vah tzah-bah-oath*)
Archangel: Haniel (Angel of Love and Harmony)
Angels: Elohim (Gods and Goddesses)
Color: Green
Crystal Ball: Malachite
Divination Information: Love; relationships; sexuality; creativity and artistic efforts; nature spirits; some money issues and endeavors.

TIPHARETH

Divine Name: Jehovah Aaloah Vadaath (*jah-hoh-vah-ay-loh-ah-vuh-dath*)
Archangel: Raphael (Angel of Beauty, Brightness, and Healing)
Angels: Malachim (Virtues and Angelic Kings)
Color: Gold or Pink
Crystal Ball: Rose Quartz
Divination Information: All health issues; spiritual insight; childhood issues; path to success; revelations of beauty in all things and situations; insight into adversity.

GEBURAH

Divine Name: Elohim Gibor (*eh-loh-heem guh-bur*)
Archangel: Kamael (Prince of Strength and Courage)
Angels: Seraphim (the Flaming Ones)
Color: Red
Crystal Ball: Garnet
Divination Information: Issues of strength and courage; tearing down of the old and building of the new; insight into all changes; insight into enemies and discord.

CHESED

Divine Name: El (*ehl*)
Archangel: Tzadkiel (Prince of Mercy)
Angels: Chasmalim (Brilliant Ones)
Color: Blue
Crystal Ball: Sodalight or Lapis Lazuli
Divination Information: The spiritual path; insight into abundance or lack of in our lives; hypocrisy and bigotry; issues of justice and how to obtain.

BINAH

Divine Name: Jehovah Elohim (*yah-hoh-vah eh-loh-heem*)
Archangel: Tzaphkiel (Prince of Spiritual Strife Against Evil)
Angels: Aralim (the Strong and Mighty Ones)
Color: Black
Crystal Ball: Obsidian
Divination Information: All mother issues; insight into sorrows and burdens; to open to the akashic records; for understanding of all things; uncovering secrets.

CHOKMAH

Divine Name: Jah (*yah*)
Archangel: Ratziel (Prince of Hidden Knowledge and the Concealed)
Angels: Auphanim (Whirling Forces)
Color: Gray
Crystal Ball: Flourite or Quartz
Divination Information: All father-type information; insight into proper course of action; reveals hidden abilities and potentials; insight into the zodiac influences.

KETHER

Divine Name: Eheieh (*eh-heh-yeh*)
Archangel: Metatron (Greatest of the Archangels)
Angels: Chaioth Ha-Qadesh (Holy Living Creatures)
Color: White
Crystal Ball: Quartz
Divination Information: All final ending and new beginning information; transition and change insights; sheds light on spiritual quest; all initiatory activities; new ideas and creativity.

Each level on the Tree of Life has certain ideas, colors, sounds, images, and symbols associated with it. This includes an aspect of the divine that manifests most strongly through that level on the Tree, and the corresponding level of the subconscious mind. We can use all of these aspects to enhance our scrying abilities with the crystal ball. We begin by determining what kind of specific information we are seeking to divine. Then it is a matter of aligning ourselves and our crystal gazing with the corresponding level upon the Tree of Life.

Earlier I described the uses of different kinds of crystal balls. While gazing with some crystal balls will elicit certain kinds of information more easily than with others, it is not necessary to have a ball for every level upon the Tree of Life, or for every type of information you are scrying for. Any quartz ball can be used to access information from any level on the Tree of Life.

The guidelines below will enable you to use any crystal ball to obtain information through Tree of Life divination rituals. All you need have is the information provided from the previous pages on the Qabala and the Tree of Life.

Begin by creating a Tree of Life divination cloth. This cloth will cover the table upon which you perform your crystal gazing. It is only to be used when you are crystal gazing. It will become your sacred cloth.

In the center of this cloth, draw the Tree of Life design, as seen on the opposite page. You may want to encircle it, so it appears as if the Tree of Life is found within its own sphere. The more significance with which you imbue its creation, the more effective it will be as a tool for you in enhancing your crystal gazing.

Make each sphere the appropriate color. You may also wish to write the name for each of the ten levels in its appropriate color. Make it special and unique.

As you work on each sphere, tone the divine name, along with the names for the archangel and angels for that sphere. Do it softly, but with intention, as if you are breathing life into each section. In essence, you are charging each level, so that when you set your crystal ball upon the appropriate level, it will awaken visions and images within the crystal ball appropriate to it.

Before you actually use your divination cloth, meditate with it. Visualize and see this cloth as a tool that will serve your own crystal gazing. Meditate upon the significance and symbolism of the tree. See it as a symbol for the human potential. The tree represents things that grow and evolve. It is the bridge between heaven and the earth, between the con-

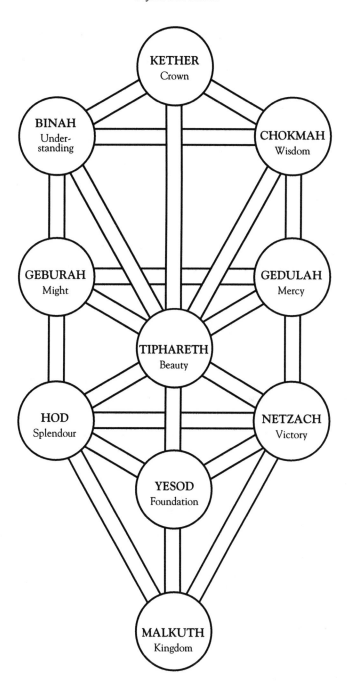

The Tree of Life

scious mind and the subconscious. Visualize and imagine this tree as a miniature channel of energy that will stimulate your own vision through the energies of the crystal ball. Know that when you place the ball, anywhere upon the tree, it will bear fruit for you.

This cloth will become an essential part of your crystal gazing ritual. Keep in mind that it is simply a tool, an outer reminder and reflection of your inner potentials. The following guidelines will help you with ritual divination, but don't feel that you have to hold strictly to them. They are guidelines only, a starting point, and if you wish your crystal gazing to truly be empowered and effective, you must take theses guidelines and adapt them in the manner that works best for you.

1. When not in use, your divination cloth should be folded and kept in a safe, undisturbed place. It should be treated as sacredly as the crystal itself. In this way, when you do take it out, it makes it more special, and it will work more effectively for you. The use of the cloth and its unveiling upon the table you will use for your gazing now becomes a physical gesture, an opening signal to the inner levels of the mind, and to the universe, that you are opening the doors for divination.

2. Having laid the cloth out on the table, determine which level of the Tree of Life is most appropriate for your concerns. For example, if you are gazing for health information, you will want to place your crystal sphere on the level of Tiphareth. Place your crystal ball, while still covered, upon that sphere on the Tree of Life. Take a few moments to relax. Now uncover the crystal ball.

3. Cup your hands gently about the sphere and take several deep breaths, allowing yourself to relax. Feel the energy of the ball, pulsing slightly, as if in rhythm to its position on the Tree of Life.

4. Now close your eyes and tone the divine name for that level on the Tree of Life. This awakens the energy of that level, and aligns it with the energy of the ball.

   As you inhale slowly, sound the divine name silently. As you exhale, sound the name audibly. See this level of the Tree of Life awakening and filling the crystal sphere with its energy. Give each syllable of the divine name equal emphasis. Don't allow yourself to get hung up on "proper" pronunciation. On the previous tables, I have provided phonetic spellings to help with the Hebrew pronunciations. As long as you are close, the divine energies are called into play.

5. Repeat this toning five to ten times. Then tone the name of the archangel and the angels. This is a way of inviting angelic influence to guard and protect your visionary work.

6. Now focus upon the issues for which you wish to gaze, and proceed with the crystal gazing as you would on any occasion, following the guidelines for such given to you earlier in the book.

7. When you have completed the crystal gazing, cup your hands about the crystal sphere once more. Again tone the divine and angelic names. This is a way of thanking the universe and your own higher self for the vision. It also serves as a closing gesture to turn off the visionary connection of the ball, and cleanses the crystal ball of the influences from that level upon the Tree of Life.

8. Now cleanse and cover the crystal ball and return it to its safe place.

9. Next remove the Tree of Life cloth from the table. Fold it and place it safely away until the next divination session.

10. Record your visions and impressions in your crystal gazing journal.

If you wish to further enhance the process, you may wish to use candles of the appropriate color for the level of the Tree of Life that you are accessing with your crystal gazing. Set the candles behind the crystal ball on the table and light them prior to the toning. At the end extinguish them after the final toning. The use of the candles adds even greater power to your crystal gazing. Experiment, and above all else, have fun with the process.

Exercise 13—
Crystal Gazing with the Angels

In recent times, the interest in angels and spirits has greatly increased, but throughout the ages—in most societies—angels and spirits have been invoked to aid in divination and protection. The functions of angels have included praising and attending to the Divine, protecting the faithful and guiding humanity. There have been angels of power, healing, home, nature, art, beauty, creation, and divination—angels associated with every aspect of life.

Angels appear in all literature and all religions. They have been written about in story and song, and can be found in half the books of the

Christian Bible. In the Book of Psalms (Ps. 91), we read, "He hath given his angels charge over thee to keep thee in all thy ways." They have been called messengers, sons and daughters of the Divine, spirits, holy ones, devas, shining ones, nature spirits, seraphim, cherubim, thrones, dominations, virtues, powers, principalities, archangels, or just simply, angels.

There have been angels associated with each day of the week, each season of the year, each sign of the zodiac, for almost every activity and natural rhythm and cycle. As we will see, knowing the various angels and archangels can be beneficial to crystal gazing work. Their influence can be invoked to empower the gazing process and make the scrying more effective. The following tables provide some of the more common associations of the angels to the natural rhythms of the universe. Although different traditions assigned different angelic beings, the following lists, unless otherwise noted, are my own adaptations and correspondences that I have found to be most effective.

Angels of the Seven Days of the Week

Sunday	Raphael
	(sometimes Michael)
Monday	Gabriel
Tuesday	Kamael
Wednesday	Michael
	(sometimes Raphael)
Thursday	Tzadkiel
Friday	Haniel
Saturday	Tzaphkiel

Angels of the Planets

Sun	Raphael
Moon	Gabriel
Mercury	Michael
Venus	Haniel
Mars	Kamael
Jupiter	Tzadkiel
Saturn	Tzaphkiel
Neptune	Ratziel
Uranus	Metatron
Pluto	Kamael

Angels of the Seasons

Autumn	Michael
Winter	Gabriel
Spring	Raphael
Summer	Auriel

Angels of the Zodiac

Aries	Machidiel
Taurus	Asmodel
Gemini	Ambriel
Cancer	Muriel
Leo	Verchiel
Virgo	Hamaliel
Libra	Uriel
Scorpio	Barbiel
Sagittarius	Adnachiel
Capricorn	Hanael
Aquarius	Cambiel
Pisces	Barchiel

Sigils for the Archangels of the Planets

Saturn ♄

Archangel: Tzaphkiel
Color: Black
Keynote: Mother information,
understanding, birth

Jupiter ♃

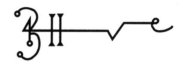

Archangel: Tzadkiel
Color: Blue
Keynote: Money, abundance

Mars ♂

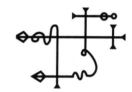

Archangel: Kamael
Color: Red
Keynote: Information on enemies,
courage, judgment

Venus ♀

Archangel: Haniel
Color: Green
Keynote: Love, relationships, sex

Mercury ☿

Archangel: Michael
Color: Orange
Keynote: Business, education,
communication

Moon ☽

Archangel: Gabriel
Color: Violet
Keynote: Changes, dreams, emotions

Sun ☉

Archangel: Raphael
Color: Gold
Keynote: Health, childhood, spiritual path

Sample Angelic Placemat

In this circle is the archangel sigil and planetary symbols for the moon. If drawn in the appropriate color (violet) or used with violet candles during the gazing, this combination enhances crystal visions of changes and emotions (keynote lunar influences).

There are many ways of using this information to enhance your crystal gazing. Many traditions speak of angelic contact through the different signs of the zodiac and through planetary influences. A general astrology book will provide basic information on the various signs and planets, and thus the qualities and energies of the angels associated with them.

There are angels working through every sign and every planet. As each month passes and a new astrological sign comes into play, the influence of that particular group of angels working through that sign also comes into play. They are more easily attuned to during that month. The astrological glyph can be a doorway to connecting more effectively with them.

The same holds true for the angels associated with the planets. The angels of the seven major planets also have sigils (symbols) associated with them. These sigils and the planet's glyph can be used with crystal gazing for information that lies within that angel's and planet's domain. For example, if you are gazing for insight into love and relationships, you would use the sigil for the archangel associated with Venus and the planetary glyph for Venus. These will stimulate images and visions along the lines of their influence within your life. To further enhance this process, use candles of the appropriate color to assist your ritual.

The table on the previous page will provide some basic guidelines that you can use to create an effective crystal gazing ritual. Use the following steps as a guideline, but do not be afraid to adapt them.

1. Begin by determining which angel's influence you require for the information for which you wish to gaze. Take into consideration the day, the season, and the astrological sign in which you are gazing. Jot all the appropriate information down in your crystal gazing journal. This information you will want to save for future references.

2. You will need to make preparations ahead of time. For this crystal gazing ritual you will need parchment paper, candles of the appropriate color, and some drawing materials. These will be used to create an angelic placemat, upon which you will set your crystal ball prior to gazing.

3. Begin by drawing upon the sheet of parchment paper a circle, approximately 4–6 inches in diameter. You may wish to make it the appropriate color for the planetary influence, or use the color for the astrological sign. Include in this magical drawing anything that has significance for your gazing.

4. In the middle of the circle draw the glyph for the planet and/or astrological sign. Along with this, draw the sigil for the archangel of the planet, and even write the name of the archangel as well. You may also wish to tone the name of the angelic influence you seek for your gazing throughout the process of making this placemat. Follow the toning directions given in the previous exercise. Give each syllable of the angelic name equal emphasis.

5. Once the placemat is completed, set your crystal ball and its stand within the center of the circle. If you are using candles of the appropriate color, light them now.

6. Cup your hands about it, close your eyes, and perform deep breathing. As you do this, visualize a being of light in the appropriate color, surrounding you, protecting you, and encompassing you and your crystal gazing. You may wish to perform the angelic toning at this point to enhance the effects.

7. Then open your eyes and perform your crystal gazing as you have learned to do.

8. When you have completed the gazing, cup your hands about the ball once more, and repeat the toning. See this as a way of thanking the angelic influences for the visions during the crystal gazing.

9. Extinguish the candles, cover the crystal ball, and put everything away. You may wish to save the parchment for future use. If this is the case, set it aside where it will not be bothered.

10. Record your visions and impressions in your crystal gazing journal. Include a copy of the design for your angelic placemat. This will serve for inspiration in the future.

Exercise 14—
Healing with Your Crystal Ball

The human body is an energy system. It is comprised of many very subtle energy fields. We can use crystal balls and their natural electrical qualities to interact with the human energy system for health, strength, and balance. The crystal ball can be a stimulus to interact with, stabilize, and correct certain physical, emotional, mental, and spiritual conditions.

Although it is not within the realm of this book to go into all of the subtleties of vibrational healing techniques, this exercise will provide a starting point at which you can apply your crystal ball to holistic health. For further information on vibrational healing techniques, you may wish to consult my earlier book *The Healer's Manual—A Beginner's Guide to Vibrational Therapies*.

Chakras are the primary mediators of all energy within the body and coming into it. Chakra comes from the Sanskrit word meaning "wheel." It refers to a spinning vortex of energy that can be found emanating from positions around the body. They mediate the electromagnetic impulses and other subtle energy impulses of the human energy system.

Although not actually part of the physical body itself, they help link the body's subtle energy fields. Often thought of as metaphysical "mumbo jumbo," modern science and technology are demonstrating that, in the traditional locations given for the chakras, there is a greater electromagnetic emanation from the body.

We can use our crystal balls to stimulate our chakras and their corresponding body parts into greater activity. The electromagnetic of the crystal ball interacts with the electromagnetic of the human body, strengthening and balancing the body's organs and systems. It provides a boost to the body.

Healing through touch has taken many forms throughout history. Massage, acupressure, etheric touch, and laying on of hands are but a few of the more commonly known examples. How healing through touch actually works is still poorly understood. There are a variety of theories, all of which may have validity.

It is important to acknowledge that when certain acts are performed, specific effects will result. We all have the ability of effecting changes in our energies, physical and subtle, even if we don't understand it, and that shouldn't preclude us from using them. Most people do not know how antibiotics or even aspirin work within the body, but we can attest to the results, and so we use them.

The first healing ritual involves balancing and energizing the chakras. On the following pages are diagrams of their traditional location within the body. Each chakra is linked to specific systems and organs of the body.

The vibrations of the crystal ball are absorbed through the chakra centers. This vibration is then transmitted into the vertebrae of the spine, and then transferred along nerve pathways to the organs, tissues, etc. to which they are linked. Imbalances are thus balanced.

The Seven Major Chakras

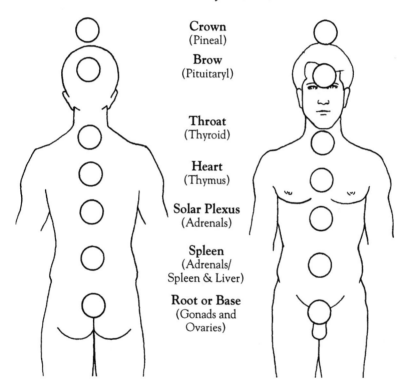

Crown
(Pineal)

Brow
(Pituitaryl)

Throat
(Thyroid)

Heart
(Thymus)

Solar Plexus
(Adrenals)

Spleen
(Adrenals/
Spleen & Liver)

Root or Base
(Gonads and
Ovaries)

The Chakra System

The chakras mediate all energy within, coming into, and going out of the body. They help distribute energy for our physical, emotional, mental, and spiritual functions. The seven major chakras are points of greater electromagnetic activity within the auric field. The hands and feet are other points of great activity.

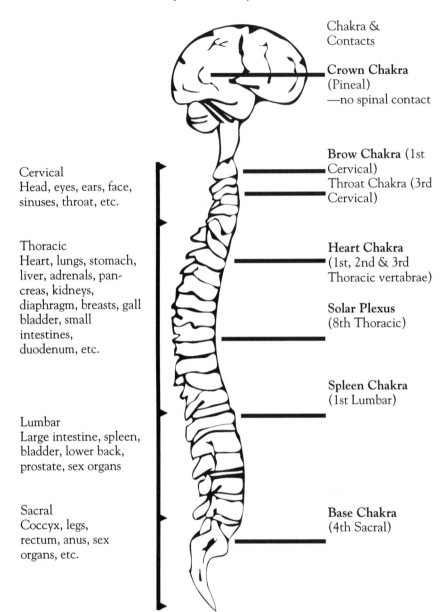

Chakra &
Contacts

Crown Chakra
(Pineal)
—no spinal contact

Brow Chakra (1st
Cervical)
Throat Chakra (3rd
Cervical)

Heart Chakra
(1st, 2nd & 3rd
Thoracic vertabrae)

Solar Plexus
(8th Thoracic)

Spleen Chakra
(1st Lumbar)

Base Chakra
(4th Sacral)

Cervical
Head, eyes, ears, face,
sinuses, throat, etc.

Thoracic
Heart, lungs, stomach,
liver, adrenals, pan-
creas, kidneys,
diaphragm, breasts, gall
bladder, small
intestines,
duodenum, etc.

Lumbar
Large intestine, spleen,
bladder, lower back,
prostate, sex organs

Sacral
Coccyx, legs,
rectum, anus, sex
organs, etc.

Spinal Contacts of the Chakras

Vibrations can be absorbed or projected through the chakras. The vibration is
transmitted into the vertebrae of the spine, then transferred along nerve pathways to the organs, tissues, etc., to which they are linked. Imbalances can thus be
balanced.

Chakra Correspondences

The following are the major chakras and their physical connections within the human body:

Base Chakra

Located in the area of the coccyx at the base of the spine. It is tied to the circulatory system, reproductive system, and the functioning of the lower extremities.

Spleen Chakra

This center is tied to the function of the adrenals, and it influences the reproductive and the entire muscular systems of the body. It also influences the eliminative system and the organs associated with it. Work with this area assists in detoxifying the body.

Solar Plexus Chakra

This center is linked to the solar plexus area of the body. It influences the digestive system and all of its organs, assisting the body in the assimilation of nutrients. Many crippling diseases, intestinal problems and psychosomatic problems are eased by working with this center.

Heart Chakra

This center influences the entire immune system, circulatory system, and all organs associated with it. It has ties to all heart and childhood diseases, and it affects tissue regeneration.

Throat Chakra

This center is tied to the functions of the throat, esophagus, mouth and teeth, thyroid and parathyroid. It affects the respiratory system and the functions of the bronchial and vocal apparatus.

Brow Chakra

This center influences the endocrine system of the body, particularly the pituitary. It has links to the immune system, and the synapses of the brain. It is linked to the functions of the eyes, ears, and the face in general.

Crown Chakra

This chakra center is tied to the functions of the entire nervous system and the entire skeletal system of the body. It influences the pineal, all nerve pathways, and all electromagnetics of the body.

1. Always begin a healing session by centering yourself. Relax. Perform a progressive relaxation or meditation prior to starting.

2. Take a seated or prone position. Whatever is most comfortable is best.

3. Take the crystal ball and cup it between your hands. Now roll it briskly between the palms for about 30 seconds. This activates the energy of the ball and the chakras in your hands, which will make it easier for you to stimulate your other chakras.

4. Lay the crystal ball against the chakra point on the body, holding it next to it with both hands. Start with the base chakra. Close your eyes and breath deeply. Try to imagine and feel the pulsing of the ball against the body. Now slowly roll the crystal ball in a circle over the chakra point for 30–60 seconds. Pause and repeat two more times.

5. Now move the crystal ball up to the spleen center, and repeat the procedure. Continue all the way up the body, energizing each chakra in turn.

6. To enhance the effects, you may wish to massage the chakra point longer. Trust your feelings with this.

7. Having stimulated all seven chakra points, return to the chakra that is tied to any particular problem you have been having. Give this point some extra work. Then return to doing all seven points once more for some extra balancing.

8. Having energized and stimulated all seven chakra points, you may wish to roll the crystal ball over the two major meridians of the body. Meridians are natural nerve/energy pathways. Two of the most important for balance and health are the governing and the conception meridians. (Refer to the diagram on the following page.) These two meridians govern the polarities of the body and affect the interrelationship of the seven major chakras.

   To run these meridians with the crystal ball, you may need the assistance of a second party. Take a prone position, and have the individual slowly roll the crystal ball up and down the spine, rolling the ball on either side of the actual spine, following the pathway in the diagram. Then turn over and perform this on the front.

9. If you wish to enhance the procedure, while running these meridians with the crystal ball, have the individual hold a quartz crystal in one

hand and an obsidian in the other. It will further enhance balancing the polarities of the body. This rolling/running of the meridians with the crystal ball can be performed with all meridian pathways in the body with great health results. All of the major meridians are depicted in my book *The Healer's Manual.*

10. To conclude the healing, allow yourself to sit up, if you haven't already. Take the crystal ball again within both hands. Close your eyes, and slowly perform some deep breathing. As you do, feel and imagine the crystal ball pulsing energy into you through your hands, and into every cell of your body. Visualize yourself stronger, healthier, and more vibrant. See yourself shining with crystalline energy—a true being of light.

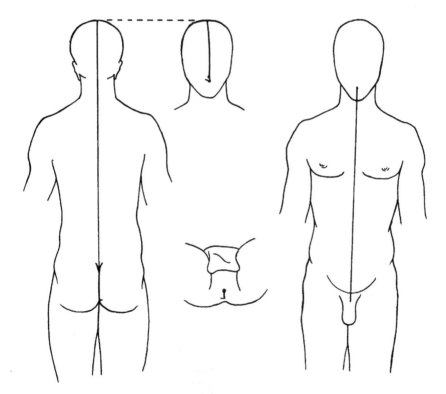

Governing and Conception Meridians

These two meridians are critical to the balance of polarity in the body. The governing is masculine, and the conception is the feminine.

Part Two

Song of the Crystal Bowl

Chapter Six

Birth of the Crystal Bowls

All life is in motion. Every atom of every molecule of every cell, in everything seen or unseen, vibrates because all life (animate and inanimate) is energy.

Vibration and the movement of energy at its most intimate levels is easily detected in physical life. Our cells change continually—growing and altering. When we convert ice into water and then into steam through application of heat, we are speeding up the vibration or the movement of atoms that comprise the molecules of water. This is known as the transmutation of energy. We alter its form and vibrational frequency for new purposes.

One of the most effective ways of transmuting our own energies, consciousness, and life conditions (physical or spiritual) is through the use of sounds and tones. Sacred sound—whether as prayer, music, song, incantation, or chants—is a vital force which permeates every aspect of creation. In all the world cosmologies and religions, sacred sound is considered the basis of existence.

The book of John in the Christian Bible states, "In the beginning was the Word . . ." According to the ancient Hebrew Qabala, the world came into being through the utterance of the sacred name of God, known as the tetragrammaton YHVH. It was for this reason that, within the Judaic faith, this name was never allowed to be written or spoken. In Ethiopian cosmology, God is said to have created both Himself and the universe through the utterance of his own name. In Egypt, Thoth used words in order to create the universe. Legends and scriptures prevail in almost all of the ancient societies of this creative power of sound. Out of the Womb of Silence came forth Sound, and with Sacred Sound came life!

Sound has always been considered a direct link between humanity and the gods. At some point, all of the ancient mystery traditions taught their students and initiates the use of sound as a creative and healing force. It has been considered the oldest form of healing.

There is occurring today a re-emergence and re-expression of the elements of sacred sound. Sound, music, and voice is being applied to aspects of life both physical and metaphysical. Music is being used to alter physical energies, alleviate pain, and to restore homeostasis to physiological and psychological states. It is enjoying new applications in the achievement of altered states of consciousness as well. (Refer to the charts on the following two pages.)

The use of sounds, musical instruments, and voice is being re-examined. Many of the ancient techniques and instruments are enjoying new-found popularity. A partnership is developing between ancient mysticism and modern science in the application of sacred sound in many of its various forms. One of these partnerships has resulted in the creation of the quartz crystal bowl.

The quartz crystal bowl is a dynamic symbol of this linking of ancient mysticism and new high technology. It is rooted in the mysticism of the past, but it is also a bridge to the wondrous mysteries of the future. It is both a symbol and a tool for the alchemical process. It can be used to assist in the transmutation of physical energies and for the raising of consciousness. It harmonizes the heart and mind—the physical with the spiritual.

Crystals have acquired tremendous popularity in the 1980s. They are the heart of the tools of the communication field—with their crystal transistors and computer chips. Aside from the technological foundation, they have been found to be excellent tools for inner communication as well—communication with our own individual creative essences.

This book does not intend to explore the scientific aspects of how quartz crystals generate and transmit energy. There are references in the bibliography to assist with that. This text is designed to show how bowls made of quartz crystal can be used as a dynamic tool of sacred sound—as many instruments in the past have been. It is designed to show how they can be used to heal, to awaken creativity, and to expand consciousness.

Metaphysical Elements of Music

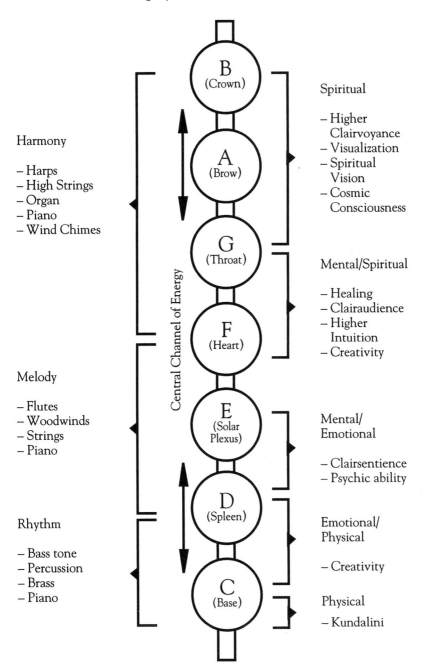

Harmony

– Harps
– High Strings
– Organ
– Piano
– Wind Chimes

Melody

– Flutes
– Woodwinds
– Strings
– Piano

Rhythm

– Bass tone
– Percussion
– Brass
– Piano

B (Crown)

A (Brow)

G (Throat)

F (Heart)

E (Solar Plexus)

D (Spleen)

C (Base)

Central Channel of Energy

Spiritual

– Higher Clairvoyance
– Visualization
– Spiritual Vision
– Cosmic Consciousness

Mental/Spiritual

– Healing
– Clairaudience
– Higher Intuition
– Creativity

Mental/ Emotional

– Clairsentience
– Psychic ability

Emotional/ Physical

– Creativity

Physical

– Kundalini

Table of Correspondences of Sacred Sounds

Chakra	Tone	Vowel Sound	Man-tram	Color	Attribute	Healing Property
Root	Middle C (Do)	ū (ooo)	Lam	Red	Vitality, Kundalini, Life force	Circulation, low blood pressure, colds and shock
Spleen	D (Re)	ō (oh)	Vam	Orange	Creativity, Reserve-energy, sexual	Muscles, reproduction, detoxifying, emotional balance, sexuality
Solar Plexus	E (Mi)	aw/ah	Ram	Yellow	Inspiration, intellect, wisdom, psychism	Digestion, laxative/constipative, headaches, adrenals
Heart	F (Fa)	ā (ay)	Yam	Green	Love/healing, balance, Akashic memory	Heart trouble, lungs, ulcers, hypertension, blood/circulation
Throat	G (Sol)	ĕ (eh) (ă/ŭh)	Ham	Blue	Clairaudience, cooling, relaxing	Throat, fevers, asthma, lungs, thyroid, antiseptic stimulation
Brow	A (La)	ĭ/ē (ĭh/ee)	Aum/Om	Indigo	Third eye, clairvoyance, spirituality	Purifier (blood), obsessions, coagulant, sinuses, headaches, stroke afflictions
Crown	B (Ti)	ē (ee)	Om	Violet	Christ Consciousness, inspiration	Soothing to nerves, stress, confusion, neurosis, insomnia, skeletal problems
*Soul Star (Transpersonal 8th chakra	High C (above middle C	——	Om	Purple or Magenta	That part of Soul linked to matter, link to our true spiritual essence	Building the Body of Light, key to burning away forms that hinder physical and spiritual health for discipleship

A Brief History of the Bowls

The quartz crystal bowl is based upon the concept of the ancient Tibetan singing bowls and bells. Unlike other bells in the world, the Tibetan singing bowls are known for their exotic sounds which hover in the air long after they have been played. It is one of the most powerful healing instruments of sacred sound, and its uses are multiple. Not much is known of their history *per se*, but it is generally recognized that they were created specifically to elicit tones for healing and ritual purposes.

The bowls are made from seven metals. These include gold, silver, nickel, copper, zinc, antimony, and iron. Some sources have claimed that the iron ore from which they are created is the iron ore from meteorites. The veracity of this has yet to be confirmed, but even if not true, it still reflects a cosmic power that is recognized—if unexplained.

Many of these bowls are 40 to 50 years old and were made by the Buddhist priests, prior to the Communist takeover of Tibet, but the bowls themselves date back centuries in their uses. The manner in which the metals are combined is secret, for the originals are all handmade. The masters that make them are no longer allowed to participate in this practice as the communists consider such a use of minerals and metals to be "frivolous."

**The Tibetan Singing Bowl and Tingshas are the basis
of using crystal bowls for sacred sounds.**

Each bowl has its own predominant tone when struck like a bell with the "wand" or striker. It also sets off a series of overtones. The bowls are also played by running the wand along the edge of the bowl, encircling it.

The tone from the Tibetan bowl balances all of the chakras and brings the subtle bodies into alignment, and synchronizes the hemispheres of the brain. It shatters any accumulated energy debris in the etheric body. The tone permeates the cells within the body to release blockages or restore vibrational balance. It breaks up rigid energy patterns and restores the circular flow of energy to the aura.

The Tibetan bowl calms the mind and balances the body. It facilitates altered states of consciousness. Similar to listening to the rhythmic pattern of a drum, the wave pattern of the bowl enables one to achieve an alpha brain wave pattern. The bowls can be used to induce trance conditions for vision quests, and many shamanic practitioners are utilizing them for astral journeys.

The other Tibetan instrument that the crystal bowl is based upon is the Tibetan Ghanta (bell) and dorje set. Traditionally, they are used by monks, nuns and lay people while performing rituals. As with many of the Tibetan instruments and tools, they are highly symbolic. The ghanta is the symbol of wisdom, while the dorje is the symbol of compassion.

The ghanta and dorje are used in religious ceremonies. The bell represents the female aspect of our energies. This is called the *prajna* or wisdom aspect. The dorje represents the male aspect of ourselves. This is referred to as *upaya*, or the method for using wisdom. (The dorje is sometimes referred to as the thunderbolt.)

As the bell is toned, the dorje is handled in such a manner as to circulate the energy about yourself. The two together help to restore the balance of male and female energies in you. In yoga this would be comparable to opening the flow of prana energy known as the

Singing Bowl

Ida and the Pingala in a balanced central channel of energy known as the Susumna.

It was from the effects of these that the idea for creating the quartz crystal bowls would unfold, which when played would follow similar patterns as the Tibetan bells and bowls, but would be comprised of the crystalline quartz energy.

The substance used in the making of the quartz bowls is silica, a sand-like, pure quartz. The sand is placed into a mold that is spinning with centrifugal force. At the proper moment, an electric arc torch is ignited, reaching temperatures of several thousand degrees centigrade, and the individual silica particles are melted into an unified whole.

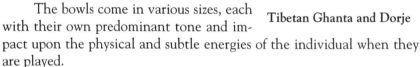

The bowls come in various sizes, each with their own predominant tone and im-

Tibetan Ghanta and Dorje

pact upon the physical and subtle energies of the individual when they are played.

They are played in much the same manner as the Tibetan bowls, but because they are made of quartz crystal, the dynamics of their energy effects upon the body and consciousness of the individual is tremendous. The human body resonates strongly to quartz energy. The electrical aspects of the quartz emanations trigger strong responses within the crystalline structures and patterns of the human body. This, in conjunction with the sound vibrations that will echo around and inside body cavities, makes for a dynamic harmonic response level by the individual to the bowl.

There are many uses and effects of the crystal bowl, as listed below and on the next page. Major characteristics will be explored in this and the following chapters.

- Balances the hemispheres of the brain.

- Cleanses the auric field.

- Creates a sacred spiral of energy which can be used for physical and spiritual purposes.

- Induces altered states of consciousness.

- Depending on the bowl, they will effect physiological systems of the body.

- Purify and cleanse water.

- Purify and charge other crystals and stones.

- Effective tools for healing in general (as will be explored in Chapter Eight), especially long-distance healing.

- Can be used to assist in astral travel and shamanic journeys.

- Are dynamic tools for manifesting through prayer or affirmations.

- Can be used to empower aromatherapy.

- Can be used to create elixirs from flowers and gems for healing and magic.

- Assist in attuning to spiritual guides, angels, and devas.

- Intensify meditational experiences.

- Can be used to explore time—past, present, and future.

- Can be used to align oneself more harmoniously with astrological influences.

- Can be used to develop the ability for scrying.

- Can be used to empower rituals.

- Can be used to create or bond relationships.

- Can be used for manifesting abundance.

Symbolism of the Crystal Bowl and the Wand

The crystal bowl is as much a symbol as it is a tool. It is the understanding of the symbolism that will empower its usage, especially for magical purposes. Just as with the Tibetan bowl and bell, there is a masculine and a feminine aspect to the bowl. The bowl itself is a symbol of the feminine energies, and the wand is the symbol of the masculine. When the male and female are brought together, creative energy is released. New birth occurs. In this case it is the birth of sacred sound, sound that will work according to the individual's programming.

All bowls, all cups, all cauldrons are symbols of the divine feminine energies of the universe. This is the energy of the womb from which new life issues forth. In the use of the bowls, the new sound is what issues forth.

The bowl's circular shape is both dynamic and complex, for it has no beginning and no end. It represents all that is unmanifest, along with all of the possibilities. The womb is the primal feminine wisdom, wisdom that manifests in silence, but is expressed with understanding. It is the symbol of illumination, intuition, and imagination, but for it to benefit our lives, the symbols must be brought forth out of the circle of the womb into expression.

The bowl is a symbol of the cyclic energies of life—this is why it has ties to the energies of the moon. The lunar phases reflect subtle energy changes. The moon has a light and a dark side, an inner and an outer expression. The bowl also has its inner and outer expressions—silence and sound.

The feminine, in its symbol of the bowl, reflects itself through mystery. It is a gate through which we may enter or leave. It is the symbol of humanity upon the earth. Through the earth energies (sound being one of them) we can be born again.

A bowl holds and contains elixirs of all kinds. It can also be used to pour them out. Learning when to hold and when to pour forth new life is part of what those who will master the bowl must learn. The bowl shapes whatever is in it according to its own shape, and yet it can always pour forth the elixirs of life.

The bowl is one of the ancient symbols for the Holy Grail. This quest teaches us that we cannot separate who we are from what we do. It is what helps us to find our spiritual essence and how best to manifest it within the circumstances of our lives.

The bowl is also tied to the symbol and energies of the cornucopia. The original cornucopia was from the horn of the goat Amaltheia, who became the constellation for Capricorn. It is a symbol of infinite supply. This serves to remind us that we can use the bowl to multiply what we have within our lives. The bowl teaches us that giving never diminishes our supplies or energies.

The bowl is the Great Mother. It is the substance of the universe; the symbol of all forms of the universe. It is a symbol of one half of the creative principle of life.

The wand is the other half of the creative principle. It is a symbol of the masculine energy. Many do not refer to the striker or mallet for the bowl as a "wand," but the term is most appropriate to the functions of the bowl. It is the activating or releasing force. When applied to the bowl, sound is created and issues forth in accordance with the will.

While the bowl is the Mother, the wand is the Father. It is what is used to draw from the great bowl of life. While the bowl holds the seeds of matrix of life or manifestation, it is the wand which brings those things forth that are desired. Wands help us to magnify and select the creative process.

Wands have been used in many societies. Most people are familiar with the magic wand of the stage magician. This is just a prop, but a true wand is one that serves a creative function in the process of transformation. When they are used with the crystal bowls, a wand will release the Sacred Sound within the bowl into physical manifestation.

Many believe that the wand used with the crystal bowls is insignificant, as long as it creates the sound. That sound, though, can issue forth with greater focus, the more we imbue our wands with greater significance. With the wands, we are manifesting sound—creating sound—where there was none. Thus they are more than just a piece of wood or metal, wrapped in leather. They have great significance. The more significance we apply to them, the more focused and directed will be that manifestation of energy according to our goals.

Wands are channels of energy, and as much care should be given to them as to the bowls themselves. Shown below are several examples of wands that can be used to play the bowls. Make them personally, if you can. If not, create a ritual or add to them in ways that make them unique and special to you.

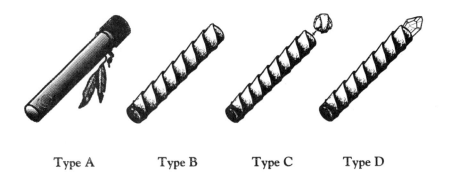

Type A   Type B   Type C   Type D

Many wands for the crystal bowls are merely wooden dowels upon which has been placed a rubber end. Simple and effective, it is a reminder to keep our energies and creation process simple at first. This simple type of wand can still be imbued with greater significance. Add to it feathers or colors, or even stones that are special to you. Some wood is easy to carve, and one of my bowl wands has the sigils for the archangels of the four quarters of the earth carved into it. Whatever you decide to do, do it deliberately. Make the wand your own, so that every time you use it, it is more than just a mallet. It is a magical instrument in the creation process.

Type B is another common form of the wand used with crystal bowls. It is simply a piece of copper tubing, capped at both ends and wrapped in suede to create friction on the bowl. It is the friction which draws out the sound from the bowl itself. Cut the copper tubing the length that has significance to you. A study of numerology and the significance of numbers can help you in creating wands of different lengths to serve different purposes. Choose a color of suede that has significance to you. With an inexpensive wood-burning set, you can also burn designs into the suede. Again it is important to make it personal and significant to you.

Type C is a variation of Type B. Its design came from a friend in Colorado named Dara Bowers, who has made the bowls a viable aspect of her life. In this one, instead of capping off both ends, keep one end open, and use a ball of suede as a plug that you can insert and take out as you desire. You can then use this by writing out, on parchment or paper, affirmations, desires, prayers, wishes, or names of those to be healed. Then insert the paper into the tube, plugging it with the ball of suede. Then as you play the bowl, the energy is directed toward the thoughts upon the paper. This will be explored further in chapter two.

Type D is a more traditional crystal wand. You can place crystal points on either or both ends of the wand. These can add power to the wands or a particular focus of energy. For information on constructing these, I refer you to the work by Michael G. Smith, *Crystal Power* (Llewellyn Publications; St. Paul, 1985).

There is much sexual symbolism in the use of the bowl and wand in creating sound. Sexual energies are physical manifestations of more dynamic spiritual energies at play. These are the creative impulses and the key to the true alchemical process. An ancient pagan ritual involves placing a knife into a cup, symbolizing the union of the Father with the Mother. This is the act of creation.

Every time you use the wand with the bowl, you are symbolically doing the same thing. Anytime the male and female unite, whether sexually or on other levels, there is a creation of new energy expressions. This energy expression is greatly determined by the focus of one's thoughts at the time of the uniting.

The wand and the bowl become an extension of your own energies. They amplify and empower. They represent the renewal of life, the union of the sun and moon upon the earth so that the Holy Child within can be born.

The bowl and wand together are the symbols of birth and initiation. It is the joining of crown and scepter, the marriage of opposites, to bring new expression and harmony. The "sacred marriage" was celebrated in many societies as the marriage between the god and goddess, the sun and moon, heaven and earth. It is this ancient symbolism of marriage that is reflected in the crystal bowls: "Marriage symbolism remains basically similar in all the world over . . . The ring represents power and dignity; it shares the symbolism of the circle as completeness, fulfillment, continuity, and, by extension, imperishableness. This completion and fulfillment, expected of marriage, binds to a new state, to a new life, but it also expands in the fullness and completeness of that life." (Cooper, J. C. *Symbolism—The Universal Language*. Aquarian Press, Northhamptonshire, 1982, p. 90.) It is this which is activated through the crystal bowl and its wand.

The Creation of Sacred Space with the Bowl

The crystal bowl is played in the same manner as was described for the Tibetan bowl. The wand encircles the bowl, the friction of the two creates a vibration that emanates from the womb of the bowl as sound. (Explicit directions on playing the bowls is covered in Chapter 7.)

This act is the linking of the male and female, as symbolized by the wand and bowl. It is also an act creating wholeness. We are all a combination of male and female energies. Often they are out of balance. The playing of the bowl creates a place and space of sacredness. It is a point where there is no separation of male and female, day and night, darkness and light, positive or negative, physical and spiritual. It creates an intersection where all possibilities exist.

The most powerful means of playing the bowl is in this circular motion; the motion in itself is highly symbolic. The circle is the perfect symbol, for it has no end or beginning. We can start anywhere within the circle and become creative. The movement of the circle brings to mind the turning of wheels, as in the wheels of life, as well as the movement of the sun and planets. The circle is the time cycle of the universe. It seals in and it seals out. It separates the inner from the outer. As we learn to move in circular spirals, we can move from the inner to the outer and back again.

The making of a circle—in dance, ritual, or in playing the bowl—is an act of creation. We are first creating a sacred space within the mind, a place between worlds where the physical and the spirtual worlds intersect and play upon each other. The creation or marking off of a circle in Wiccan beliefs is referred to as the raising of a cone of power. The circling creates a vortex.

As the bowl is played, you will hear and feel the sound circling around you. It cleanses all within the circle, strengthens it, and opens the doors to new experiences of energy.

The circle playing of the bowl is a symbol of the sun and the moon—the male and the female together. When the inner and outer, the sun and the moon, are joined, the dance of life begins. Thus the playing of the bowl is an ideal rite of preparation before meditations and ritual. It creates a sacred space, one of higher creativity.

The playing of the bowl is the sexual act for ritual releases of creative energies. There have been many symbols of this process around the world. One of the most common is the union of moon and sun, as in the illustration here. To further enhance this creation of sacred space, place symbols intimate to your highest aspiration upon the bowl and the wand. This enables the creative act to work even more effectively. Placing the symbol of the sun and moon upon the wand and bowl will amplify their creative aspects.

**Union
Symbol**

Just as you need to make the bowl and the wand your own through personalizing them with symbols and energies intimate to you, you can draw on the bowl's symbols and images appropriate to your ritual playing. As you play them, the energies represented by the symbols on the bowl are manifested and set in motion. (Some bowls are smooth and clear, and it is easier to draw on symbols and wash them off. Other bowls, especially those larger than ten inches, are opaque and have rough surfaces. It can be difficult to remove symbols drawn on them, even when using water soluble colors.)

When you play the bowl, you are releasing energy along the lines you have determined by your thoughts and your focus. Those thoughts and focal points are facilitated and concentrated through symbols and images, or words and phrases, that are appropriate to your goals. The energy you release through the playing creates a sacred space beneficial for and appropriate to your design(s).

Exercise 15—
Invoking the Empress of the Crystal Bowl

As you begin to work with your bowl and experiment, you will be drawn into contact with a great archetypal force that works through and behind all of the crystal bowls. As we will explore later, there are spiritual guides and devas that will assist you as you work to become the priest/ess of your bowl, but this archetypal force operates even beyond them. It is a force that I have come to call the Empress of the Bowl.

In the ancient mystical Qabala, there are 10 levels at which the divine operates within the world and within the consciousness of the individual. Two of these represent the seats of the primal male and female forces within us (represented on the Tree of Life by Binah and Chokmah).

An example of designs drawn upon the bowl to more pointedly direct the energy. These designs are those appropriate to amplifying the joining of the male and female forces for new expression.

The bridge to linking them is a path associated with the Empress card in the tarot. When you work with your bowl, you are sending a message to the universe and to deep levels of the subconscious mind which mediate the primal male and female forces that operate within your life.

It is often difficult to determine specifically how these archetypal forces will manifest in any single individual's life, as archetypal energies express themselves in accordance with the individual's own unique energies. When you play the bowl for any purpose, you are releasing those energies and they will manifest in the physical life. The bowl sends out a call-signal to that archetypal force, symbolized by the Empress, to draw her energies more dynamically into your life.

In the tarot, the Empress is pictured as a pregnant woman, full of life and expression. It is she who brings the blessings into our lives. She awakens opportunities for us to acknowledge our own blessings and to give thanks for them. It is she who helps us to understand that through the feminine (the illumined soul), the Christ within is born. It is she who helps us to recognize our own ability to create and give birth within our lives. She teaches us, through the bowl, the universal processes of joy and love and reproduction—physical and spiritual.

Rest assured that when you get your bowl, new birth will be initiated. Doors and opportunities you have not seen nor considered will open. Hidden talents and abilities will be born. The opportunity to merge the imagination with reality will arise. Whether or not you take advantage of such opportunities will be your free choice.

It is important to know that this is set in motion from the moment you take possession of your bowl. It is important to honor this energy. Meditating upon the tarot card of the Empress is one such way. Visualize yourself stepping into the scenery of the card itself, and allow the Empress to greet you. Give your thanks to her for the assistance. Let her show you ways in which you can apply the bow uniquely within your own life. As a prelude, you may wish to place the Empress card inside the bowl before playing it and entering into the meditation. (This can actually be done with any tarot card. It deepens the effect, and it helps you in connecting with the essence of the cards.)

Reading and meditating upon myths and tales of birth, especially those involving the birth of the goddesses, is a way of acknowledging and honoring the process you are setting in motion.

Yes, the bowl is a wonderful, joyful instrument, but it is also a powerful invocation. Such an invocation opens new adventures and greater responsibility. It opens the door to learning the creative power of the

Logos—Sacred Sound. As you begin to work with it and develop greater facility for its use, you will encounter healing, blessings, and opportunities to assist others. You will learn what you need to transmute within your own life and you will be given choices as to what you wish to give birth. You will meet the guides and angels of song and sound, and, even more importantly, you will ultimately encounter and experience the great archangelic force that I have come to call the Empress of the Crystal Bowl.

1. For this exercise, as with all within this book, make sure that you will be undisturbed. Remove phones from the hook, etc.

2. Make sure you have read chapter two before working with this exercise. It is important that you be familiar with your bowl and have cleansed it prior to this invocation. Take time to work with the "Crystal Energy Absorption" exercise described in Chapter Seven. Take time to play with your bowl and become familiar with its tones and some of its effects on you.

3. Having familiarized yourself with the bowl, perform a cleansing of it. You may even wish to do the "Crystal Bowl Ritual Bath" prior to this exercise. Keep in mind the significance of every aspect. The more significance you imbue to it, the more you empower it to work its magic.

4. Review the significance of the Empress, as described earlier. If you have books on the tarot, you may want to read about the Empress.

5. Having cleansed the bowl and reviewed some of the major significance of the bowl and wand symbology, retire to your meditation area with your bowl, wand, and the Empress card from your tarot deck.

6. You may wish to light a candle to help set the tone. Use a green-colored candle if you can. Green is the color of growth and new birth. If you do not have a green candle, a white one will do.

7. Assume a comfortable seated position. You may set the bowl on the floor in front of you. Place the wand inside of the bowl, as if in a state of preparation. By the light of the candle, contemplate the image and scenery of the tarot card, keeping in mind that all aspects of it are symbolic of the archetypal energies of new birth and reproduction.

8. Having assimilated the picture, withdraw the wand from the bowl with your right hand, and place the tarot card in the bowl itself. Tap the bowl three times, softly, on the side. This "ringing" is a call to attention and a ritual opening of the sacred space.

9. Hold the bowl in your left hand (feminine hand) and begin to encircle it with the wand in a clockwise direction. (For a bowl larger than ten inches, allow it to sit on the floor—holding it will be awkward.)

10. As the bowl begins to sing, allow your eyes to close. See and feel the sacred sound circling around you, spiralling and creating a vortex of energy. When you can feel and hear the circling of the sound, visualize—imagine—a door forming itself before you. As it forms, there is a life-size painting of the Empress tarot card upon the door. When the door is formed, stop playing the bowl, and as the last sounds fade, place the wand within the bowl, and the bowl upon your lap.

Invoking the Empress

You stand before this door, and you begin to realize that it is not truly a painting of the Empress upon the door. Rather it is an open door through which you can see the scenery of the Empress card in real life. You know that you must walk through the door, for this is the same as encircling the bowl with the wand.

You step across the threshold, and you find yourself enveloped in darkness. For a moment there is anxiety, as you were sure there were grass and trees here just a moment before. Then you smell the sweetness of a summer day. The darkness brightens and you find yourself standing naked within a field of green grass.

In the distance are the sounds of a waterfall and birds singing. The grass beneath your feet is soft and luxurious. A stream flows through this open meadow. Flowers of every color and fragrance fill your senses. In the distance, sitting upon a crystal throne, enjoying the beauty of life continually born anew within this meadow, is a woman of great beauty—pregnant with life herself. Upon her lap rests a scepter, in the shape of the orb of the full moon upon the equal-armed cross. At her feet lies a crystal bowl. Engraved into the bowl itself are ancient symbols of the united male and female forces of the universe. Some you recognize, while others are not in the least familiar to you.

You sit quietly before her. She places the scepter within the crystal bowl and she speaks. Although you do not understand all she says, her words touch your heart with love and joy.

"To give birth is to discover the great song of harmony. One who gives is a catalyst in the lives of all they touch. To give birth is to harmonize opposites. It is to be the priest or priestess of your life. It is to be master of the Sacred Sounds of life. Each of you must find the way to bring creative harmony and birth in the manner best for you. Although you may all use this creative power, the way of one is not the way of another."

She looks into your eyes and withdraws the scepter from her crystal bowl. She taps it three times, and music fills the meadow. For a moment you can hear the song of the stream and the chorus of the trees. She leans forward and sings a single word softly into your ear—a word for you alone—a word that will lead you to your own crystal song and life harmony.

She gently cups your face in her hands, and, with a soft kiss, she fills you with the breath of new life. Then she turns, walking back across the meadow until she is lost to sight amid the flowers and trees.

You turn around, and you see the door through which you entered. On the other side of the door you see yourself sitting with the bowl before you. There is a golden glow about your physical body that was not there before, and somehow it all makes sense. You step back through the door, and you find yourself sitting once more in a meditative pose. The door with the painted picture of the tarot card is again before you.

You breathe deeply, allowing yourself to feel more grounded within your body. You pick up your wand and you begin to encircle the bowl, playing it again, only in a counterclockwise direction. As you do the door begins to fade and your full awareness of your surroundings returns. You are grounded, balanced, and energized. You are blessed with new life that you brought forth from the sacred space and your encounter with the Empress of the Crystal Bowl.

As you tap the bowl three times again to close the ritual, you hear that private word sung once more into your ear—a reminder of the new life and new direction for you and your own bowl.

Chapter Seven

Crystal Bowl Basics

For longer than humanity has kept records, crystal has been used to allow people to access, amplify, and project energies not normally available. There have been an endless variety of uses in clearing, healing, and communicating.

These multi-use, high-tech, high-energy bowls, primarily created for the semi-conductor industry as a medium of intense energy for growing crystal silicon chips, have evolved into a multi-purpose, high-energy medium for our personal use.

The bowls come in various sizes, ranging from six inches in diameter to 20 inches in diameter. Each has its own predominant tone, and the tones will vary in accordance with the manufacturing. Although there is a predominant tone, there are overtones given off by the bowls as well. Overtones are tones that issue forth simultaneously, but are not usually audible. For example, if we were to remove the felt pads and strike the piano key for middle C, by feeling along the inner piano wires, we would discover that wires other than the middle C wire would be vibrating.

Overtones, or harmonics, are very important in understanding the significant influence of these bowls. Every musical sound has overtones, unless electronically produced. Four to five overtones are usually acknowledged and detected in music, but overtones extend a great deal further than the human ear can follow. Thus, when we use music or words or prayers or sound of any kind to enhance our life or our attunement, we need to be aware of the effects of the overtones.

What we consider one tone, sound, or word, is in reality a complex combination of tones. The overtone series is not continuous. It is formed by what modern physics terms quanta, the energy state of molecules. The atoms are not distributed continuously, but in jumps, such as from the primary tone of middle C to the overtone of G, as opposed to following the chromatic scale of middle C, D, E . . . . It is because of these overtones that manifest as a result of our prayers and affirmations that we may get more than what we asked for, or we may manifest it within our lives in a strange manner.

It is important to keep this in mind with the descriptions of the bowls and their effects. Do not limit yourself solely to what is described. There will be overtone effects. These will vary somewhat in how they affect the individuals.

The musical tones of the bowls are rich in harmonics. When their intense, pure tone impinges upon the ear, it generates new vibrations and tones within the ear itself. These new, supplemental tones are called aural harmonics. We hear frequencies that do not exist in the original sound because the ear and the human body is a complex transducer. This same process occurs when we open up and heighten our own spiritual vibrations. As we work to develop one gift, we find that other gifts open themselves to work for us as well. These are our spiritual harmonics. This is why the crystal bowls are such a dynamic tool to use in the unfoldment process.

The crystal bowls also come in an opaque and a clear form. Usually the opaque forms can be any size within the range discussed. I have not seen a clear crystal bowl over the size of ten inches in diameter. This is due to the difference in the heating process and manufacturing. The clear bowls are thinner, and as the diameter of the bowls gets larger, the thickness of the bowls must increase as well.

There is a slight difference in the tones that are emitted from the opaque and the clear bowls, but one is no better or worse than the other. I am often asked which is more effective, or which is more powerful, or which is more useful. My stock answer is "whichever one you are drawn to." In an 8-inch clear bowl and an 8-inch opaque bowl, there is a difference in the tones emitted. Much of this depends upon the height of the individual bowl and its thickness.

Regardless of its clarity or opaqueness, there will be overtones that can be employed by the individual to create harmony and to use for any of the exercises or rituals within this work. All crystal bowls are adaptable to

Part of the author's collection of crystal bowls that he employs for music therapy, meditation and the making of elixirs.

the situation. All can be used for healing, for ritual, or for any other purposes described. All crystal bowls are easily programmable to your individual purpose. Thus you do not need to run out and spend a fortune trying to buy all of the different sizes of bowls; just find one whose sound resonates with you. As anyone who has worked with crystals can attest, you will soon discover that the bowls will call out to you. You will be drawn to those in which there is a strong resonance. It is the same way with the balls.

Keep in mind, also, that the bowls are musical instruments. The more you work with one, the more you will discover ways to use it not described within this work. You will also discover easier and more direct methods of employing it for the various purposes described. We can learn to play the bowls so that a variety of sounds, rhythms, and effects can be achieved. It is always better to be a master of one, rather than a dabbler in many.

How to Play the Bowls

There are two predominant ways of playing the bowls. They can be played by tapping the wand on the side to create a bell-like sound. This particular method is effective for opening and closing rituals and meditations. This will be explored more fully in Chapter 8. The bowls can also be played by rotating the wand around the outside or the inside of the bowls, creating a spiral of energy that sings out and can be directed for particular effects.

1. Using the rubber end of the wand or the leather-bound area, strike the inside of the bowl softly three times. (Three is the creative number and is appropriate to the energy of the crystal bowls. The female force, plus the male force, will always create a third force from their union. It is an excellent ritual to establish as a prelude to playing the bowl at any time.)

2. You may rub either the inside or the outside of the bowl, slowly encircling the circumference, until the bowl sings at the level of intensity you desire. Intense vibrations created by playing the bowl too loudly for too long can cause the bowls to break. More is not always better, especially with crystal bowls.

3. As you learn to play the bowl and make it sing, you will find that you can create two predominant audible tones. One is deeper and more

natural to the bowl. The other is a higher tone that can be created. It has been my experience that this tone is a higher octave of the original tone. The vibrations raise the energy to a higher level of intensity.

Do not be upset if you cannot create the higher tone at first. It takes time to discover it. It is also more easily created with bowls that are ten inches or less in diameter. I have also found that in performing some healing techniques on an individual, the bowl will not sing the higher song, no matter how I work at it; yet with some other individuals in a healing session, the higher tone was predominantly sung by the bowl. It took me a while to discover that the bowl knew what intensity the individual could and could not handle better than I did.

4. In some bowls there is a difference in the tone that emanates from playing the inside of the bowl and from playing the outside. Symbolically, there is also a difference. Using the wand on the inside of the bowl is a symbol of bringing the assertive male force into the feminine energies to create a new energy by their union. It is symbolic of the act of spiritual intercourse, an intercourse that assists in withdrawing from the outer so that exploration of the inner can occur more easily. It is powerfully effective for learning to go deeper into your own feminine energies—to touch the womb of your own inner self.

    Playing the bowl by using the wand on the outside is a means of bringing the new energy out into greater expression in your physical life rather than to go within to your spiritual sources. Instead of entering into the Divine Feminine, we work to bring the Divine Feminine out into greater expression. Meditation on the variations of these aspects will reveal even more to you.

5. Do not hit the bowl with the wooden or metal ends of the wand. Also do not "boom" the bowl by striking it too hard or playing it too loud. The bowls are strong, but they can also be shattered.

6. Do not play two or more bowls too close in proximity to each other. The bowls will pick up the sounds of each other, and too many vibrations can cause a shattering or breaking of the bowls.

7. Do not lay bare stones, rings, and other jewelry inside the bowls while playing them. The vibrations of the bowls will cause them to rattle, setting off a second discordant vibration that can crack the bowls. An effective means of charging rings, small stones and crystals inside the bowl is to place a small circular pad of leather (approximately 3–4

inches in diameter) inside the bowl and place the rings and other items upon it. This prevents the rings from rattling and setting off a discordant vibration, and it does not interfere with the singing of the bowl.

8. Some bowls, because of their light weight, are difficult to play unless they are being held. The pressure of the wand upon the bowl causes it to slide and move. This is easily prevented through the use of O-rings that can be inexpensively purchased at any hardware store. Purchase an O-ring and set the bowl upon it. This stabilizes its movement and does not interfere with its sounds.

9. There is often some question about which direction to rotate the wand upon the bowl, clockwise or counterclockwise. Either way, a spiral of energy will be created. This spiral will rotate in different directions and will result in different effects.

    Clockwise direction, or a deosil movement, is activating of the energy. It invokes and releases. It is considered more masculine, more outwardly energizing. It has a centrifugal effect, pulling energy from the inside to the outer. It draws into the physical what we need from the spiritual. It charges, strengthens, and stimulates power. In healing with the bowls, this movement energizes the aura and strengthens the overall balancing process. In meditation work it is effective for opening new realms and energies, and invoking them into play within your life.

    The counterclockwise rotation, or widdershins movement, is an inward or receptive energy. The spiral created is drawing. It draws the outer consciousness into the inner. It facilitates going within oneself—especially in exploring time and past-life connections. It activates more strongly the feminine energies. It awakens a greater sense of timelessness, and it can open awareness of the interrelationships of the past, present, and future. It can be used in healing to draw negative energy patterns out of the body and the auric field. It is grounding and balancing.

    It is interesting to watch people when they first hear and play the crystal bowls. You do not have to be psychic to see the effects. They are very noticeable. People are drawn to the exotic sounds of the bowls. Often, when an individual first plays the bowl, they will play it in a counterclockwise direction for a few moments. Then they will move to a clockwise direction. Unconsciously, they are grounding themselves before they energize. Something has spoken to them so that the song of the bowl will most effectively work for them.

It is also interesting to watch the effects of the playing upon people as they walk by. Almost everyone will pause as they draw close to the bowl. Bodily expressions say much about the effect of the bowl's song as they walk away. The steps are lighter, the eyes are more alert, and tension seems to just melt from their faces. There is a noticeable difference in the appearance of the individual, even if they are not cognizant of it. The playing of the bowl demonstrates how healing should be ideally accomplished—through a powerful exchange of energy, without any fuss or muss.

10. Take time to listen to the sounds of the crystal bowl after playing it. Remember that every cell in the human body is a sound resonator and has the capability of responding to the bowl. The sounds of the bowl are absorbed primarily through the cells, and the spine, in conjunction with the chakra centers. (Refer to Chapter Eight for further information on the absorption through the chakras as it occurs with vibrational healing methods.)

How to Purify and Energize

The crystal bowl is an effective tool for purifying and energizing in a variety of ways. It is strengthening to the auric field of anyone within its range when played. It stabilizes the field and balances the individual.

It can be used to charge crystals and stones. As mentioned earlier, you must be careful about placing objects within the bowl while it is being played. This can set off a secondary vibration which can cause the bowl to crack or break. Use a felt or leather pad inside the bowl to set small stones, crystals, rings, and other jewelry pieces upon, in order to cleanse and charge them. The combined effect of the energy of the crystal and the sound emanating from it will penetrate to the primal energy pattern of the piece and will shake loose and shatter any negative energy pattern that has accumulated around or upon it.

For larger pieces, you can hold the piece in your hand and, while playing the bowl, simply lower it. This can be awkward to do while playing the bowl in the rotation manner. Using a tapping or bell-ringing sound is easier and just as effective. You may even wish to tie a string or cord around the piece and dangle it within the heart of the bowl while it is playing.

The bowl is also effective in charging and cleansing water. Much of the water that we drink today has contaminates and chemicals. Using the bowl is an effective way of "sweetening" the water. An easy experiment is to take a small paper or plastic cup and fill it with water from your taps. Taste the water, so that you will be able to recognize the difference. Place the cup of water into the bowl. Tap the bowl several times, allowing the tones to fade out before tapping again. You may wish to play the bowl by rotating the wand. This is not always possible, depending upon the size of the cup and its weight.

Remove the cup from the bowl and taste the water. It will be sweeter. The negative effects of any chemicals will have been transmuted, and the sound will have charged it with greater force and nourishment.

The bowl can also be placed in the middle of the dinner table and played while all the food is set out. This charges it and strengthens the nourishment of it. It also eases the stress of those sitting at the table so that the digestion process occurs more beneficially.

The sound and the crystal emanations together work to transmute the negative and heighten the effects of the positive. This can be applied to almost any aspect of our life in which there may need to be a cleansing and an energizing.

Just as with any crystal or stone, the bowls also need periodic cleansing and charging. This cleansing is two-fold. It should be a physical cleansing. Any dirt and dust within or upon the bowl will have its energy set into motion with the playing of the bowl. The energy of the dirt will be absorbed by the individual. This may be more easily understood when we discuss ways of using the bowl to give power to prayers and affirmations later in this chapter.

The second is to cleanse the crystal bowl of negative energy it may have absorbed. With all crystalline structures, there is electromagnetic energy. This means that the structure has the potential of releasing (electrical) energy as well as absorbing it (magnetic). This is especially important when working with the healing aspects of the bowl discussed in the next chapter. The bowl should be cleansed after each healing, so that the old negative vibrations are not released to be absorbed by someone else, especially yourself.

In cleaning it physically, use distilled water and a mild detergent. Biodegradable is best. A soft cloth is effective to use on the clear bowls. Use a toothbrush or soft brush of any kind on the granular surface of the opaque bowls. After washing and rinsing thoroughly, set the bowl outside to dry. You cannot cleanse the wand in the same manner. Using an incense or oil as described in the next step is the best way to purify the wand.

To cleanse the bowl of the more subtle energies that can accumulate, any method of cleaning quartz crystals is effective. These include but are not limited to the following:

1. Use a smudge or incense that is purifying. Frankincense is effective, as is a combination of cedar and sage.

2. The use of pennyroyal flower essence is also cleansing to quartz crystals, especially the bowl. Take a small bowl of distilled water and place 5–7 drops of pennyroyal flower essence into the bowl. With a soft damp cloth, bathe the bowl, inside and out, with the solution.

3. Sea salt is also a very effective cleanser of crystal bowls. The sea salt draws the negative energy out of the bowl. This particular method is elaborated upon in the "Crystal Bowl Ritual Bath."

4. After cleansing the bowl, it is always good to charge and energize it. The most effective manner of doing so is to place it outside in the sunlight and let it sit for 24 to 48 hours. If done at the time of the full moon, the charging is especially effective. We are using nature's energies of the sun and moon (male and female) to re-energize the power of the bowls; every few months or so is effective.

   The bowls do not have to be charged often. If they are being used regularly, the playing itself serves as a charge. If you perform a lot of healing work, you may wish to cleanse and charge the bowls more frequently than every couple of months.

Exercise 16—
Crystal Sound Absorption

1. Find a time and a place in which you will not be disturbed. place the bowl in your left hand, if it is small enough to be handled comfortably, or place it on the floor in front of you or upon your lap.

2. Close your eyes and feel the silence surrounding you.

3. With the wand in your right hand softly tap the side of the crystal bowl once. Listen to the sound issue forth into the silence around you. Wait a few seconds and repeat a second and then a third time.

4. Begin rotating the wand against the bowl and make the bowl sing. As the sound builds, you may wish to slow your rotations down so that

the sound remains steady. Feel the sound circling around you. As you hear and feel it circling the entire room, feel it pass through every atom of your beings.

5. As you continue to play the bowl, pay attention to yourself. Do you feel the sound more strongly in any particular part of your body? Do you associate any particular colors with the sound? Does it stir any emotions, thoughts, or ideas? How does the sound make you feel? What is your breathing like? Can you visualize or imagine the sound in a physical form, encircling you? All of these thoughts will provide insight into other possibilities of the effects and uses of the bowl at a later date.

6. Now rest the wand upon your lap next to the bowl, sit quietly, and allow your body to absorb the sound. You may want to see yourself as a sound magnet, drawing the crystal bowl's vibrations into your own energy system. Feel yourself becoming charged and balanced as you absorb the sound. Again pay attention to where you feel the sound

The wands or strikers for the bowls are as important as the bowl itself. Different types serve different purposes.

most strongly, as this may provide insight into areas that may need extra work in the future.

7. Experiment with the bowl. Instead of just making it sing, use it in a bell form, softly tapping out a series of tones. Pay attention to the different effects it has. Notice how it does not circulate as much as it pulses. How does the pulsing affect you?

8. Play the bowl inside and outside, and observe the difference in the way the bowl sings and in how the sound is absorbed by you. Is there a difference in the way you feel? If so, what is it?

9. Set the bowl at your feet upon the floor. Play the bowl and make it sing. As it begins to sing strongly, lie back and feel how the sound affects you. Repeat the playing, but this time lie down so that the bowl is at the top of your head. What is the difference, if any. Then place the bowl on each side of you and play and absorb it from those aspects. You are trying to attune to your bowl and understand its effects upon you. As you come to understand how it affects you in the way it is played, and by how it is placed in association with your body, you will come to understand how you can use it with others for healing and for heightening consciousness.

10. Have fun with the bowl. It is an instrument of music and joy, and it should be a pleasure to experience. It lets you know that even though there must be persistent effort in the unfoldment process, we can learn to enjoy it.

Exercise 17—
The Crystal Bowl Ritual Bath

This ritual cleansing is effective as a preparatory rite to any ceremonial work. It is also beneficial to do this periodically, regardless of personal rituals, as it is a dynamic and powerful cleanser to the bowls.

1. Fill your bathtub with your regular bath water.

2. Make sure that you won't be disturbed.

3. Place around the edge of the bathtub any personal crystals and stones that you use. Clusters are very empowering to this exercise.

4. You may wish to set an atmosphere by lighting candles and a purifying incense. You may wish to place a few drops of an essential oil into the bathtub as well. Use your own imagination in this process.

5. Take one cup of sea salt and pour it into the tub. Stir the water, so that the salt dissolves and distributes itself.

6. Tap the bowl softly three times and step into the bath water.

7. Play the bowl so that it sings. When its sound begins to reverberate through the bathroom, lay the wand aside and lower the bowl into the water.

8. You may choose to either lie down or sit up in the bath water. Keep in mind that this is a ritual, and everything you do should have significance to breathe power and magic into the act. See yourself as the wand, and the bathtub and the water as the bowl. You are the male force uniting with the female force.

   Place the bowl between your legs, the seat of your creative, sexual life force. It is from here that we draw forth energy to bring forth new birth.

9. As you rest within the bath, meditate upon the bowl and its creative energies. Meditate on the bowl as a symbol and extension of your own creative life force. See and feel yourself being cleansed and purified. Just as the sea salt will draw off the negative energies of the bowl, it will also draw them out of your own energy system. When you feel as if you and the bowl have been cleansed, raise the bowl out of the water, and again make it sing until its sound reverberates around you.

10. Stand and rinse yourself and the bowl off. Tap the bowl three times, saying a silent prayer of thanks for the cleansing and the blessing of the bowl. You can then move on to the actual ritual, if this was used as a preparatory rite, or you may go on about your normal business, knowing that you are cleansed and energized—physically and spiritually.

Exercise 18—
Crystal Bowl Prayer Techniques

Because the crystal bowl works with sacred sound, it is an excellent tool for manifesting the energies of our prayers and affirmations. We can use it in a variety of ways that include, but are not limited to, those that follow.

It is important, though, to understand how manifestation works. Because we are multi-dimensional, we must place energy into the manifestation process on all levels. We must place mental energy, the visualization and imaging process. We must see what it is that we hope to manifest as if it is already ours. Think of it as picking something out of a catalogue. You must see it in as much detail as possible.

Because we are also emotional beings, we must place an emotional energy in manifestation as well. This is not the emotion of desire, though. It is the emotion of anticipation. It is comparable to the feeling of having placed a catalogue order, and anticipating it being delivered by a parcel service.

Because we are also physical beings, if we don't do anything other than visualize and anticipate, what we hope to manifest will either never arrive, or will be so delayed and hindered that ultimately we may decide it's more trouble than its worth. We must do whatever we can in the physical to assist the process. The physical activity grounds the mental and emotional energy into play. If we are trying to manifest a job and we only visualize and anticipate it, and if we never fill out applications, resumes, etc., we will never get the job.

Working with the bowl is a way of doing something physical to set the mental and emotional energy into play more strongly. The three of them combined make up the spiritual process of manifestation.

Even if we apply energy on all three levels, if we do not pay attention to one of the natural laws of the universe, we can still block or hinder the entire process. This is what is sometimes called the Law of Receiving. We must be willing to receive whatever it is that we are asking for. This law is set in motion from the moment you begin to affirm or work with manifestation in any way.

When we use the crystal bowls, this law is even more dynamically set in motion. What usually happens is that the bowl grounds the energies into activity, and the universe begins to respond. If we are trying to manifest greater abundance, usually within a week there will be signs that the process has been set in motion. Someone may offer to assist you with a project. Others may pay you compliments. Someone else may bake you something. It is important to honor those things. Accept them. Receive them graciously. Don't shrug off the compliment. Don't say you can handle the work by yourself. Accept the assistance, the compliments, or whatever is presented to you. If you don't receive the little things, the universe will not send you the bigger. As you receive the little, a magnetic pull is initiated which draws the bigger to you. This applies to anything that you affirm, pray for, or try to manifest with any of the techniques that follow.

1. As described in the previous chapter, use a wand that has a removable plug in one end. Place within the wand a wish, an affirmation, a specific prayer, that you would like to see manifested within your life. As you play the bowl, visualize the affirmation being sent out into the universe and then rebounding back into your life, being fulfilled. Visualize it as if it is already happening. Give thanks for its manifestation. Visualize ways in which it is going to help you and others within your life.

2. For manifesting abundance, place something gold into the crystal bowl, and the wand if possible. By playing the bowl, you send the male force of gold out with the female force of gold to create a new expression of gold and abundance within your life.

3. Another technique for abundance is to use a gold-colored candle. A small votive candle is most effective. Light the candle and place the candle within the bowl. (Use a dripless candle.) As you play the bowl, the energy of the candle and the bowl combine in a force of sound and light to release the energies of abundance. (This is also adaptable to healing techniques that will be discussed in the next chapter.)

4. Write your prayer or affirmation upon a piece of paper and set it within the crystal bowl. As you play the bowl, it releases the energy to work for what is written upon the paper.

5. There are also fragrances which are effective for the manifesting a certain kind of energy vibration. These can be vibrations for physical, emotional, mental, or emotional purposes. They will be elaborated upon in the next two chapters. For now, though, it is possible to rub a particular fragrant oil or flower essence onto the lip of the bowl. As the bowl is played, the vibration of the fragrance and/or the flower essence is released to begin the process of manifestation.

6. Combining techniques is even more effective. When working with vibrational techniques, the energies, when combined, take on a synergistic effect. They increase their potency exponentially rather than arithmetically. For example, if we are trying to increase abundance, we can place gold into the wand and bowl, use a written affirmation, and, placing it within the bowl, anoint the edge of the bowl with bayberry fragrance and use a gold candle in the bowl itself. We now have four methods that we are employing to set the energy of abundance in motion. This does not mean we have four times the effect. Rather, the energy increases on an exponential level, which in this case is the same as 2^4 (2 to the fourth power). The energy amplification is 16 times as great as using only one modality.

Exercise 19—
The Spirits of the Bowl

As you work with your bowl, it is going to serve to open the veils between the various worlds. There are those spiritual guides, teachers, angels, and devas that work with humanity through music, and thus through the crystal bowls.

Remember that the bowl creates sacred space, and where ever there is a vortex of intersection, there is the potential of linking the human with the divine, and the physical with the nonphysical.

As you attune to your bowl, you will find that the energy created is different with each particular method in which you apply it. It is not unusual to find different spiritual guides for each type of sacred sound application. There is usually one primary guide that will work with you through the crystal bowl.

Even today, the idea of spiritual guides and beings makes many individuals—even those in the metaphysical and New Age movement—uncomfortable. The truth is that their reality and their assistance to those of us in the physical have been a part of every major religion in the world. Whether we refer to them as angels, saints, ancestral guardians, guides, teachers, or whatever, mystical experiences involving those of the spiritual realms are a part of the entire global evolution.

One of the most common phenomena of working with the crystal bowls is the subtle dimension contact that it opens for the individual. Because it employs sacred sound, there is usually activated a higher functioning of the throat chakra energy. This particular energy center is tied to our functions of communication and creative expression. It also has links to the gift of clairaudience (the hearing of sounds and the communication with other beings and planes). As you work with your bowl, you will become more sensitive to the subtle communications often ignored or unrecognized by most. Whether we call these intuitive communications or spirit guide teachings is unimportant. What is important is that we begin to acknowledge and utilize this communication appropriately.

This does not mean that whatever insight or energy with which we connect through the bowl should be accepted as inscribed in stone. All things must be discriminated and discerned, especially communications from realms to which we are generally unfamiliar. Just because an entity says they accomplished something, or are part of a particular society, does not make it so. The purpose of all metaphysical study is to expand the consciousness in a manner that we can resynthesize the experiences of our lives, learn to independently test the knowledge and reexpress them in the manner that is most creative and productive for your own life circumstances. As I have often told students concerning spiritual guides, "If death were the only criteria for wisdom, none of us would be alive."

Do not pick up the bowl expecting the guide to instantly appear. It does not work that way. As you learn to work with the bowl, you will be drawn into a gentle, and yet increasing, realization that you are receiving assistance. The source of that assistance will reveal itself in time.

When you do meet the guides of your bowl, take extra care to balance and clean your own energy on a daily basis. This prevents static information and distorted energy flows. Keep yourself grounded at all times. Contact with nonphysical states has a tendency to draw the living from the plane of objective life, even when the entities are of the highest type.

Request your guides' presence, one at a time. Allow them to identify themselves in the manner they feel suited. This may be in the impression of a color, a particular touch, a feeling, etc. Allow them to behave as individuals. Don't allow any preconceived ideas to interfere. Discriminate and test all that comes through them. Those that are your true guides will expect this and will not be offended by such testing.

Their presence will be experienced by ordinary and nonordinary senses. Remember that the bowl creates a vortex that thins the veil between the physical and nonphysical worlds, and thus they are more likely to be experienced with it.

Many may show themselves as distinctly male or female, but this may vary according to the use of the bowl and to your own receptivity. Many are actually androgenous—neither truly male or female.

If any display a quality or temperament that you do not like, dismiss them strongly. Just as you can choose who you associate with in the physical, you can do likewise with the spiritual.

Use the bowl to establish an atmosphere that will enable you to more easily develop a relationship with them. Use the bowl as a prelude to spirit guide meditations. Ask them in these meditations for messages for friends. Ask for favors and information. Set reasonable time limits on the fulfillment of these favors. (This is a good means of testing.) Ask for ways to use the bowl that are most beneficial to you and to those within your life.

The guides that work for you through your association with the bowl will have a marked atmosphere of their own. There will be a love and compassion that is markedly different—more dynamic and powerful. The guides will help influence powerfully the feelings of all those participating in any bowl-related activity. Remember that the bowl is a catalyst for transmutation and transition. Those guides that will work through it will have that same dynamic effect. They have powerful creative energies which stimulate our own inner imaginative and intuitive capabilities. The bowl and the guides that work through it have an energy for initiating the process for a fully conscious union with the supersensible realms and their energies.

Exercise 20—
The Wheel of Life

This is an exercise which can help you learn to control the energies of the crystal bowl. It teaches you the power of creating sound, using the clockwise and counterclockwise movement. It reveals the significance and the ties between the past and the present, and the present with the future. More than anything else, it can be used to set the wheels of your own life into motion more effectively.

This is an exercise of flux and flow, of learning to use sacred sound to attune to the rhythms of the universe, to work within Mother Nature's patterns. It can be used to counter the periods of limbo and to restore movement in various areas of life. It can be used to open the veils that allow you to see the purposes of the highs and lows of your own life.

The wheel of life is an image appropriate to the crystal bowl. We have discussed the significance of the circle, but one of its associations is also the turning of the wheels of life. As you play the bowl, you are learning to turn those wheels which control the manifestation and the learning within your own life circumstances. You are learning to ride the wheel of life, not as a roulette wheel, but as a wheel that spirals higher and higher, with less and less chance of failure.

Learning to control the manifestation and use of sacred sound in such a manner is not easy. It does take time and persistence, but working with the crystal bowls is one of the most effective ways of doing so.

The wheel of life is sometimes referred to as the wheel of fortune, also depicted in the tarot deck. As with all wheel symbols, it represents a mixed bag of energies. Learning to sort them and control them can be difficult, but using the crystal bowl in the process facilitates it.

The tarot card and its imagery, when used with the crystal bowl, releases the energies for opening the doors to fame and fortune. This opens the doors to help us to use the rise and fall, and it can teach us the importance of synchronicity—things happening in the time and manner and means that is best for us as individuals. Everyone has his or her own individual rhythm, and success in life requires that we recognize it and use it to our benefit.

This exercise can be used periodically with the crystal bowl to help you to recognize the rhythms that are operative in your life at any given point. It is also an exercise that will increase your sensitivity, so that you can recognize such rhythms. It teaches you that seeds do not grow unless planted, and that they require a gestation and a root-forming period before the growth may reveal itself.

This exercise can also reveal the patterns of your past so that they are not repeated in the future. More than anything, it creates choices. The success of the choices within your life is determined by how much you choose with your heart.

We can use the bowl with this exercise to begin the process of recognizing the divine laws as they operate within the physical. It helps you in understanding the significance of the highs of your life, as well as the lows. It teaches you the importance of those limbo periods, while revealing creative possibilities for moving out of them.

1. Choose a time in which you will be undisturbed.

2. Meditating upon the tarot card of the Wheel of Fortune can be a good preparatory rite.

3. For this exercise, you will need to visualize and be able to use the bowl at the same time.

4. Allow yourself to relax. Perform some rhythmic breathing or a progressive relaxation.

As you relax, softly tap the bowl 12 times, as if a clock is chiming in the distance. As the sound of the bowl fades away, begin playing it by circling it in a clockwise direction. Circle the bowl 12 times. Allow the sound of its singing to fade, and then play it in a counterclockwise direction for 12 rotations.

As the bowl begins to sing through all of this, visualize yourself being surrounded by colors of rich, deep blues and purples. See spirals of purple within spirals of blue forming all around you. Visualize the movement of time as it reflects itself in nature.

Once more turn your playing of the crystal bowl to a clockwise direction. As you do, against the backdrop of the blue spirals, you see a sun shining upon a tree that reflects the seasons passing from spring to summer, to autumn, and then to winter. As the sun moves across the sky, the leaves begin to bud. Then they turn a rich green, only to be painted with the colors of autumn and then fall to the earth. The bare limbs of the tree are covered with snow, and then the snow melts, revealing the first buds of spring. See one season passing into another. One year after another. They all follow the same pattern. They all have the same rhythm and cycle. You begin to notice that the season changes in accordance with the spiraling of the blue and purple colors. As the colors spiral, the tree changes.

You cease the clockwise movement of the wand against the bowl and allow the sound to fade. As it does, so does the image of the sun and the tree. Then there are only the purple spirals of energy. You begin a counterclockwise movement of the wand against the bowl. As you do, the moon begins to rise up against the backdrop of colors. As you continue playing the bowl, you see the moon move from new to full and back to new—passing through every stage in between. You begin to see the rhythm of it as it moves within the spirals of the purple time.

You cease the playing, and as you do the image of the moon fades. Again you softly tap the sides of the bowl 12 times. With each ringing of the bowl the scenery shifts, becoming more clearly distinct. The sky and earth is filled with shades of blue and purple. It is as if you have found a void in which everything upon the earth rests in limbo. Above you are the sun and the moon. Surrounding you upon the earth are clocks of all shapes and sizes: grandfather clocks, cuckoo clocks, watches . . . they hang upon trees and are encased in the stones. The entire landscape is surreal, and looks like a painting of Dali.

On some of the clocks the hands turn clockwise, clicking off the minutes. Others turn counterclockwise. Some spin round and round, never stopping. Some seem not to move at all. As you move closer, you see that in the face of each clock are episodes of your own life. Some reflect the seasons of learning. Some reflect the patterns of relationships. Some reflect monetary movement. Some reflect the movement of one incarnation to the next.

Within these time pieces are the patterns and rhythms of your entire life. Only as you bring them all into harmony does true spiritual enlightenment occur. As you work to move the hands of the clocks in synchronicity, so does your "luck" change.

You begin to touch the clocks, and with your fingers you force the hands of several clocks to move in synchronicity. You guide the hands, slowing some down and speeding others up. As you do, you look about you. There are so many clocks, so many rhythms. There is so much to do. And then you understand that, as you learn to control the rhythms, you will have all of the time in the world.

With this realization there begins a deep chiming, as if the great timepiece of the universe was ringing for your perception. You raise your eyes to the heavens and you see the sun and the moon blending together. It thrills and excites you. It reminds you that all is possible, that the only limits are those you impose upon yourself, or allow to be imposed upon you.

As you bring your attention back to the earth, you find the clocks have disappeared. You are left standing in the vortex of blue and purple spirals of energy. You softly tap the bowl again 12 times. With each tap, the blues and purples fade, and you find yourself back within your own room and your own rhythms; rhythms that in the days ahead will begin to work for you, rather than against you.

Chapter Eight

The healing Magic of the Crystal Bowls

everything in our world is energy in one form or another. When similar energy vibrations link, we have what constitutes matter. All matter is composed of particles called atoms. These atoms, in turn, are comprised of subtle electromagnetic energy vibrations called protons and electrons. They are in constant motion, whether they are the atoms that comprise a stone, the atoms which comprise the air molecules, or the atoms that comprise the human body. These atoms draw to themselves similarly vibrating atoms, and then they link, forming molecules which ultimately comprise all matter within our universe.

All of the organs, tissues, muscles, etc. within our body are comprised of similarly vibrating atoms. If something such as a wrong food substance enters the body, it can alter the normal vibrational pattern of the organ, the system, or the entire body itself. At those times, the body needs something to restore it to its original vibratory pattern. Only by restoring balance to the discordant or dis-eased area will the body be able to reestablish true health.

If we can determine what vibratory pattern is "normal" for the diseased area, we can then project a vibrational frequency to the area to help it regain homeostasis. Different sounds, colors, thoughts, stones, or fragrances all have different vibrational frequencies that can be utilized in the restoration of health. By projecting an appropriate focus of energy upon the problem area, we can temporarily restore balance to it. The body can then more effectively rid itself of toxins, negativities, and other energy patterns that hinder the system's life processes on all levels. We restore a proper circulation of energy.

We are a biochemical/electromagnetic energy system. We can no longer treat the body simply as one or the other. We must begin to examine the interaction of both aspects of our energies. Just as there are biochemical processes going on within the body, there are also electromagnetic processes and emanations as well.

Vibrational remedies operate according to several principles. The first is the Principle of Resonance. Resonance is the ability of a vibration to reach out and trigger a response in anything of a similar vibration. Different organs and systems in the body will resonate with different vibrations. Specific colors, sounds, or electromagnetic frequencies can be used to affect those organs and systems. If an organ or a system is out of balance—out of its normal vibrational frequency—we can use a vibrational remedy to bring it back into its normal pattern. Forced resonance is the use of a stronger or primary vibration upon a different or weaker frequency to "force" it into a different pattern. In this case the stronger vibration forces the weaker into a pattern more appropriate to the health of the body.[11]

In vibrational healing, this method is used to create entrainment. The two vibrations come into step or phases with each other. With the crystal bowls, the oscillation of the sound, and the resonance to it by the body, effects a micro-massage of the systems, tissues, and cells of the body. This, in turn, effects balance and improves blood circulation, metabolism, endocrine balance, chakra balance, and alignment with our higher self.

Vibrational remedies are one of the most effective means of working with both aspects of the human energy system and for restoring the normal flow of energy in and through the system. Vibrational remedies projected to us from the outside (as with the crystal bowls) or taken internally (with flower and gem elixirs, as described in the next chapter), follow a specific path in the restoration of homeostasis. From external sources, such as sound and color projections, the vibrations enter through the subtle energies surrounding the physical body. These subtle energies are sometimes called the subtle bodies. The vibrational remedy aligns and balances them so that greater energy can be drawn through them into the

---

11 This aspect of resonance explains the sympathy and antipathy toward those in our lives. It is this quality that can be used to alter our personal vibrations to attune to the frequencies of those in the more spiritual realms and dimensions.

physical. The remedy then interacts with the chakras, establishing a balanced rate of vibration. From the nadis within the chakras, the energy passes through the meridians and through the nervous system of the body. It is here that it interacts more intimately with the physical body itself. An electromagnetic current is stimulated, creating an intimate partnership between the circulatory system and the nervous system. Then it is passed on to the problem area to restore balance. (Refer to the charts on the following two pages.)

In essence, the vibrational remedy triggers a rippling effect that moves through the outer energy bands surrounding the physical, and into the particular area or system of the body to which it most strongly resonates. There it restores balance. For remedies taken internally, such as with the flower and gem elixirs, the vibration begins inside and ripples outward, restoring energy, alignment, and balance.

Through vibrational remedies, blockages of energy within any of the particular energy frequencies are removed. If the remedy is being applied to a physical condition, this process releases the toxins that have been built up in the problem area. These toxic frequencies may then actually be pushed to the outer limits of the auric field for purification. They may also be pulled back into the body by the mind. This is why counseling and increased awareness of the causes of dis-ease is so critical to the healing process. Work must be done on emotional and mental levels to correct the patterns that helped create the situation.

The chakras, as discussed in Chapter Five, are the keys to working effectively with vibrational healing, especially with the sounds of the crystal bowls. The chakras are the primary mediators and distributors of outside energies with the physical body and its systems. They are tied to the physical body through the endocrine and nervous systems, and although they are not a part of the physical body, there is an intimate connection to it.

There are actually hundreds of energy distribution centers connected to the physical body, but there are seven primary ones, along with some very important secondary centers as well. There is often confusion as to their actual location—depending upon whether you are oriented to the Eastern or Western traditions. The differences exist simply because people in different parts of the world utilize their energies differently.

The chakras or "wheels" in Sanskrit (notice the symbolic connection to the bowls) take our normal life force and direct it into areas and functions of the physical body. They help take the energy from the food we eat and the air that we breathe, and assist the body to distribute it for its various activities. Energy is thus flowing in and around us at all times, creating our own unique energy field.

The chakras, because they are centers of electromagnetic energy, are extremely susceptible to the influences of vibrational remedies. By learning which functions of the body are affected by which chakras, we can utilize the vibrational remedies to restore homeostasis to physical conditions.

This is a critical point in working with vibrational healing. If a problem exists within the physical, an imbalance within the normal flow of energy (either a blockage or an overactivation), the body then has a double task. It must first restore balance to that area, and then it must set about correcting what created the imbalance. Vibrational remedies, especially those associated with sound, are dynamically effective in this process.

The chakras are linked to the neurological ganglion along the spine and to the endocrine glands, and, thus, the energy they mediate extends from them to the organs that are associated with them. The chakras extend both in front and behind the body, and they are actually small vortices of energy that are scientifically measurable. The vortex of energy for each rotates, when healthy, in a clockwise direction, circulating and distributing energy for the physical body's uses. If they are not balanced and working correctly, this rotation is slowed down or can even become a counterclockwise direction. Physical, emotional, and mental imbalances will result. The crystal bowl is effective in restoring proper movement and function to the chakras.

Effects of the Individual Bowls

The sounds created by the bowls will vary according to shape, size, clarity, and how the bowls are played. Keep in mind that they are musical instruments, and can be used to elicit different tones. All crystal bowls are adaptable. Just as quartz crystal stones can be programmed for any particular function, so can a crystal bowl. Yes, some bowls may have a greater facility at creating a specific effect, but all can be programmed and used in any of the methods described in this book. Thus, the individual does not have to purchase an entire set of bowls.

Although we will discuss particular effects of individual bowl sizes, it is important to remember that these are guidelines, and that the particular size bowl simply has a greater facility at eliciting the specified effect. With practice, any bowl size can be used to create such an effect.

It all depends upon your willingness to work with your bowl and attune to its energies.

Six-Inch Bowl

The six-inch bowl gives a high, clear tone that facilitates the clearing and opening of the crown chakra and the third eye. This allows energy and higher wisdom to flow from the crown down into the throat and heart centers of the body. Its energy frequency can be too intense for some people, and should be taken, initially, in small doses to allow oneself to become used to it.

This is a bowl whose tone is effective in activating an important minor chakra center located at the stem of the brain, at the medulla oblongata. At this point in the physical body there are 12 nerve passages, three of which extend down into the heart, and the others into areas of the brain. This center is one which creates what the ancient Egyptians called "intelligence of the heart"—a linking of the mind and the heart in a new expression within the individual's life.

This bowl activates the upper four chakra centers—heart, throat, brow, and crown. Since many people work and function in their daily lives from the lower centers, initially, its vibration may be too intense. It can be used to pull the powerful life forces up from the lower centers into a higher and more dynamic expression through the upper. For those not used to working with the higher frequencies, the bowl's sound can create anxiety, agitation, and nervousness.

With the six-inch bowl, a little can go a long way. More is not always better. Use it sparingly in the beginning, until you become more acclimated to its vibrational frequency.

Seven-Inch Bowl

The energy of the seven-inch bowl is protective and balancing, especially to those who work with astral energies and phenomena. This would include psychic activities, out-of-body experiences, various forms of mediumship, and other psychic phenomena which derives its manifestation from the astral level.

The seven-inch bowl aligns the astral body with the physical, so that imbalance does not occur through misuse or overuse of psychic energies. It is balancing to the emotions, so that physical problems do not result. The crystal sound energy from this bowl neutralizes disruptive energy in the astral body of the individual by absorbing and transforming discordant vibrations into light energy.

This bowl temporarily aligns the seven major chakra centers. It is also an excellent bowl for working with children, up through early adolescence. Once puberty has been experienced, the dynamics of the bowl will alter in its effects on children. In the early years, the chakras are becoming activated and developed. The seven-inch bowl assists this chakra activation and development. It provides a nourishing and gentle coaxing of their opening. After the age of puberty, it serves more to balance and align, so that the individual's own creative activation of the chakras can occur in accordance with his/her own unique life experience.

Eight-Inch Bowl

The eight-inch bowl is one of the most adaptable and creative. It activates the throat chakra, our center of higher creativity and abundance. This is the center that is also tied to the gift of clairaudience, and assertion of the creative will-force.

The sound of this bowl has ties to the universal "OM"—the sound from which all sounds came forth in Eastern philosophy. It can be used universally as a healing and a meditational tool, and it stimulates the creative imagination. It is effective in meditational work, in helping the individual to access the library of past-life experiences from the time of the soul's inception. It can also be used to draw to the surface disruptive memories to release the emotional attachment to them. (Many individuals that have undergone child abuse fail to remember the experience. This is an excellent tool in counseling and therapy to assist the individual in bringing them out so they can be dealt with.)

This bowl opens the veil between the finite world and the infinite. The 8 is the symbol of infinity, standing vertically. This is a bowl which can be used to develop the ability to stand between the two worlds. Such a path is difficult, and requires tremendous will-force and creativity, both of which are activated by the crystal sounds of this bowl.

This bowl also has ties to what is often called the eighth chakra or "soul star." This is a chakra point, approximately six inches above the crown of the head. It is tied to the functions of the astral body. The eight-inch bowl helps to activate and strengthen this center so that the astral body can, in turn, be strengthened and used as a separate vehicle for consciousness, i.e., consciously controlled astral projections or out-of-body experiences. It also has ties to the process of lucid dreaming and dream alchemy—learning to control, transmute, and re-create dream scenarios.

Nine-Inch Bowl

The nine-inch bowl creates a universal healing sound. If un which sounds or bowls to use in a particular healing situation, you can rarely go wrong with the nine-inch bowl. Its sound activates all of the chakras, but its effects upon the lower is unique. It stimulates our basic life force and draws it up through all of the chakras, strengthening them in fighting off the illness, and in restoring balance.

The nine-inch bowl is also effective in nervous and psychological imbalances. It effects the minor chakra at the stem of the brain, as does the six-inch bowl, but it differs from the six-inch bowl in that it seems to have a more dynamic effect upon the nerves and processes of the brain than upon those nerves which extend into and are associated with the heart.

The nine-inch bowl raises the entire vibrational energy of the individual and his or her auric field. In meditation, it elicits a tone that enables the individual to perceive and access the universal principles and truths operative within the individual's life. As with all of the bowls, it can be used as a powerful tool for interdimensional traveling as well. It raises the entire energy of the individual in a way that can make you more conscious of the subtle interpenetrations and influences of other energies and dimensions with your own.

Ten-Inch Bowl

The vibrational energy of sound from this bowl enters the body most strongly through the solar plexus chakra. This particular center is a personal power center for most people. Thus, this bowl can be used for exercises and meditations for self-empowerment. It awakens those energies within our lower selves and brings them out into manifestation.

The solar plexus chakra is a center for much psychic energy. For those wishing to open to their innate psychic abilities or to strengthen them, the ten-inch bowl is extremely effective. The solar plexus center is associated with the psychic ability of clairsentience—"clear feeling." In this case, it is the subtle feelings about people, events, etc. that do not always reveal themselves on a conscious level.

The ten-inch bowl combines the qualities of smaller and larger bowls, as it has the ability of producing both high and low tones. It also balances excessive left brain activity, and it facilitates applying the rational mind to intuitive responses.

This is an excellent bowl for manifestation. It is effective in using with the prayer and affirmation techniques described in the previous chapter. The solar plexus was known to the ancient Essenes as the lower womb. It is through the lower that we give birth to the higher. It serves little benefit, if any, to awaken and stimulate the higher faculties if the lower are not strong and balanced. The ten-inch bowl strengthens and balances the lower, while initiating a stimulation of the higher. This enables the growth and unfoldment process to occur in a gentle manner, rather than through trauma and distress.

Twelve-Inch Bowl

With the twelve-inch bowl we move into those that are almost entirely opaque. There may, in fact, be clear crystal bowls in the larger sizes, but I have yet to uncover any. Because of the size of the bowls, the manufacturing process makes the clear form more difficult to produce in larger diameters. This does not limit the usefulness of the larger bowls, and, in fact, most of the bowls readily available to the general public are usually the larger ones.

The larger bowls do have an advantage over the smaller ones. Because the thickness of the bowls is greater, they can be played for a more extended time than the thinner, smaller diameter bowls. This does not mean they are impervious to breakage or cracking. Care must be taken with them, as with all the bowls, in playing them too extensively at a high vibration.

The twelve-inch bowl is powerfully effective in enveloping the body in sound that touches the core of the physical being and stimulates a higher consciousness of our physical essence and our chakra system. It can be used to attune to the influence of the twelve signs of the zodiac and all astrological influences. One technique for this will be explored in Chapter Ten.

The twelve-inch bowl is also effective in initiating the change from the seven chakra system to the 12 chakra system of the modern spiritual disciple. There are really 12 major energy centers to be fully awakened and utilized if we are to release our highest capacities. The 12 centers are as much symbolic as actual, and the number 12 has always had much symbolism attached to it. These 12 centers of the body can be likened to the 12 lights surrounding the manger and the 12 signs of the zodiac. In the ancient Greek mysteries, 12 was the holy number. In the East these are referred to as lotus blossoms, but in the esoteric Christian world, they represent roses upon the cross of the body. When fully activated, they create the "golden Wedding Garment" of Biblical scripture.

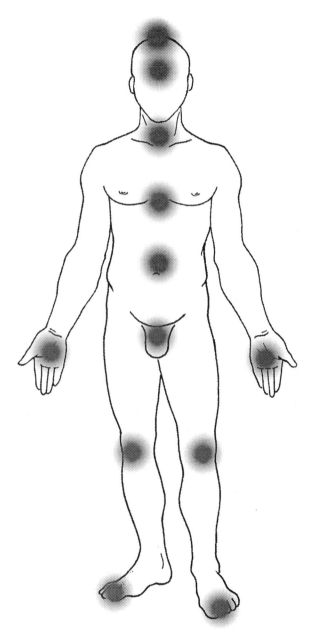

The Twelve Chakras of a Spiritual Disciple

These 12 lights are latent within the body of every person. They are 12 energy centers which, when awakened and functioning, become the 12 glorious body lights.

The twelve-inch bowl, one of the most common available, has great use in awakening any or all of these chakras. Meditating upon the qualities essential for their awakening while using the bowl assists the process. Those centers in the feet are awakened through dedication of our life in service, and by walking in the steps of the masters—never becoming weary of well-doing for others. Those in the knees are awakened after much prayer and meditation, through kneeling to help others, and when humility becomes a keynote of our personality. The centers in the hands awaken through service and assistance to others. Meditating upon greater, more loving service assists their awakening.

As our life becomes purified and spiritualized, the center at the base of the spine is awakened. This aids in the transmutation of the entire body. The center in the solar plexus (a joining and balancing of the mental and emotional energies) awakens with greater reverence toward the physical body as a temple for our spirit, and as our outer activities are harmonized with spiritual principles. The center in the heart awakens when compassion is extended to all living creatures. Life in every form must become sacred. The center in the throat will not bloom into a true power center as long as hasty, unkind, or destructive words are uttered. When activated, it emits a soft blue radiance, to which aspiration will add silver tones. The twelve-inch crystal bowl assists in these developments.

The upper two chakras are also affected by the twelve-inch bowl, but these two centers are also affected by every crystal bowl. These are the male and female centers that we have previously discussed. The female center is the brow chakra and the male is the crown center.

Work with the 12 centers of light—both inner and outer—must proceed simultaneously. We should not work on one center to the exclusion of others, simply because we may think one is more powerful or glamorous than another. The twelve-inch bowl helps us to balance the energies and activities of all 12 centers, so that one is not overly stimulated, while others are understimulated. It stabilizes our entire energy system as we unfold and develop.

Fourteen-, Sixteen-, and Twenty-Inch Bowls

The larger size bowls are most effective in balancing the physical and in stabilizing its energies in preparation for work on a higher consciousness level. Contact with new energies can tend to draw the consciousness away from the physical, which is where we need to remain focused. Our task in the unfoldment process is to bring the spiritual out into the physical. The larger bowls help to keep us grounded.

Any of these three larger bowls can be used for this grounding process, and, although their tones are different, the effects of their tones vary only in the intensity and depth of experience. They all strongly affect the chakras within the feet, helping the individual to stay connected to the earth's energies. Anyone who has a tendency toward flightiness can benefit from these bowls.

These bowls are also effective in shamanic journeying. They serve to link the individual's energies to those of the earth, so that the more subtle energies of the earth itself can be discovered. Anyone wishing to help themselves attune to nature in any form could benefit from work with these larger bowls. Their vibrations help bring the individual's vibrations into synchronization with the energies of nature or an element of it.

In meditation they can be used to awaken a realization of ourselves as a microcosm of the universe. Their deeper tones are strengthening and powerfully protective.

Exercise 21—
Aura Balancing

The crystal bowls have great potential as healing instruments. The sounds and the overtones created by them serve a number of healing functions. As the bowl is played, it balances and strengthens the entire auric field of the individual. It also restores the circular pattern of the flow of energy around and through the individual.

It can be used to impact greatly upon the functions of the chakras. Some bowls are more effective for specific chakra centers, but the universal effect of all bowls, regardless of their size, is that they can be employed in restoring function of any chakra center. The energies of the bowl are created in accordance with the purpose and the mind focus of the healer.

The crystal bowl can be used to restore the proper rotation of the chakras. The bowl can be used to strengthen chakra activity, and to cleanse the center, to draw out negative energy patterns that may have accumulated and which may be contributing to ill health.

Aura balancing is the easiest healing aspect to employ with the bowl. Playing the bowl in a clockwise direction will align all subtle energies, and stimulate a greater energy flow in and around the physical body. It also is balancing and strengthening to the entire circulatory system.

Sit with the bowl either in your lap, on the floor in front of you, or in your left hand. Tap the bowl three times to awaken the energy, and begin to play the bowl by rotating the wand around its edge. Continue to make the bowl sing for several minutes or as long as you are comfortable. As the sound of the bowl builds, it will resonate with your own energy, and entrainment will occur. Your own auric field will become more vibrant.

If you are using the bowl on someone else, you may wish to have the other individual seated or prone. Move the bowl around the perimeter of their body as you play it. If the bowl is too large to hold in your hand and play, simply begin by setting it in front of the individual if he or she is seated, or place it at his/her head if they are lying down. Play it for several moments in this position, and then move it until you have played it on all sides of the individual.

You may wish to do this several times in the course of one healing session. As you employ other healing techniques, the energy you release or balance in a problem area may move to some other part of the physical or subtle energy field. Playing the bowl helps to keep the auric field stable so that this does not occur.

Individuals that are somewhat hyperkinetic can benefit from a counterclockwise playing of the bowl. This slows down the activation of energy through the chakras and within the auric field. Care must be taken, though, not to reverse the clockwise movement entirely. This can also be effective in obsessive and compulsive behaviors. A study of the chakras and their ties to emotional and mental aspects can help you in determining which specific chakra to focus upon in the healing session and the application of the crystal song of the bowl.

Exercise 22— Chakra Songs

The bowl can also be used to specifically work on each individual chakra center. One effective means of doing this is by having the individual prone upon the floor, and holding the bowl directly over the chakra center of the spine while playing it. This enables that particular chakra to be impacted upon more strongly by the crystal tones.

You can set specific stones and crystals associated with a chakra upon the spinal contact point. Then, while the bowl is played, the chakra effect will be amplified. (Some specific stones and their chakra alliances are examined in the next chapter, in learning to make gem elixirs with the bowl.)

The Effects of Colors and the Crystal Bowl

(These colors have physiological properties as well as spiritual. When used with the crystal bowl, they awaken healing and higher consciousness.)

White   The color of purity and truth; amplifies the effects of other vibrations; awakens creativity.

Pink   Stimulates the heart chakra; awakens purity of intention; opens a vision of truth and success; immune system.

Red   Stimulates the base chakra; good for circulation and overall energy; can be used to stimulate change and sexuality; effective color for colds and mucus ailments.

Orange   Spleen chakra; muscular system of body; affects adrenals; affects emotional health; communication; opens awareness to laws of magic; can be used to reveal deceptions.

Yellow   Solar Plexus chakra; left hemisphere of the brain and mental activity; clarifies dreams; digestive system; activates adrenalin.

Gold   Heart chakra; abundance and prosperity; all healing activities; can open a higher sense of devotion; restores harmony; strengthens immune system.

Green   Heart chakra; harmony and growth; prosperity; ties to the nature kingdom; awakens artistic inspiration; can be used to open understanding of love and relations; has calming effect; bright greens leading to the blues are healing; should NOT be used in cancerous or tumorous situations as it makes things grow; awakens compassion.

Light Blue   Throat chakra; soothing and healing, especially to children; calming and quieting; affects respiratory functions; has an antiseptic effect; opens intuition and imagination, and ability to perceive on new levels; has a cooling effect; good for fevers.

The Effects of Colors and the Crystal Bowl (continued)

Indigo   Brow chakra; the color of devotion; connected to the endocrine and reproductive systems; purifies the blood; high spiritual energies.

Violet   Crown chakra; healing to the skeletal and nervous systems of the body; effective for many neuroses; cleansing to the aura; stimulates energy of independence and intuition; good for stimulating dream activity and for recognizing tides of change.

Purple   Purifying on physical and spiritual levels; awakens ambition; opens deep spiritual understanding; awakens energy for overcoming business obstacles.

Gray/ Silver Energy for initiation; helps attune to astrological influences; awakens all moon or feminine influences; assists in realizing innate abilities.

Brown   Awakens energy of discrimination; grounding; can stimulate movement; awaken consciousness of lost items.

Black   Protective and absorbing of negative energies; can be used to stimulate awareness of secrets; assists in opening understanding of burdens and sacrifices; all mother information and energies opened through it.

In the foregoing chart, specific tones and colors are given for each chakra. We can use the color references to more strongly direct the crystal bowl sounds to a chakra center. There are a number of ways of doing this. You can simply place a colored paper or film in the bottom of the bowl; as you play it, the sound and the color will more strongly resonate with the corresponding chakra. For example, if we wish to increase the effect of the bowl upon the base chakra, we can place red filter paper in the bottom of the bowl. As the bowl is played, the red color is linked with the sound, and a greater stimulation of the base chakra will occur.

In the last chapter we discussed placing a candle in the bowl and then playing the bowl. The candle color will determine greatly the effects of the sound. The candle and sound together will impact more strongly upon the particular chakra. On pp. 170–171 are some guidelines to the effects of colors when used with the crystal bowls.

If you are able, you may wish to set the bowl directly upon the back of the individual while they are face down, lying in a prone position. Set it on the chakra points of the spine and play the bowl on them. This serves two dynamic functions. First, it creates a balancing of the aura, and second, it dynamically affects the chakras and the physical organs of the body.

The spine is a dynamic sound resonator. The vertebrae pick up the sound vibrations and then distribute them along the nerve pathways to the organs to which they are connected. The physical vibration of the bowl, in conjunction with the sound, impacts powerfully on the spine. The individual receives a physical micro-massage, along with a sonic one.

Exercise 23—
Long Distance Healing

The crystal bowls are wonderful tools for employing long-distance healing. Often people are asked to send prayers and healing to others who are not present. The crystal bowls can be used to amplify such energy exchanges.

The phenomena of long-distance healing is nothing new. It does transcend logical thought processes, but it in no way transcends reality. Energy operates on all levels and in many ways not yet understood. What is often referred to as psychic energy is the creative life force of all substance. It surrounds us, penetrates us, and is a part of us. It can be controlled and directed, molded and shaped, stored or used. It can be controlled by the mind.

We know that the human body is a biochemical, electromagnetic energy system, but our psychic energy is the basic building block of these. The biochemical and the electromagnetic aspects are the physical expressions of our psychic life force. It operates on a level that transcends physical time and space.

Quantum physics has done much to explain the phenomena of psychic energy. It teaches us that all life and all energy expressions are connected; and because we are energy, operating on many levels and in many forms, we can't move without influencing everything in our universe—even if we don't recognize the influence initially. It teaches us that even observation will change ourselves and what is being observed. With higher expressions and focuses of energy, time and space are transcended.

Thus, in long-distance healing, we experience the individual in an immediate proximity regardless of the actual time and location.

The crystal bowls are tools for employing a more active form of our psychic energy in this manner. It assists us in concentrating, tuning, and transmitting the healing energies and tones. The sound waves sent out by the bowl strengthen the entire etheric body of the individual, so that physical illness will be blocked, balanced, and/or eliminated.

The crystal bowl also assists us in achieving a transcendent level of consciousness, so that we can employ a more concentrated focus of our psychic energy. It assists us in a controlled use of the mind through the power of sound.

For long-distance healing, it is beneficial to have a witness. A "witness" is a term that has come to be associated with the field of radionics. It is "anything which will psychically represent the subject."[12] A witness can be a photo, a signature, a blood specimen, hair clipping, nail clipping, or anything which can provide a link between the bowl and the person to whom you wish to direct the sounds. A polaroid photograph is considered most effective by many people, in that it will capture the entire positive and negative ion field around the individual, while one developed from a negative will only capture half of the field. Thus, it is not considered as strong a link.

The witness helps us to link the rational and intuitive levels of the mind, thus serving to awaken the process of sending energy at a distance. It assists you in creating a thoughtform and in directing it toward the individual. Through the witness, you are more easily able to establish resonance. It serves to awaken the connection beyond a physical level. It brings the individual "to mind." The healing energy can then be sent, regardless of space and time.

Procedure:

1. Always clean the bowl inside and out before doing a healing, long-distance or otherwise. Dust within the bowl can have its vibrational frequency transmitted along with the sound. The cleaning also helps to establish the proper mindset for the procedure.

2. Place the witness inside the bowl. Meditate briefly on the energy you wish sent, and visualize it as if it has already been accomplished. This helps to create a thoughtform which will be sent out with the sound, to resonate with the individual.

---

12 Cosimano, Charles W. *Psionics 101*. Llewellyn Publications, St. Paul, 1986, p. 82.

3. You may even wish to place a healing affirmation in with the witness. Write on a piece of paper what it is that needs to be healed. You do not have to be complicated with the process. Something as simple as "Heal and strengthen _____." You may wish to get even more specific, in accordance with whatever the condition may be.

4. You may wish to place a flower or gem elixir in with the witness, so that, as the bowl is played, the sound will carry the vibrational remedy of the elixir to the individual as well. (This will be covered in greater detail in the next chapter.) Using aromatherapy is also beneficial in long-distance healing. Dabbing the witness with the fragrance and then playing the bowl sends the sound and the fragrance vibration to the individual as well (pp. 177–178).

5. Tap the bowl three times to activate its creative energies, and then begin to play the bowl. The longer the bowl sings, the stronger is its energy projection, but be careful not to play to the point of rupture of the bowl. Ten to 15 minutes is very effective. The bowl need not play constantly during this time. Play it. Rest. Play it some more.

6. Be sure to visualize throughout it all. See, feel, and experience the sound resonating with the individual, restoring balance and health. The individual will experience changes. Noticeable effects will be experienced within 24 hours.

7. It is always good to affirm that the healing manifest "for the good of all and according to the free will of all," in order that the healing occurs in the manner most beneficial to the individual's growth. We do not have the right to intrude upon the free will of others, and this is a dynamic way of affecting others in very subtle, although often unnoticed, ways.

   Opinions differ as to whether we should project healing toward another without their permission. I am of the school of taking great personal responsibility for one's life and actions, believing that the only one who knows what is ultimately best for the individual is that individual. Everyone has the right to make mistakes, and it is often through our mistakes that our greatest growth can occur. If we interfere, we may rob the individual of a learning experience critical to his or her evolution. Besides, it takes little energy to ask someone if you can help.

   These are not hard and fast guidelines. Obviously, if there is someone under our care—such as children—we act in accordance with what we as adults know is best. There are always exceptions, but we must make our decisions, being willing to take full responsibility for the consequences of our actions—positive or negative. If we cannot do this, then we do not need to be dabbling in such matters.

8. At the end, give thanks for the healing and the opportunity to serve as a channel or aid to the process. Tap the bowl three times again and remove the witness. (Some may find it beneficial to leave the witness in the bowl at the end, and to place the wand inside the bowl with it overnight. This is symbolic of the creative force continuing to work for you through the hours until it is next needed.)

9. Keep in mind that we are not practicing medicine, as there are many laws against diagnosing and prescribing. We cannot prescribe sounds as we can medications. When we use the crystal bowls and other tools of vibrational healing, we are simply employing preventive care, along with holistic maintenance. Taking money for using the bowl on someone must be approached very cautiously, as the laws are very strict about practicing medicine without a license. I personally do not charge for my healing and therapy sessions, nor do I take "donations." I make the request that the individual either donate to a favorite church or charity, or pass a favor on anonymously to someone else. I do know a number of licensed massage therapists who employ the bowl in their work, but it is used as a tool within their massage work, and as they are licensed, there is no problem.

10. Do not be afraid to experiment. The extent of the crystal bowl's healing effects are as yet undetermined. I personally feel they will never be truly defined, in that they can be used to enhance any method of healing—traditional or nontraditional—that is employed by the individual.

Exercise 24—
Aromatherapy with the Crystal Bowls

Aromatherapy has gained greater popularity in the past decade. It is being employed in holistic healing practices around the world. Traditionally, it involved the senses of touch and smell through massage with oil or lotion. In magical aromatherapy, the senses of smell and sight are linked through visualization enhanced by fragrance. "Magical aromatherapy is an offshoot from the holistic branch . . . It isn't necessarily directed toward healing (though it can be) and its aims are much broader."[13] The crystal bowl can be employed in both healing and magical aspects of aromatherapy to amplify the effects.

We can combine aromas and sounds from the crystal bowl to enhance both healing and magical effects within our lives. Combined, they are a powerful form of transmuting energy on many levels. They provide a powerful catalyst for change. They can be used for meditation and ritual practices, and they are beneficial for all healing experiences. They are also effective for long-distance healings.

Historically, essential oils have most often been used for several purposes at once. The first is therapeutic, as an aid in healing and in restoring bodily health. The second is for spiritual upliftment. The oils alter the vibration of the individual and the environment according to the quality and characteristic of the oil. This it has in common with crystal bowls.

This work does not intend to explore all the varieties of oils and their qualities and individual characteristics. Again, I refer you to my earlier work, *The Healer's Manual*, for more information on aromatherapy. There are also several works in the bibliography which can assist you with that process. Keep in mind that conventional holistic aromatherapy can become quite complicated when trying to create specific physiological, psychological, and spiritual effects. In spite of the potential complexity, aromatherapy, along with the crystal bowls, are wonderfully enjoyable tools for growth. Through them we learn to work and to grow, and to have fun while doing so.

1. Choose the oil for the effect you wish to elicit. Do not always go strictly by the source, as the vibration of the oil may interact with your own individual energies uniquely.

2. With a cotton ball, anoint the rim of the bowl with oil lightly. As you play the bowl, the fragrance will combine with the sound and fill the room with the vibration. It will also resonate with your own auric field, facilitating the effect you wish to manifest. Visualizing with this will amplify it even more.

3. For long-distance healing, you may wish to anoint the witness that you are placing in the bowl. This way, as the sound grows, the sound and the fragrance will reach out to the individual to be healed.

---

13 Cunningham, Scott. *Magical Aromatherapy*. Llewellyn Publications, St. Paul, 1989, p. 5.

4. You may wish to simply inhale the fragrance prior to playing the bowl, keeping in mind your own particular purpose, be it magical, healing, or otherwise. Allow the fragrance and the sound to carry you up and out, or to balance your energy in the manner desired.

The combined use of the fragrance and the sound serve to transfer awareness from the conscious mind to the intuitive levels, where we may access more dynamic energy and set it in motion with greater force. Through this combined use we are able to bypass the rational mind, which can so easily block our psychic and healing energies. We can more effectively open to those levels of our mind that control and direct our most creative and powerful energies.

Exercise 25—
Creating Healing Chambers

I have heard of individuals creating healing chambers for work with the crystal bowls. These are supposed to be glass-enclosed areas of specific dimensions, with crystal sounds being played outside as well as inside the chamber. I have not encountered them personally, but it would not be difficult to set up.

Almost any room can become a healing room. All that would be needed would be an empty room. Furnishings could be limited to maybe a rug or a chair, or table, upon which the individual could rest. The less cluttered the room, the less the sound would be disrupted as it begins to circulate.

In the middle of that room would be placed the individual to be healed. Bowls could be set in the corners of the room, or in a circle around the individual. Each could be played singularly, and then in unison, if there were enough people.

Other tools and symbols of healing could be used to decorate the room. A mat, designed with figures and symbols of healing throughout the ages, could be used to place the crystal bowls on as they are played. The more significant you make it, the more powerful will be the effects of the sounds.

Other possibilities would be using pyramids with the bowl and within your healing chamber. Many pyramids are on the market, constructed of copper tubing, and large enough to sit under. Playing the bowl while in the pyramid, or by having another play it on the outside, could be very effective.

There are no limits to creating healing chambers, particularly those effective for crystal bowls. A room that has quartz crystal and other stones in various areas will enhance the effects. Plants and herbs within the room add to the overall energy. The chamber should be treated as a healing temple. The more you can do to add to the significance of that temple, the more powerful will be the effect.

There are many experiencing visions of establishing holistic healing centers, and yet they have no knowledge on how to begin. They do little work with healing themselves. Turning a room or a corner of your home into a meditation and healing chamber is a dynamic first step. Each time you use that area you add energy to it, so that as you sit there, or work to heal another, it becomes easier. The energy is initiated before you even begin. You create a sacred space, one that exists in the physical environment you create for it. The more you use it, the more sacred and strong it becomes.

Remember that the sound of the crystal bowl creates a sacred atmosphere by which we can transcend the usual aspects of physical energy. The more you use the bowl in your own healing manner, the more your own aura becomes a sacred healing space, one that is felt by anyone who comes in contact of its field. You become a crystal bowl that can sing into creation a healing chamber, wherever you may be.

Chapter Nine

Creating Flower and Gem Elixirs

ealth is, in actuality, the ideal balance between all major parts of our being—body, mind, and soul— in connection with our environment, our associations, and all that we encounter in our individual incarnations. The word "healing" has its roots in the Greek word *holos*, the same word from which we get "whole" or "holistic." Healing is an expression of wholeness. Health is wholeness. It is not simply physical, or mental, or emotional. It encompasses the whole of our being. Because of this, the crystal bowl is a dynamic symbol and instrument of holistic healing.

Just as all paths of spiritual development tell us to look within, so for our own healing must we look within ourselves. ALL HEALING COMES FROM WITHIN, AND THE BODY HEALS ITSELF. The quickening may come from without, but the healing from within. Before any true healing can occur, there are two prerequisites. We must first understand the basic cause of our sickness on all levels—physical, emotional, mental, and spiritual. We must also be willing to surrender to our deepest wisdom and implement whatever possible alternatives may appear to be helpful.

There are always alternatives. There exist many methods of healing, many therapies, and many remedies. There is no universal one while we are in physical form. We must seek out and use the method or combination of methods that suits our own individual development and energy.

Sometimes that means we borrow from several sources and therapies to come upon a synthesis that is uniquely our own. The important factor in healing is discovering that method(s) which will be most beneficial for you at the time you need it.

In discovering what will work for you, you must consider all aspects of your being. The emotions, the thought life, and the spiritual flow are as important to health as is the physical state of the various organs and tissues. Whether we are concerned about being healthy, regaining health, or moving to a level of greater health and energy, the whole being—both the physical and the subtle—must be involved.

Flower and gem elixirs assist us in this process. They are simple and effective in helping us to bridge and link all aspects of our energies in creating homeostasis on all levels.

Our bodies maintain a steady, internal state, where activities such as temperature, blood sugar level, and other variables are kept within certain limits. This operates not only on a physical level, but also in connection with the subtle energies of humanity as well. This is called homeostasis, or balance.

We incarnate under various circumstances that will test this homeostasis on all levels of our being. That is why there are trial and error and countless changes within our lives. By learning to flow with the rhythms of change and maintain our balance, we grow and we establish ever higher states of energy and health. When we hold ourselves back from experiencing the changes we have chosen to encounter, when we oppose the changes, we manifest the primary causes of our sickness.

The yearning for an ideal on any level is what helps propel us through changes. To do so with balance is what we are striving for, and is what the crystal bowl and the elixirs we can make with it can assist us in doing. Together they help us to develop the consciousness that opens higher awareness of our being.

It is essential to realize that every disease has a positive aspect. The ailment informs us of our resistances and our imbalances. It helps us to see the negative energies that we are cultivating. Through the healing process we can learn the lessons and the body is brought back into a natural state of balance. If we fail to see the lessons, we may bandage the symptom, but the illness is likely to remanifest in some other way—perhaps even more strongly.

We put ourselves in situations that cause illness for a number of reasons. First, it does help us to grow and learn. It often occurs as a means to foster compassion in ourselves and others. It can be a means for making the transition we call death. It can occur as a means to get attention and love. It can be a means of cleaning out old debris we have been holding onto within our systems. There can be as many reasons as there are illnesses. We must remember, though, that things such as bad diet, accidents, self-neglect, and other "causes" of sickness are themselves just reflections and symptoms of the true sickness or imbalance we are experiencing.

A disease healed naturally leaves a person stronger. In the natural process, we come to understand our weaknesses and learn to replace them with true strength. How many times do we hear people say "I'm never going to do that again. I'm going to start getting myself back in shape." Usually, as soon as the discomfort of the illness fades, so does the resolve.

The human energy system knows how to maintain itself; unfortunately, we often get in its way. It is not unusual to discover a person who initiates a process of change, i.e., eating right, exercising, proper rest, etc. Three to four weeks later, that individual may find himself or herself down with a cold or flu. Then they wonder how this could happen when they were working so well to improve their health.

This is known as a healing crisis. It is triggered by the appropriate care of the body. When we do not care for ourselves appropriately, it is like muck settling at the bottom of a river. When we strive to improve our health, all of that muck gets stirred up and brought to the surface. The result is the runny nose and all of those other uncomfortable symptoms. This is simply the body's way of cleansing itself.

Unfortunately, many people at such times turn to over-the-counter and prescribed pharmaceuticals to stop this discomfort, not realizing they are also stopping the cleansing process of the body.

Modern pharmaceuticals act swiftly and powerfully to remove symptoms of the disease, bringing superficial relief. This is, in fact, little more than a "fast food" remedy. It relieves the individual from the responsibility of taking care of his or her own health—physical or otherwise. The remedies can, in fact, create more trouble down the road for the individual, for the warning signals are pushed aside, the cleansing is stopped, only to be buried with the potential to surface later even more intensely.

The highest form of ancient healing involved sustaining the individual through methods that allowed him/her to heal themselves—from within and completely. Any attempt to offer a remedy that would stop the body's natural process of healing was a breaking of integrity with the individual.

It is important to treat the whole person, not just the symptom. This involves utilizing methods that promote the natural functions of the physical body in relation to all other aspects of our being. Unfortunately, in our society, we have relegated the responsibility and care of OUR bodies to other individuals. This is not to say that doctors are not needed, as all aspects of medicine can be beneficial. It is saying that we each need to learn more about our bodies and learn to maintain stronger and more natural standards of health.

There are times, when we have ignored and abused our energies for so long, that we may cross that "point of no return." Even then, though, there are alternatives that we can employ to help rebuild some of the body's natural strength and resiliency against disease. We must learn to build and strengthen our own immune systems, rather than relying only on pharmaceuticals; otherwise our systems will become weaker. To assist us in this process we can use any of the modern "energy medicines"—two of which are the use of sound and flower/gem elixirs.

Even though I had been working with the healing forces of sound, music, and voice, when I first came across the crystal bowl I was more excited about using it to create my own flower and gem elixirs than I was about its tonal aspects. I had been employing flower and gem essences in a limited manner with healing sessions with others, although I was using them extensively with myself. I believed it would be more beneficial and effective to make my own—using the flowers and plants from my own environment and by using the crystals and stones that I had personally collected.

I experimented with them, using some of the herbal flowers from my yard, and using just a glass bowl in their creation. Because lead and other chemicals in the glass bowls prevent the full light spectrum from penetrating, the power of the essence was limited. With the quartz crystal bowl, despite its hard consistency, almost the full light spectrum can penetrate and infuse any liquid within the bowl with light energy. Researchers are presently testing the restructuring process of water and other liquids within crystal bowls (through spectra-analysis and other methods).

Flower and gem elixirs are energy "medicines." They can be made by anyone with a crystal bowl, and they serve dynamic functions in the entire holistic healing process:

- They can assist the individual in understanding the lessons of a particular illness or dis-ease being experienced.

- They help restore physiological balance, as well as helping to balance the emotional and mental states that aggravated the condition.

- They can be used to help us open to new levels of awareness—and not just to those associated with health. This includes psychic, creative, and spiritual states of awareness, and their integration within physical life circumstances.

- They assist us in attuning to our environment. Because they are made from the elements of nature, we begin to recognize through their use the intricate interplay of nature and humanity.

- They assist us in aligning and attuning to our more subtle energies and their impact upon our physical life.

- They assist us in developing a deva consciousness, an awareness of the archetypal patterns of energy which operate in and through nature. It is these patterns which enable each flower, plant, stone, and crystal to grow and form in its own unique manner, and yet do so in harmony with nature and humanity.

- Flower and gem essences are catalysts for transformation—emotional, mental, and spiritual, and thus repercussing into the physical as well. (They do not act by way of the roundabout route of the physical body, but rather they act upon the energy system at the root of and surrounding the physical body.)

Through energy medicines, especially those created and charged through the crystal bowl, we can learn more about ourselves and our relation to all aspects of our environment. They teach us the significance of the words of Lao Tzu in the *Tao te ching*: "A person will get well when he is tired of being sick."

Understanding Flower and Gem Elixirs

In the 1930s, Dr. Edward Bach of London gave up a very lucrative practice to explore and develop remedies in the plant world that would restore vitality. The flowers were picked from various plants and trees, and processed into medicines that would treat negative states of mind. He strove for simplicity, wanting to first identify the state of mind, mood, or personality, and then to pick an appropriate flower remedy for it.

The 38 remedies were discovered by trying them on himself. He was considered an extremely sensitive man—so sensitive that if he placed the bloom of a flower upon his tongue, within a short time he would experience the exact states of mind that it would serve to heal.

This reinforced his homeopathic training and its primary axiom of "like cures like."

Unlike medicinal herbology, flower essences do not use the physical material of the plant. Instead the energy behind and operating through the plant is extracted in a simple alchemical procedure (to be explored later in this chapter). The flower remedies are truly "simples" as Dr. Bach referred to them. They stimulate no physical discomfort. They use only the pure and beautiful elements of nature. The plants used in their making grow wild and free, and most are accessible to anyone willing to search them out. Ideally, they are made from plants grown in natural conditions, without chemicals.

Flower and gem essences are absolutely benign. They are not harmful, nor do they conflict when taken with other medications. They can never produce an unpleasant reaction under any circumstances. I have encountered individuals who have complained of the side effects of their use, the most common being "I can't handle the energy." In these cases, the individual is encouraged to examine the motivation for being ill and whether there is a desire to truly get well. Remember, every illness and our response to it can teach us something about ourselves. The worst they can do is nothing. The best is to heal and enlighten.

There are as many uses for flower and gem elixirs as there are flowers and gems. Every flower has its own personality. Each flower and gem has its own vibrational frequency, its own life energy pattern. They each have their own unique function and effect upon the individual. It is that energy pattern which is infused within a liquid. The liquid is then used to alter, transmute, or create new vibrational patterns for the individual— ones that will assist the individual in achieving particular functions and purposes.

In the last chapter we described briefly how vibrational energies can be used to heal and how they interact with an individual's own energy system—whether taken internally or when projected from outside. However taken, the flower and gem elixirs are benign, although the course they take in individual cases is not always predictable. Many experience immediate effects, with tension being relieved. Others find themselves able to confront aspects of the personality which helped the particular condition to manifest. Some may not see effects for up to seven days. Regardless of individual response, self-examination and even counseling are of tremendous help in working with the flower and gem elixirs.

It is important to recognize the link between the psychological make-up and the physiological responses of the body— for good or bad.

The elixirs assist with this. Healing is not just removing physical discomfort or suffering, but it is also coming to terms with the significance of the illness. The remedies stimulate opportunities for this self-encountering. If we want to return to true health, we must expect to change. Unfortunately, many of us are resistant to change. The elixirs open the consciousness to the higher self, bypassing personality resistances and blockages, to initiate the holistic healing process.

On the following pages are several lists of flower and gem elixirs. It is by no means complete, as there are hundreds of flower remedies available. The first is the list of Dr. Edward Bach's 38 remedies, and the basic qualities and lessons associated with them. Following the 38 remedies is a list of other flower remedies, and some of their psychological and spiritual properties. Next is a list of gem elixirs beneficial for each of the seven chakras. Their descriptions, effects, and qualities are skeletal at best, but it does provide a starting point for your own use and exploration of them. In the bibliography are several works which provide in-depth information on individual flower and gem elixirs. (Although there are commercial sources for flower and gem elixirs, it is beneficial to make your own at least once, as it helps to attune you to the alchemical processes of nature and their application to you.)

The 38 Bach Flower Remedies

Agrimony—for inner torture behind a facade; awakens inner peace.

Aspen—for anxiety/apprehension; awakens openness to new experiences.

Beech—for criticalness; awakens acceptance and tolerance.

Centaury—for weakness of will; awakens inner strength.

Cerato—for lack of confidence; awakens trust in inner guidance.

Cherry Plum—for fear of collapse/shock; awakens courage under stress.

Chestnut Bud—for repeating same mistakes; awakens awareness of life's lessons.

Chicory—for possessiveness and martyr syndromes; awakens appropriate giving and receiving.

Clematis—for dreaminess and lack of attention; awakens a grounding and practical inspiration.

Crab Apple—for feelings of uncleanliness or shame; awakens harmony and an inner cleansing.

Elm—for feelings of inadequacy; awakens self-confidence.

Gentian—for discouragement and self-doubt; awakens perseverance and confidence.

Gorse—for despair and hopelessness; awakens faith and hope.

Heather—for self-absorption and failure to listen; awakens caring for others and ability to listen.

Holly—for jealousy, hate, and revenge; awakens compassion.

Honeysuckle—for dwelling in the past; awakens letting go of the past.

Hornbeam—for lacking strength to handle daily activities; awakens confidence of energy and ability.

Impatiens—for impatience and irritability; awakens patience and understanding.

Larch—for lack of self-confidence and inferiority; awakens confidence and creative expression.

The 38 Bach Flower Remedies (cont'd)

Mimulus—for fears and shyness; awakens courage and confidence.

Mustard—for gloom and depression; awakens joy and peace of mind.

Oak—for despair and despondency; awakens brave perseverance and strength.

Olive—for mental/physical exhaustion; awakens renewed vitality.

Pine—for guilt and blame; awakens positive self-acceptance.

Red Chestnut—for excessive fear and anxiety; awakens calm detachment.

Rock Rose—for terror and panic; awakens courage to transcend self.

Rock Water—for inflexibility and self-denial; awakens flexibility, spontaneity, and self-nurturance.

Scleranthus—for uncertainty and indecision; awakens stable decisiveness.

Star of Bethlehem—For all shocks and trauma; awakens healing of trauma.

Sweet Chestnut—for despair and the last of endurance; awakens faith in darkest of times.

Vervain—for fanatical straining and over-enthusiastic; awakens relaxation and moderation.

Vine—for domineering and inflexibility; awakens sensitive leadership and respect.

Walnut—for transition and change and over-sensitivity; awakens objectivity and freedom of perspectives.

Water Violet—for excessive pride and superiority; awakens humility and service.

White Chestnut—for unwanted thoughts and worry; awakens quietness and clarity of mind.

Wild Oat—for dissatisfaction in achievement; awakens clarity of life direction.

Wild Rose—for apathy and resignation; awakens enthusiasm for life.

Willow—for resentment and bitterness; awakens acceptance of responsibility and releasing of blame.

Examples of Other Flower Remedies and Their Effects

Angelica—opens one to the ministrations of the spiritual realms and angelic influences.

Blackberry—for manifesting creative inspiration and for opening to new levels of consciousness.

Calendula—awakens the healing power of words.

California Poppy—for higher intuition; assists in connecting with the nature kingdom and in seeing the aura.

Chaparral—helps one to experience deeper levels of psychic awareness and perception through dreams; helps in detoxifying the system.

Indian Paintbrush—stimulates artistic and creative expression.

Iris—stimulates creative imagination and inspiration; awakens artistic abilities.

Lavender—soothing to nerves and to over-sensitivity to psychic and spiritual experiences.

Lotus—for inspiration, intuition, healing; amplifies the effects of other essences.

Mugwort—awakens greater awareness of spiritual influence and understanding of dreams; assists in making you more conscious of your psychic energies.

Rose—awakens love and inspiration; helps attune to the angelic hierarchies and the divine Feminine.

Rosemary—assists in controling out-of-body experiences; stimulates mental faculties.

Sage—assists in awakening to inner world experiences; slows aging process; understanding life experiences.

Saint John's Wort—opens one to divine guidance; activates ability for lucid dreaming; increases psychic energies; assists in out-of-body experiences.

Shasta Daisy—spiritualizes the intellect; assists in seeing the entire picture.

Other Flower Remedies (cont'd)

Star Tulip—makes one more receptive to spiritual realms and astrological influences; awakens feminine aspects of imagination and intuition.

Sunflower—balances the ego and awakens the inner light of divine inspiration; assists in realizing capabilities of the soul.

Violet—attunement to the fairy realms; for awakening warmth and greater spirituality.

Wild Rose—for overcoming apathy and for integrating the spiritual in the physical; tonic for longstanding illness.

Yarrow—for psychic protection and oversensitivity; strengthens the aura; gives emotional clarity; eases stress.

(For other uses of these and other flower remedies, consult the bibliography.)

Examples of Gem Elixirs and Uses

Base Chakra

Smokey Quartz—This elixir stimulates and purifies the base chakra. It channels the energy of the crown chakra so that it can be expressed more practically in the physical life of the individual. It also draws the love from the heart center to the root center so that it can be grounded and utilized. This elixir helps to bring more light force into the entire auric field, as it dissolves negativity and other auric debris.

Spleen Chakra

Carnelian—An elixir made from this stone helps awaken the creative and artistic forces of the individual so that they can be used by all aspects of his/her being. It awakens the energies which assist in the manifestation process. When used with meditation, it helps you to focus energies on your goals and intentions. It activates the magnetic aspects of your energy field so that you are able to draw more energy in. It can also be used to tap into past-life records of yourself and the planet.

Solar Plexus Chakra

Citrine—Citrine elixir helps to balance the rational mind and to open a bridge between the higher mental and intuitional levels of consciousness. It awakens a greater sense of wisdom and peace. It also activates the magnetic aspects of your auric field in a manner that can assist in drawing riches or new opportunities for their acquisition. It can immerse you in the illusions of the pleasures of the earth, if care is not taken with its usage. It can assist you in seeing your higher goals, along with the best ways of manifesting them.

Heart Chakra

Rose Quartz—Rose quartz elixir is a strong and gentle healing tonic. It helps in releasing negative emotions being held within the heart. It awakens a greater sense of inner peace and self-fulfillment. It can be used effectively for internal wounds revolving around past giving and receiving of love. It can be used for emotional release, and for cleaning out forgotten memories and energies that are blocking growth. It is calming to the emotions in times of turmoil.

Malachite—A gem elixir made from malachite awakens creativity and the energy and ability for change. It helps to bring out your true aspects, and it can be used in meditation to focus on single problems. It can be used to stimulate the aura so that it triggers opportunities for new growth and balance.

Throat Chakra

Turquoise—Turquoise gem elixir balances emotional and creative expression. It heightens sensitivity, and it can be used as an aid to developing the ability of clairaudience. It protects those who work and live in negative environments, and it promotes healing on all levels.

Brow Chakra

Sodalite—Sodalite is the densest and most grounded of the dark blue stones. When used to make an elixir, it elicits deep thought and a clearing of the mind so that it can function properly. This elixir assists the individual in thinking and responding intelligently in all situations, and in reaching logical conclusions. It opens one in meditation to new sparks of spiritual light by balancing the mind.

Lapis Lazuli—An elixir made from this stone serves to cleanse the mind and the aura. It can be used to break down subconscious blockages to deeper levels of consciousness. It assists in the development of telepathy, and in seeing the spiritual path that is best to follow in this incarnation.

Fluorite—Fluorite also makes an excellent elixir for the brow chakra. It is multi-dimensional in its uses. It awakens the aura to increase opportunities to advance the mind. It can be used to help in understanding and assimilating abstract ideas. It balances the yin and the yang, when used as an elixir. It balances the hemispheres of the brain for more creative functions. Blue fluorite stimulates mental calmness. Purple fluorite in an elixir awakens the devotional aspects of the soul so that communion with the divine is easier. Yellow or gold fluorite elixir awakens wisdom and helps in understanding life's experiences, so that understanding can unfold into wisdom itself. White fluorite gem elixir is purifying on all levels. It also assists the mind in uniting with the creative forces of the universe.

Crown Chakra

Amethyst—Amethyst stones make excellent gem elixirs. They are cleansing and purifying on all levels and can be used for all illnesses and disease. Amethyst awakens deeper understanding and intuition when used in meditation, and awakens a greater sense of humility. It can also be used in helping the individual develop the ability to control astral projections and to overcome their fears of such.

Other Important Gem Elixirs

Clear Quartz—Clear Quartz can be used to augment the effects of all other gem and flower elixirs. It is effective in balancing and energizing all of the chakra centers. The elixir awakens the pure light of the soul and helps to draw it into the physical life of the individual. It balances and energizes the aura, and is one of the easiest and most powerful of those elixirs made from the crystal bowls.

Moonstone—An elixir made from moonstone can be used by almost everyone upon the planet, just as quartz elixir can. Moonstone elixir balances and soothes all emotional states, and it assists the individual in moving from the lower emotional expressions to higher aspiration. It assists in transforming psychic energy into spiritual energy.

This elixir assists in guarding us against thresholds we are not prepared to cross in our psychic explorations. For women, it is helpful in maintaining physical and emotional balance during the menstrual cycle. Moonstone elixir assists men in becoming aware of their feminine aspects. Overall, it is an elixir which assists in experiencing calmness and

peace of mind. It can also be used in ritual work for awakening the ability of invisibility.

How to Determine the Elixirs You Need

Determining the flower or gem elixir to use is fairly straightforward. If
working on altering a behavior pattern or personal characteristic, self-
observation and common sense are the keys. How do you respond to various situations and people within your life? What qualities and abilities
do you wish to work on developing? Asking yourself such questions can
assist you in determining the elixir or combination of elixirs most beneficial to you.

Ideally, self-determination of the essences is encouraged, as opposed
to having another choose the essences for you. Counseling sessions and
flower/gem essence readings can be effective, but ultimately it is the individual's responsibility. "Know Thyself" was a precept of the ancient mystery schools, and this is the precept behind the use of the flower and gem
elixirs. They demand greater self-observation and personal responsibility
if they are to be as dynamic a tool of healing as possible. They teach the
individual to get in touch with his/her inner levels. Self-determination of
the essences needed forces the individual to articulate those changes that
are necessary, and to affirm the qualities desired.

In essence there are predominantly two methods for determining
the elixir(s) to use. The first is a rational approach and the second is more
intuitive. A third would be a combination of the two. Under each of
these, there are specific techniques that can be employed.

The rational approach is done through the self-observation and
questioning already determined. Look at the patterns of your life. What
mistakes do you tend to repeat? How do you respond in various situations? How do you react to the people in your life? What are your predominant moods from day to day? Observe yourself. Listen to yourself.
Assess your needs, challenges, and growth. Keep in mind, in the rational
approach, the qualities of all of the essences probably apply to all of us at
some time in our lives.

Remember that Dr. Edward Bach worked to demystify medicine and
develop a system that could be understood and used by anyone seeking
better health. Read through the various descriptions of essences in this
work, and in those listed and described in the works found in the bibliography. Make a list of those remedies which correspond most to your

personality type, or the stresses and emotions you are going through. List all those that are tied to qualities you wish to develop.

Having made your list, decide which are most urgent or immediate. If undecided, rate them on a scale of 1–10 (with 1 as the lowest priority and 8 to 10 as the highest). You do not have to limit yourself to a single remedy, as they can be combined. It is best, though, to limit the combinations to seven or less. This allows the remedies to work more effectively together.

Other methods of choosing fall under the category of the intuitional approach. This includes such methods as using meditation to determine the essences and elixirs needed. Applied kinesiology can be used, and some individuals use etheric touch, running their hands through the aura of an individual or over the tops of the essence bottles to feel the magnetic attraction or repulsion. One of the easiest of the intuitional is the application of radiesthesia.

Radiesthesia ia a method of dowsing or divining involving the use of a tool to determine the radiation of the essences and their compatibility with the individual. The tool may be a pendulum, willow branches, or dowsing rods. Radiesthesia involves the process of divining—of connecting to our divine nature which knows what we need. For it to work, the mind must be kept objective, but it is a method that anyone can easily learn and develop to high degrees.

Using a pendulum is the easiest. A pendulum is made by attaching a symmetrical object to the end of a thread or chain. It is then dangled over the object in question. It provides answers in accordance with its movement.

Steps to Using a Pendulum:

1. Draw a circle on a piece of paper. You can place horizontal and vertical lines through the circle. You may also draw an inner circle in which you can place a witness (if you are divining for someone else) or a particular remedy that you wish to determine how effective or important it is to you. Refer to the diagrams on the following pages. With a little ingenuity and practice, you can turn this circle into a powerful diagnostic tool for yourself.

2. Decide what each direction of movement will mean. If the pendulum swings in the vertical direction, is it an affirmative answer? If it swings horizontally, is it a negative response? Whatever you decide the movements will mean, hold to that whenever you use the pendulum henceforth. You are laying the ground rules for your intuition to

communicate to you through the symbology of the movement. Common movement assignments are:

—Back and forth along the horizontal line = NO.
—Back and forth along the vertical line = YES.
—Clockwise circling = YES.—Counterclockwise circling = NO.

Movement of the
Pendulum along the
axis of the circle
gives yes or no
answers.

Witness or
Essence to be
checked is placed
in the inner
circle.

3. Practice with the pendulum before using it on yourself and others to
   determine flower and gem elixirs. Set the circle flat upon a table. Rest
   your elbow on the table so that your hand is above the circle. Hold
   the pendulum thread between the thumb and the first finger, with
   the weighted end of the pendulum dangling an inch or two above the
   heart of the circle. Ask yourself some yes or no questions that you
   know the answer to. Initially, move the pendulum in the direction of
   the right answer. At this point you are simply sending messages to
   your more intuitive levels of consciousness, letting it know how to
   communicate through the pendulum.

4. Next set the elixir in the circle, and hold the pendulum over it. Make
   sure it is not moving. Then simply ask appropriate questions: "Do I
   need this flower/gem essence?" "Does _____ need this
   flower/gem essence?" The movement and the strength of the movement will give you your answer. Remember that it is the intuitive levels of the mind which is interacting with the energy of the essence
   and causing the movement of the pendulum in response.

   If you wish, you can also hold the essence in one hand, while
   testing it with the pendulum with your other hand. You can also
   determine essences for someone at a long distance. Place a witness for
   the individual into the circle, along with the essence, and then simply ask the appropriate question. Remember these are guidelines to
   help you develop a quick attunement to your more intuitive levels.

Place elixir within the inner circle, hold the pendulum over it, and ask your questions about its appropriateness to your condition.

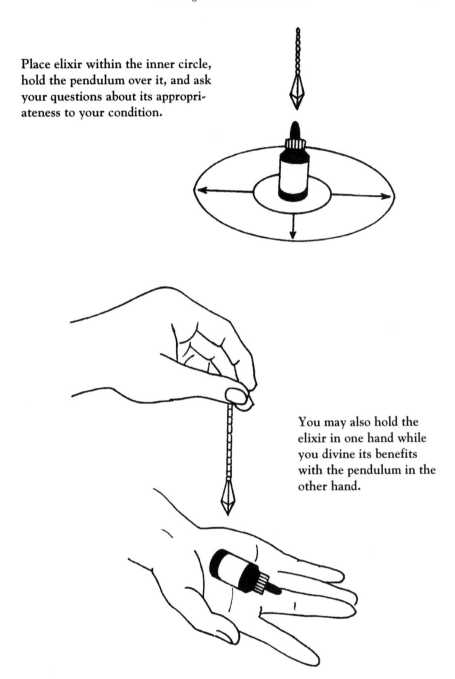

You may also hold the elixir in one hand while you divine its benefits with the pendulum in the other hand.

Using the Pendulum to Divine the Elixirs

5. You can also use the pendulum to determine dosage and combinations that are most beneficial. It all depends on the questions you ask. Be specific and phrase in a "Yes or No" pattern. "Do these three essences work well together for me?" "Should I take this essence four times a day?"

6. Having determined the essence needed, it can be taken four times a day—just several drops per dosage. For someone who is at a long distance, place the witness of the individual into your crystal bowl. Place the flower essence bottle (use your felt or leather pad) also within the bowl, next to the witness. As you play the bowl, the essence is sent to the witness through the etheric upon the sound waves. The sound waves carry the vibrations of the flower/gem elixirs to the individual, to interact with his/her energy field. You can also place several drops on the rim of the bowl. As you play the bowl, the vibrations interact and are carried to the individual.

   How long to play the bowl and send the energies to the individuals is a common question. There is no set answer. Ten minutes is often more than enough, but do not limit yourself to this. Use the pendulum to help you determine how long to send the energy of the essence through the witness to the individual. "Is five minutes long enough to send this elixir with the bowl?" The effects of the elixirs are always amplified when used with the force of the bowls.

7. Having determined your essence(s), you can also use the crystal bowl to fill your environment with the vibrational frequencies of the elixirs. As you play the bowl, the frequencies of the sound and the elixirs combine, filling the air with its vibrational energies. These energies then interact with your auric field while you are within that environment, providing a more constant healing for you.

8. Remember that the pendulum is a tool for communicating with the subconscious mind—the seat of our intuitive energies. The subconscious intuition communicates through the nervous system, giving signals that make the pendulum move. Through the nervous system, the brain gets all of its data from the external and internal senses, and then transmits the appropriate messages back.

   The swinging of the pendulum is an ideomotor response—an involuntary muscle reaction caused by the subconscious mind. Any muscular action creates electrical impulses which are transferred in this case to the pendulum, causing it to move in the appropriate manner.

9. Children respond strongly and more effectively to vibrational remedies such as the essence than do adults. Their energy system is more magnetic, and thus they absorb the outside vibrations into their system effectively. The flower and gem elixirs are dynamic tools for preventative medicine with children. They can be used to strengthen and build the child's immune system and to keep the child balanced and attuned to those more intuitive energies that are so natural as the child grows. With children, it is beneficial to lessen the number of essences within combinations, as their systems respond very strongly to these elixirs.

10. Elixirs can also be used with the treatment of pets for illness and personality quirks. Adding the elixirs to their food and water is the easiest method.

Exercise 26—
Preparing Your Healing and Magical Elixirs

Flower and gem elixirs are prepared by placing flowers in a crystal bowl of water in full sunlight for several hours. They can also be made by lightly boiling the flowers and gems together. Both methods will be explored in greater detail later. This process extracts the life essence and energy matrix of the flowers and gems to form a potentized elixir. This is known as the MOTHER ESSENCE, or MOTHER ELIXIR. Brandy is added to this elixir as a preservative.

From the Mother Elixir will come STOCK BOTTLES. Two drops of the Mother Elixir is added to one-ounce dropper bottles of good water (non-chemically treated). To this is added a teaspoon of brandy—again as a preservative. From these stock bottles will come individual DOSAGE BOTTLES. The dosage bottles are also one-ounce in size. Two drops are then taken from the appropriate stock bottle and added to the dosage bottle with water and brandy.

Mother Essence   Stock   Dosage

Once the dosage bottle is made up, the individual can either take the elixir straight from the bottle itself or add drops to a glass of drinking water. Four to seven drops at a time is all that is needed. Most recommend that this dosage be taken four times a day.

The flower and gem essences actually become potentized in this dilution method, in much the same manner as homeopathic medicines. Dr. Ernst Lehrs, in the book *Man or Matter* (Faber and Faber), gave a description of the potentizing process as applied to homeopathy. "The method of diluting or 'potentizing', is as follows: a given volume of the material is to be diluted in nine times its volume of distilled water. The degree of dilution thus arrived at is 1:10, usually symbolized 1x. A tenth part of this solution is again mixed with nine times its bulk in water. The degree of dilution is now 1:100 or 2x. This process is continued as far as it is necessary for a given purpose . . .

"We can carry the dilutions as far as we please without destroying the capacity of the substance to produce a physiological effect. On the contrary, as soon as its original capacity is reduced to a minimum by dilution, further dilution gives it the power to cause even stronger reactions, of a different, and usually opposite, kind. The second capacity rises through stages to a variable maximum as dilution proceeds.

"What this potentizing process shows is that, by repeated expansion in space, a substance can be carried beyond the ponderable conditions of matter into the realm of pure functional effect. The potentization of physical substances thus gains a significance far wider than that of medical use."

It is for this reason that the primary principle of homeopathy is that "like cures like." Disease symptoms are treated with highly diluted substances which produce similar symptoms if ingested in normal quantities. In the potentizing process, the substance moves from cause to an effect. The symbol of infinity reflects this process. As a substance is diluted and potentized the inverse occurs, where the cure or effect is elicited because the primal core of the energy is released. We are brought into touch with an archetypal pattern of energy.

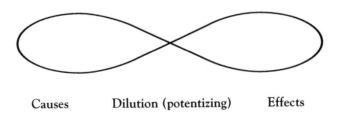

Causes   Dilution (potentizing)   Effects

Those who take flower and gem elixirs often have to change old ideas about medication. More is not better when it comes to these elixirs. Taking them upon rising, when going to sleep, and several times in between is all that is necessary. Also, with flower and gem elixirs, increasing the frequency of dosages is more effective than increasing the amount of each dosage. More frequent dosages are recommended for acute conditions, and for accelerating the transformation process.

When you set out to make flower and gem elixirs you are participating in alchemical processes. Within a crystal bowl of flower or gem essence, the alchemy of nature is created. The four elements of nature are combined in the process to touch the fifth element of ether or spirit life. The fire of the sun plays upon the water within the crystal bowl (an earth tool), the essence in the bowl is surrounded by the air, and, through the sound of the bowl, the energy of the air is used to charge the essence/elixir.

All of this occurs upon the earth. When the process is completed, the life or spirit essence—the archetypal matrix—of the flower or gem is released alchemically into the liquid within the bowl.

1. Clean your crystal bowl. Performing the ritual bath is beneficial.

2. Take time to meditate and attune to nature. Sitting and meditating outside, near the area of the flowers you will be using, or outside with the gems and stones you will be using.

3. If you intend to make the gem elixirs, it is better to use stones in their raw and uncut form. If you do not have any in this form, do not be upset, just make sure that the stones and gems are cleansed thoroughly of any previous programming. Setting them in sea salt for 24 to 48 hours before you make your elixir will serve to erase any programming and negativity.

4. For the flowers, make sure you pick them in their full maturity, and do so early in the morning. The early sun is more vitalizing. Usually from noon on, the ultra-violet rays become more intense, and the basic prana of the air is diminished.

5. Have on hand appropriate water to use. Crystal spring water that is not chemically treated is most effective for the flower essences. Distilled water is most effective for the making of gem elixirs.

6. Set your crystal bowl in full sunlight. Make sure it is a day in which there are no clouds. Add approximately 12 ounces of water to the bowl. Chime the bowl softly. I recommend 12 times, to represent

the movement of the sun and the signs of the zodiac. Remember that the more significance we can add to the process, the more empowered the essences become. Ringing the bowl also serves to cleanse the water within it of any outstanding pollutants or thought contaminates.

7. Pick the flower blossoms and float them immediately upon the sur-face of the water. (Some people recommend that you handle the flowers by a leaf or the stem, rather than with your hands. Some also recommend avoiding touching the water.) Float the flowers until the surface of the water is covered, making sure each blossom is touching the water. Place the bowl in the sun where shadows will be unable to touch it for several hours. You may wish to cover the bowl with plas-tic or such to keep bugs and dirt from it.

8. After at least three hours—or until the flowers begin to fade, careful-ly remove the blossoms from the water. Use stems from the flowers or longer crystal points to pick the flowers out. I recommend that the blossoms then be laid around the shrubs and plants in the yard as a sign of reverence and as a blessing of the return to Nature.

   For the gem elixirs, you may wish to leave the stones and gems in the sun a little longer. Some recommend using brandy in the bowls with the stones and gems, believing it to draw more energy from them than just distilled water. Either way is effective, although using the brandy does help in purifying the stones. With raw cut stones, it is easy for dirt to become wedged in crevices in the stone. Using brandy helps to prevent contamination.

   (Also be careful of ringing the crystal bowl when stones are inside it as it may cause a discordant vibration that can crack the bowl. Either ring it very gently or use a pad, as discussed earlier.)

9. Ring the bowl again. This will charge the essence and will help to cleanse it of any impurities that may have entered. Then, using a clean funnel, empty the contents into a dark brown bottle. The brown bottles help preserve the life and energy of the essence more than do clear bottles.

10. Add brandy (approximately one-fourth to one-half of the amount of the elixir). This is your Mother Essence. From it you will be able to make the stock and dosage bottles.

11. On days that are less sunny, or in times of poor weather, the boiling method can also be used. In this procedure, the flowers are picked on

as sunny a morning as possible. Fill the cleansed pot with blossoms and then add enough pure water to cover them.

12. Bring the water to a quick light boil, simmering for about half an hour, with the pot uncovered. Then set it outside to cool.

13. When the pot has cooled, cover it with a piece of cotton muslin and pour the liquid through the cloth into the crystal bowl. The cotton serves to filter out sediment that occurs through the boiling. You may wish to pour from one pot to another several times, using the cotton to filter all the sediment before pouring the water into the crystal bowl.

14. Play the bowl for about five minutes, visualizing it being charged with awakening the essence of the flowers of the stones. Then set it outside for about an hour, regardless of the amount of sunlight. This will help to rejuvenate any energy that was lost in the boiling method.

15. Repeat step ten and create your Mother Essence Bottle.

You will find as you work with this process, you will have ideas for variations. Follow them. Flower and gem essences help us to attune to our more intuitive and subtle energies. It is important to learn to act upon them. Your own personal attunement and variations will help to form a foundation for more dynamic use and response to the elixirs you prepare.

Exercise 27—
Charging and Storing Your Elixirs

1. Place your elixirs in brown bottles. This helps to filter out extraneous light (particularly artificial) which can leech the energy from the stored essence.

2. Before using, shake the bottle of elixir. This keeps the energy active, and prevents it from becoming dormant when not in use. Periodically shaking the bottles is beneficial.

3. Use dropper bottles. This reduces waste and enables your elixirs to last a much greater length of time. Many pharmaceutical companies sell empty dropper bottles. The primary sources for commercial essences, as listed at the end of this chapter, often sell empty bottles you can use.

4. When taking your dosage from the bottle (i.e., four drops under the tongue), be careful not to touch the tongue with the dropper. This can serve as a transfer of bacteria to your dosage bottle. Occasionally, it is good to hold your bottles up to the light. If there is anything floating in them, they are probably contaminated, and you shouldn't use them.

5. Periodically use the crystal bowl to charge the essence. Simply playing the bowl around them serves this purpose. If you wish, you can lay each elixir bottle on the pad inside the bowl and charge them with the bowl in that manner.

6. Some people will place their elixirs under a pyramid to charge them periodically, to make sure they are at maximum energy frequencies.

7. As you are making the elixirs, surround your crystal bowl in the sun with other quartz crystals and stones. This will enhance the effects in accordance with whatever stones you utilize.

8. Another effective way of charging the elixirs is by placing small pieces of quartz crystal inside the bottles. Quartz crystal is a dynamic amplifier of energy.

9. The mother elixirs and the stock bottles should be charged and cleansed about every three months. This keeps their energy active. Simply playing the bowl around them for about ten minutes after having shaken the bottles will serve this purpose effectively. The energy effects of the elixir can last indefinitely by doing this.

10. Make sure you clean the bowl and any other items after making an elixir and before making a different kind. Otherwise, traces of one will be carried over and combine with the new. Although the combination may be compatible, you will not be able to determine properly and utilize the effects. The catalytic factor of the elixirs may vary in ways you could not otherwise anticipate.

Chapter Ten

Crystal Bowl Ritual Songs

O ne of the most powerful ways of applying music to enhance our lives—especially the music of the crystal bowls—is through ritual. It does not require much work to discern how effective the bowls are in the healing realm, but they are also extremely dynamic tools for heightened levels of consciousness and perception. They can be used ritually for inducing altered states, facilitating astral projection, trance, vision quests, and the opening of higher clairvoyance; and they can assist us in attuning to nature and the beings and life within it. Crystal bowls can be employed in every facet and ritual of our life.

Mention the word ritual to a dozen people, and you will receive a dozen different reactions. There are even varied and confusing reactions among those of the metaphysical and spiritual fields. When it comes to the application of sound in relation to ritual and other "mystical" aspects of our unfoldment, misconceptions abound. It is amazing how many people still think along the lines of spells, incantations, and charms in association with anything metaphysical or psychic. Most of these perspectives have their origin in the fabric of imagination—what has been stimulated by distorted views through television and movies over the past 25–30 years.

The general public has little knowledge of how sacred sound—such as through the medium of the crystal bowl—is used in ritual to align our individual energies with the highest energies of the universe.

Most information on ritual and the "magical" use of sound is conceived—and performed—by the dabbler or the psychic thrill seeker who has little true knowledge. They often invent practices just to cover their own misbehaviors. They use such practices to proclaim themselves as something they are not, or they use them for self-gratification. Unfortunately, this is what gets attention and publicity.

It was once considered that ritual and the mystical use of sound concerned themselves only with the demons and angels, but we use rituals in our actions and our words every day. We get up, shower, drink coffee, and go to work. We follow the same routine or ritual every day. We walk into the work environment and someone says, "Good morning." We say, "Good morning," in return. It may be rote, and it may not seem to have much energy attached to it, but it is ritual.

We have personal rituals, social rituals, military rituals, religious rituals—rituals associated with every aspect of human expression. Those religious groups that would condemn any ritual activity would do well to look upon their own religious practices. Their services follow a specific order to create a specific atmosphere within the church. They employ ritual techniques of sound through music, bells, and prayers.

What this chapter will focus upon is how the sounds of the crystal bowl can be used in mystical and ritual ways to expand our consciousness. Bells, gongs, and clicks are ancient instruments in ritual attunement, and the modern crystal bowl can serve their functions as well as others. We can easily learn to use the crystal bowl as an effective tool to cross thresholds to higher, more divine energy.

A soft tapping of the wooden or metal end of the wand against the side of the bowl while holding the side of the bowl so it cannot vibrate will provide the "ritual click." (It must be gentle because the bowls are susceptible to cracking.) The purpose of the click in ritual is to focus attention from silence into sonics, bringing all points of consciousness together in unison. It links the unmanifest with the manifest in a natural way. There is no shock. It can be incorporated to allow the ritual participant(s) to adjust to conditions that are about to change within the ritual itself. In this way there is no drastic movement which could break concentration and shatter altered states.

Rhythmic clicks and knocks are a part of many rituals. One method of employing them for magical purposes is to associate the rhythms with definite ideas or experiences. You can establish a clicking pattern for emotions, for different inner levels of consciousness, etc. Ritual clicks and knocks serve to clarify and not mystify. They are calls to attention.

Remember that the more significance we can apply to every aspect of our rituals, the more magically empowered they become.

An example of using the clicks and knocks upon the crystal bowl for ritual purposes can be found in the mystical Qabala, discussed earlier. In the ancient Tree of Life of the Qabala, there are ten spheres, or levels of consciousness. Each level of consciousness has its own energies that can be released when we learn to access those levels. We can use clicks and knocks to serve as a call to attention to the conscious mind that we are going to enter ritually a particular level. If we intend to do a ritual to enter into the fourth level, known as Chesed, so that we can open to greater abundance and prosperity, we could use four clicks or taps upon the bowl to initiate the ritual, and then later to close it.

The clicks help move the mind's attention from one level of awareness to the next. In this case, it initiates the process of moving from the conscious mind to that level of the subconscious symbolized by Chesed on the Tree of Life, and then back again.

The crystal bowl can also be used as a bell or gong in any ritual work. The bell or gong in traditional rituals serves a different function than the click or tap. The sound of the bell or gong causes reverberation, with diminishing resonance fading into silence. A reverberated sound is one which re-echoes many times. These reverberations impinge upon the ear and the body, giving the impression of being in a sea of sound.

It is this effect that was created through strong repeated invocations and chants, filling the temple or room with the energy or force being invoked. This is what the crystal bowl also does. The reverberation from it helps to create a space acceptable for an actual manifestation of a particular energy, or for the altering of consciousness of the individual.

The individual learns to follow the sound into silence. The bell or gong aspect of the bowl, as well as its singing aspect, initiates a transference from the audible to the inaudible energies—from the physical to the more subtle dimensions. The bell aspect is used to direct outward attention to inner meanings. In playing the bowl as a bell or gong, it should be slow and repetitive. The sound needs a good period of reverberation to be most effective.

The bell or gong aspect of the crystal bowl is effected by tapping the wand against the side of the bowl. Making and using a special wand for this is recommended. A simple wand can be made with a doorstop, found in any hardware store. Fasten a small, hard rubber ball (such as can be found in most pet stores) onto the screw end, and you have a wand.

The bell or gong capabilities of the crystal bowl can induce an altered state just as effectively as its singing aspect. The gonging should be allowed to reverberate to its maximum before each repetition. With practice, you will develop a rhythm appropriate to your ritual. The number of gongs will vary also, according to the ritual. The more significance you add, the more power it will invoke, and the easier it becomes to follow the sound to the inner realms of awareness and energy.

Gongs and bells of any kind are often considered the highest and most spiritual of not only the percussion instruments but of all instruments. Their single tones give off one and many tones at the same time. These tones reverberate. The tone can be thought of as being dormant within the crystal bowl, and as it is awakened it creates harmony with its release. We also are bound within the crystalline structures of our bodies. As we learn to release our energies, we can create harmony within our lives.

Altered States and Shamanic Journeys

The tones of the crystal bowls can be utilized to facilitate the touching and entering into new levels of consciousness. The tones trigger dramatic effects within the body and the consciousness. When you learn to combine the tones with specific imaging, you will begin to touch levels and dimensions of life that cannot be as easily touched without the bowl.

Guided imagery, as found in many forms of meditation, produces altered states of consciousness. If concentrated and focused through the sounds of the crystal bowl, these images can lead us into connecting our individual energies with the more archetypal energies of the universe. The archetypal images reflect the primary energies of the universe, i.e., as they were in the beginning. The archetypes are the primordial source of energy, the first point where the divine begins to take upon itself a concrete form or image. All guided imagery and symbols are derived from archetypes, and at some point within our evolvement and development they must lead us back to them. If we do not try and get back to the archetypes, we do not progress beyond a certain point. Guided imagery in meditation, when applied with the crystal bowls, assists us in merging our finite minds with the infinite mind of the universe.

The use of tones in meditation can facilitate a deeper response within your consciousness. The sounds of the crystal bowl can be incorporated into meditations to enhance the effects of your imaging. One way of doing this is through the magical journey. This is a variation of the

Qabalistic technique known as pathworking. It is a method which opens the doors to the astral plane and to other dimensions. The imagery employed in the meditation is that of a journey. You simply visualize yourself going on a mythical or magical journey. This is more commonly known today as a shamanic journey, although in reality there are slight differences. The purpose of the journey will determine what you encounter along the way.

A question often asked is how to differentiate a true shamanic/magical journey from an imaginative visualization. Both involve visualization, but with the shamanic/magical journey we become a part of the process, experiencing it as if it were real—much in the manner of our dreams at night. The visualization and imaging in our meditations—with the use of the bowl—energizes and strengthens us so that we can open to that full experience.

We use the bowl to initiate the journey and to assist us in focusing the consciousness. We learn to ride the sounds to deeper levels of consciousness, where the imaging can be used to release energies into manifestation within our lives. Through the magical journey with the crystal bowl, we learn to align ourselves with the forces of the universe to enhance our lives, rather than being at odds with it. We work more fully with the ancient Hermetic Principle of Correspondence: "As above, so below; as below, so above." What we do on one level affects us on all other levels. They are inseparable. The effects may not be immediately visible or discernible, but their manifestation into a corresponding physical life circumstance is inevitable.

When we create a magical journey, we create a series of images and actions that we play out within our mind while in a relaxed (altered) state of consciousness. This relaxed state enables us to activate greater inner energies which are then focused and directed by our thoughts. These energies will ultimately play themselves out on a physical level somewhere within your life. The magical journey utilizes the creative imagination and the use of sacred sound in a concentrated, controlled and directed manner to elicit specific responses within our physical life. The journey visualization can be seen as a symbolic representation of that which you are manifesting or wanting to manifest. This can be anything from greater abundance to prosperity, to clairvoyance, to new love.

The imagination is one of our greatest assets. It is a human quality that can be developed to enhance and augment our lives. It is not an escape tool, but an enhancement tool. It is the directing of specific images in a controlled process to manifest what we need within our lives. The crystal bowl is a dynamic tool to assist us.

With the shamanic/magical journey, we build a story—much in the manner of a normal daydream. The difference, though, is that we will be a part of it, and it will follow a set pattern. We will also use the crystal bowl in a ritual manner to activate the energies into your life that are symbolized by the story. You can construct your own magical journeys, utilizing mythical figures and symbols. The ancient figures and symbols are steeped in energy. They have a powerful thoughtform connected to them, so that when we utilize them, we invoke that energy into play within our life.

The simplest way to begin this process is to use the legends, myths, and tales of the past. Most of the ancient scriptures and stories had cloaked within them esoteric teachings and energies that could be invoked by those willing to put forth the effort. Familiarizing yourself with the legends and myths and their esoteric significance will assist you in this process. If there is a particular mythology or culture for which you have an affinity, go to the stories and legends within it. Find those that reflect what you seem to be going through in your life, or that you want to accomplish in your life. By working with those that seem to coincide with your own particular purpose, you will more easily open to and access the archetypal energies and forces behind the images in the story.

If you have reached a stage where you wish to begin and take on higher initiation, you could use, for example, the Greek tales of Hercules and the Twelve Labors. You could use the tale of Jason and the Argonauts as a basis for your own magical journey to rewards, as symbolized by the golden fleece. Substitute yourself in the role of Hercules or Jason, or any of the other characters in the myth that you may feel more drawn to. The bowl can then be used to enhance and assist you in opening to the energies reflected in the tale you choose.

Even when using ancient tales and myths, remember to also use your own imagination and construction. You do not have to hold to the letter of the tale. Adapt it. Construct it to meet your own particular needs. A degree of spontaneity is vital, if it is to work for you magically and release energies to manifest as specific conditions, experiences, and opportunities within your lives.

Before you place yourself in a meditative condition of any kind, know exactly what you wish to have happen within this journey. Construct it and adapt it so that the outcome will meet your own purpose—and then stick to it! You will find, as you gain experience in this process, that images will arise that may distract you or lead you astray on your journey. Spontaneity is vital, but CONTROL is even more vital. Make sure you reach your destination before you end your meditation.

Learning as much as you can about symbology—especially arche-typal symbols—will help you to utilize them to empower this meditation-al process. In the chart below is a description of basic archetypal energies, their characteristics and the symbols associated with them.

The Basic Archetypes of Carl Jung	
Archetypes	**Characteristics and Symbols of Archetypes**
Self	• deals with energy of the ego/individual • sacred symbols include temples, homes, books, star, egg, weeds, lit candle, births, gifts, weddings
Feminine	• in life and pathworking, this energy creates relation-ships, flow, beauty, birth, receptivity and acceptance • symbols include vessel, cave, womb, queen, doorway, priestess, wells, moon, veil, scabbard
Masculine	• in life, it deals with fathering, making, directing, organizing, building, active and asserive, penetrat-ing; it initiates • symbols include kings, unicorns, phallus, sun, sceptre, sword, tools
Heroic	• deals with facing difficulties and the insurmount-able, conquers, heals, etc. • symbols include battles, struggles, teachers and new knowledge, youth, shields, healing balms
Adversary	• "All is Change," the agent of change, destroys or wounds what is, brings unexpected, tearing down of old, uses anger, morose • symbols include monsters, tyrants, beasts, demons, suffering, walls, and the abyss
Death/Rebirth (Transition)	• deals with the end of one and beginning of another, crisis, change bring sacrifice and new life • symbols: Solstice and Equinoxes, rite of initiation, altar, clock, dance, prayers
Journey	• deals with movement forward, development, aging, building on previous, new directions • symbols include Tree of Life, winding roads, ascent mountains, staff, guides, rivers, streams, vacations, pilgrimages

Perform the journey as often (no more than once a day) as is necessary for your own life experiences to begin to take on the same tone reflected within the experiences of your magical journey. Usually only three times is necessary before you are able to release the energy into your life strongly enough for it to be recognized. If done three days in a row, within a week to 10 days the energy will be experienced to some degree. (Depending upon the symbology that you utilize, your ability to concentrate, and your individual purpose, the time element for its manifestation may vary.)

It is important to take time to evaluate and assess correlations between your life circumstances and your magical journey after performing the ritual. Otherwise, you will not know how to adapt it for greater or lesser effects in the future. At the end of a week, look back over the events of your life that you have encountered since performing your magical journey. Are there similarities? What seems to be the predominant emotion you have experienced during this time? What has been your attitude? Has anything new or different occurred? Working with the magical journey teaches us that everything in our life is significant. It teaches us that we can empower our thoughts and images with sound and concentrated direction to release certain energies into play within our lives. We are not at the mercy of our life circumstances. We can change them and direct them. We are co-creators of our life.

When we employ the crystal bowls in the magical journey ritual, the effects are amplified and their manifestation is accelerated. It stimulates a balancing of the hemispheres of the brain, deepens the emotions and the associations with the symbols and images of the journey. The rhythms, sounds, and patterns of the bowl deepen your altered state of consciousness and facilitate the movement to a full magical immersion into the energies of the journey.

Exercise 28—
Magical Journey into the Crystal Womb

In this ritual, we will learn to use the crystal bowl with guided imagery to elicit dynamic effects within our normal life circumstances. This exercise can be adapted to the individual, and to any magical journeys to be created in the future by the individual.

Read through the meditation first, so that you are familiar with the basic imagery involved. Because it is an exercise to awaken the birth-giving potential within ourselves, you may wish to read and study other works that describe the Feminine Archetypal energies and those of Death/Rebirth.

Part of the purpose of this exercise is to show how to use the bowl in ritual meditations, but also to show how the use of the crystal bowl will accelerate the manifestation process in your physical life circumstances. The guidelines given should be applied to any magical journey and adapted according to your own purpose. Part of the magical process involves attaching greater import and significance to every thought, word, and action.

The crystal bowl is a dynamic tool in any ritual of manifestation, but for it to work fully, there must be a better understanding of just what manifestation is. It is not making something out of nothing. It is not a process that is workable only by a select few. It is a change of energy, a change of form, or a change of condition of being. It is a process that involves more than just things and money. We can learn to use the magical journey to manifest new ideas, health, opportunities for overcoming obstacles, creativity, higher levels of consciousness, etc. We are learning to translate energy from one level to another, from the more ethereal to the physical in a controlled, directed and accelerated manner. It is not just bringing things down and out into the physical; it is also a raising to the spiritual.

In any ritual of manifestation we must pay attention to the Law of Receiving. The Law of Receiving is one of the twelve natural laws of the universe.[14] This is a law that says we must be willing to receive if we wish to manifest. Often, individuals will work to manifest something and ignore this law, which will hinder or block the entire manifestation process.

The Law of Receiving starts the magnetic pull of that which we want to manifest into our lives. For example, an individual may perform a magical journey to manifest greater prosperity. As a result, others may pay the individual compliments in the coming days. Others may offer assistance with various tasks and endeavors. It is important to pay attention to these seemingly little gifts. Do not shrug compliments off. Do not say, "I can handle it myself." Receive all that comes to you following the

---

14 THE TWELVE NATURAL LAWS OF THE UNIVERSE:

1. Law of Thought	5. Law of Increase	9. Law of Sacrifice
2. Law of Supply	6. Law of Compensation	10. Law of Obedience
3. Law of Attraction	7. Law of Non-Resistance	11. Law of Success
4. Law of Receiving	8. Law of Forgiveness	12. Law of Love

magical journey ritual. If we don't accept the little things, the universe will not send the bigger. Receiving the little things starts the magnetic pull that brings the greater manifestations!

1. Decide what it is that you want to have manifest or be born within your physical life. Initially, choose something simple so that you will be able to verify it. Increased prosperity is a simple effect to manifest.

2. Choose a time in which you will not be disturbed.

3. You may wish to enjoy the ritual bath, as described earlier, as a preparatory stage to the ritual.·

4. Review and familiarize yourself with the meditation, the myth, or the legend you intend to use. You may wish to be so familiar with it that you will not have to refer to a script during the ritual itself, although some find it beneficial to have a printed copy nearby. In cases such as this, read it in sections—out loud—and then close your eyes to visualize yourself in that particular scenario.

5. Decide ahead of time where you will use the crystal bowl, and in what form (clicks, bells, gongs, and singing). Do not hold strictly to the guidelines for its use as outlined here. Adjust them to yourself and to your own magical journey.

6. Assume a comfortable seated position. Do a preliminary progressive relaxation. Rhythmic breathing and visualization of warm, relaxing feelings to each part of the body are very effective. The more relaxed you are prior to the magical journey itself, the more deeply will you access the subconscious mind and open to stronger energies.

7. Have your crystal bowl and script (if necessary) all within reach. You may wish to set the bowl either upon your lap or in front of you.

8. Breathe deeply and while holding the bowl tap its side three quick times. This is like a conductor calling the orchestra to attention. This is the clicking sound made by tapping the wooden or metal end of the wand against the bowl, while holding it with your free hand to prevent it from vibrating. Three is the Mother number and rhythm. It is the number of new birth and creation. It is this creative process we are participating in by using the bowl and the magical journey.

9. If using the bowl like a bell, gong it softly 12 times. Twelve is the number for a cycle of the universe and the clock. It is a reminder that

the bowl and the magical journey will enable us to work free of the physical restrictions of time and place. It begins the process of opening the veil to the more subtle dimensions. Allow the bowl to reverberate fully between each gonging.

10. As the gonging reverberates, see within your mind's eye a door beginning to form before you in the distance. As the door begins to take shape with each toning of the bowl, know that you are creating an astral doorway through which you will be able to walk between worlds whenever you use the crystal bowl. Visualize it and imagine it in as much detail as possible. See engraved into the surface of the door a crystal bowl surrounded by 12 stones and gems. As you tone the bowl for the twelfth time, visualize the bowl and the gems engraved upon the door beginning to glow with a brilliant light. As this light pours out from the engravings, see and feel the door opening in invitation to you.

Begin to play the bowl by rotating the wand around its sides. As the bowl begins to sing, allow the sound to pass through you, lift you up, and carry you to the doorway you have visualized. Feel the sound as if you are riding upon a soft cloud. Allow yourself to be carried through the open doorway and set gently down on the other side. Continue the playing of the bowl for a moment, allowing the crystal door to close behind you. Then visualize the following scenario, or your own magical/mythical journey, inserting the sound of the crystal bowl where appropriate:

Your Journey

You find yourself standing in an open meadow. The colors of the wildflowers stand out against the rich greens of the grasses. Surrounding this meadow are mountains, cupping the meadow as if it were the heart of Nature's Bowl.

You move across the meadow, stepping across a small, crystalline stream that cuts the meadow in half. One end of the stream disappears into the distant mountains, and the other empties into a small pool of water, surrounded by exotic trees laden with ripe fruit.

They are very tempting, and you cannot resist the urge to pick some and taste them. The juice spills out as you bite into the fruit. It is sweet, and it makes you feel a little giddy, almost as if the juice has fermented upon the tree within the fruit itself. It is intoxicating. You raise your head to the sky and laugh heartily, filled with a new sense of joy and wonder at the magnificence of Nature and what she can create.

(The bowl is gonged three times at this point.)

The sound of the bell surrounds you, as if in response to your joy. It seems to emanate from the pool itself, and you draw close to its edge and peer into it. You see your reflection, and there seems to be a glow about you. You are not sure if it is really your own glow or the reflection of the sun upon the water.

(Begin to make the bowl sing by rotating the wand around the circumference of the bowl in a counterclockwise direction.)

The water seems to take on a life of its own. It ripples, distorting your reflection, and then it begins to swirl downward. It becomes a whirlpool, swirling in a counterclockwise direction. Its motion is hypnotic. As it whirls, it begins to recede, drawing away from the surface of the earth, deeper into the heart of the meadow itself. As it recedes, an ancient stone stairwell is revealed beneath its surface. The stairs also spiral downward around the edge of this pool. You hesitate only a moment, and then you step carefully upon the wet stones and follow the receding waters.

Round and round you slowly move downward. Each step reveals more intricate stone formations. A myriad of colors and shapes attest to the creative forces of Mother Nature. It is like a descent into a kaleidoscope, each step creating a shifting of the colors and forms. Soon you see the bottom, and you step off onto the solid crystal floor.

(Stop the rotations of the wand and allow the singing of the bowl to diminish. Use the bowl as a bell again, chiming it softly three times. Then set the wand inside the bowl, symbolic of your being inside the womb of the earth.)

Before you is a pool of whirling waters, spinning round and round and round. You know that it is the same water that receded from the surface, but now it is different. This pool is deep and black. The crystalline clarity of the water is no longer evident.

Behind the pool is a small cave. A few feet into the cave you see a woman sitting upon a crystal throne. She is dressed in black. Her head is lowered and the hood of her robe is pulled up over her head, hiding her face. She raises her head as if in acknowledgement that you are present. Slowly she lifts the hood of her robe off her head, dropping it onto her shoulders. She is a matronly woman. Her eyes peer out at you with warmth. There is a strength about her that seems unparalleled by anything you have ever experienced. It has a depth and gentleness that is infinite. You know she can be nurturing or stern—however the situation dictates. She is the Dark Mother.

Her voice is soft as she speaks: "Out of the blackness of the womb comes new life and new light. The creative forces live within you as they do within all life. What you are experiencing now is a reflection of your own creative forces coming alive. We each must learn to embrace this creativity if we wish to manifest it within our lives. All of our creative forces have an ebb and flow, just as the water which led you here. As you learn to reach within the womb of your own life, you will learn to give birth to your hopes, wishes, and dreams. Now look deep within the pool of your own soul and see that which you will give birth to within your own life."

She stands and steps to the mouth of the cave. She extends her hands over the whirling black pool. The water gurgles in the center and then stills itself. It becomes like an ebony mirror, smooth and deep. On the surface you see your dim reflection, and as you gaze into it, your image fades, and you see that which you are desiring to manifest within your life. The image of it fills the entire pool. It is alive. It is real. You are drawn into it and back out of it. It fills you with joy to know that what you dreamed can become reality. The image remains still upon the surface of the water.

"Now take this image, charged in the creative waters of life, out of the womb and into birth in the outer world."

(Ring the bowl as a bell three times.)

The pool with the image of your dreams begins to whirl slowly again. The colors of the image melt and blend and distort, but do not disappear. The image has turned itself into energy that will be drawn up into your life as you return to the surface.

The Dark Mother smiles upon you, warming you and filling you with the confidence of your creative abilities. She returns to her throne and seats herself. With a final look of love, she pulls the hood of her cloak over her head and lowers it so that her face is no longer visible. She is at rest until called upon again.

(Begin playing the bowl, again making it sing, by rotating the wand around the circumference of the bowl. This time you play it in a clockwise direction.)

Mentally you thank her, and you turn to the stone stairs, beginning your ascent. As you climb, the water rises from the pool below, now following your lead. You are drawing it to the surface of your life. You are drawing it out into manifestation.

As you step onto the surface, you turn and watch as the pool fills again. The whirling slows and the water comes to a rest. The water is again clear and crystalline. The image you saw within the black depths of the womb stands out sharp and clear within it. Again you give thanks for being shown the first steps to activating your own birth-giving abilities. As you do, the image fades. (Chime the bowl three times again. This activates the release of the creative energy for outer world manifestation.)

As the image fades, you again see your reflection in the still crystal waters. Reflected also is both the sun and the moon, who now share the sky. You look up from the pool, at the sky and at the meadow around you. It is either dusk or dawn. You are not sure. It is one of those powerful times of the day when night and day intersect, in which the veil between the worlds is thinned. It is a time when the Unmanifest becomes the Manifest. It is the sacred time of birth. Knowing this heightens even more the creative forces you now feel active within your life.

(Slowly begin to chime the bowl 12 times, as you did in the beginning. Allow the sound to reverberate fully in between each chiming.)

As you hear the distant chiming, you look back across the meadow, and you see that door through which you entered. The chiming nudges you gently in its direction. As you approach, the engraved door swings open, and you step through. You allow yourself to settle, balanced and energized, into your seated position. As the last of the 12 chimes reverberates around you, you breathe deeply, feeling your awareness of your body and your surroundings awaken fully.

(Very gently tap the sides of the bowl with the wooden or metal edge of the wand three times to end the session.)

Chapter Eleven

Other Songs
of the
Crystal Bowl

As discussed earlier, the bowl is a symbol of the male and female forces. Whether we call them male/female, yin/yang, electric/magnetic, or even sun and moon, is not really important. What is important is that we find some way of harmonizing and directing these forces within our own life. It is this direction that enables us to create and to mold our lives according to our own goals, wishes, hopes, and dreams. It is what enables us ultimately to create within whatever circumstances our lives may fall. I once heard a quote, whose source I could not determine, but which epitomizes what the crystal bowls can lead us to: "There is nothing so rare as an act of your own."

The ritual use of the crystal bowl enables us to employ original acts of creativity. We learn to recognize that there is an aspect of ourselves that we may have ignored or allowed to be blocked from our view. It helps to re-establish our connection with those primal forces within ourselves, and in directing them into a imaginative and productive manifestation within our lives. It is a dynamic tool to assist us in discovering the creative possibilities within our limitations and the creative ways of overcoming those limitations.

The bowl assists us in reaffirming relationships with ourselves. It creates a sacred space where the physical self and the spiritual self can come together and introduce themselves. It enables the desire aspect of our essence to meet the creative aspect, so that those desires and hopes can find a means of fulfillment.

The sun and moon aspect of the crystal bowl and the wand has intricate ties to many ancient symbologies. Most strong of those is the ancient symbol of the serpent, particularly in the form coiled in a circle, with its tail in its mouth. The snake is often seen as a masculine symbol (phallic) and as a symbol of the solar energies. It is also symbolic of wisdom, a feminine aspect. The snake lives underground, in water, and in trees—all feminine symbols. When viewed in conjunction with the bowl, we see it as an alchemical symbol, opposing forces which can work in conjunction. It is symbolic of the transforming power of the male and female.

The circular motion of the playing of the bowl is an activation and joining of the solar and lunar aspects, separate and yet always together. The snake is the creative life force, always present within us, but not always activated. The playing of the bowl is an activation of this force. It awakens the kundalini. The snake, like the bowl, represents the opportunity to renew ourselves. It is a symbol of eternity and reincarnation, the continuing cycle, and the attunement of our soul to that cyclic flow of life.

The playing of the bowl is symbolic of awakening spiritual power and wisdom, clairvoyance, and vision. it is the awakening of enlightenment that facilitates the use of our creative force.

When we play the bowl, we activate the inner spiritual serpent of wisdom. We bring to life the sun and moon aspects, so that the creative force shines whenever we desire. It enables us to form transformations of ourselves and our life circumstances. It creates the change of relationship between the outer and the inner, the physical and the spiritual. They can no longer be separate dimensions and energies, but are joined into a mutual relationship and influence. The ways in which we apply these energies create the many songs symbolized by and found within the playing of the crystal bowls.

Exercise 29—
Relationship Rituals

Because the crystal bowl works with the opposites' energies and brings them together in harmony, it is a powerful tool for any ritual involving relationships between two people, providing a means for activating energies for harmony and balance in all relationships. It can be used to set the energy to motion, to provide opportunities for establishing relationships, and can be used in meditations to open to past-life connections of present relationships as well. There are few limitations in its application in this avenue.

The bowl is a tool that can join the energies of any two people in harmony. For this to work, we must understand that the bowl is a catalyst. It affects a change in the auric fields of both individuals. They are brought into entrainment—a harmonized blending. This can result in greater sharing, more openness, and greater acceptance.

Most people are drawn to those who have fulfilled something they may be lacking or searching for. There are qualities that the other partner possesses which you hold in esteem. We choose others often because some part of them reminds us of our own inner self. This exercise brings out those common bonds, drawing them to the surface, but the exercise is not limited solely to couples who are lovers. It can be adapted to other partnership situations, to break down barriers and to build rapport. It can also be adapted to one-on-one teaching situations, to help raise the energy and more strongly bring out the potentials of another.

1. Sit upon the floor close to each other, face to face. Sitting cross-legged with the knees touching is effective for this.

2. If the couple involves a male and a female, simply have the woman hold the bowl upon her lap. The male will handle the wand. If it is a couple formed from two males or two females, you will have to decide who is to hold the bowl and who is to hold the wand. If there is difficulty deciding, alternate, as this is an exercise that can be repeated as often as necessary. It is an excellent one to perform at least once a week, or in accordance with the phases of the moon.

    If it is a couple where one is more dominant in the relationship than the other, have the dominant individual hold the bowl and the other handle the wand. Remember the wand is the symbol of the assertive, outgoing masculine, while the bowl is the symbol of the receptive, feminine. IT IS IMPORTANT TO WORK OUT THESE DYNAMICS BEFORE SITTING DOWN TO PERFORM THIS RITUAL! KNOW THE REASON AND SIGNIFICANCE OF EVERYTHING YOU PLAN TO PERFORM WITH THIS EXERCISE.

3. As the one individual holds the bowl upon his or her lap, the other will hold the wand. Chime the bowl three times to activate the energy. The partner with the wand then begins to play the bowl while it rests in the other's lap. It is good for the individual holding the bowl to be touching the other in some way. Laying your hands upon the other's knees is effective. It completes the circle so that the sound can encircle and entwine both of your energies.

4. As the bowl is being played, visualize your energies entwining and spiraling together. After approximately five minutes of playing, allow the sound to diminish. As it diminishes, lay the wand within the bowl and the bowl between both individuals. (If you are sitting with your knees touching, there is formed a small open area between the knees that will cradle the bowl.)

5. Join hands and visualize the two of you joining together, each bringing his or her own energies to create one dynamic and united force. Meditate upon what can be done to make this combined force more effective and harmonious. Meditate upon additional ways in which this newly created force can creatively and productively be applied to the partnership situation, and to other areas of life as well.

6. The effects of this can be amplified if the individuals visualize streams of light connecting the chakra points as the bowl is being played. Begin with the base center and visualize a crystalline stream of red connecting the chakras of both individuals. Then do the same with the spleen (orange), solar plexus (yellow), heart (pink or gold), throat (blue), the brow (indigo), and the crown (violet).

7. If it is a love relationship, you can come together at the end in loving intercourse to ground the etheric energy created. This helps to pull that newly created and harmonious energy into manifestation more dynamically within your lives. At the end, reassume the seated position and move to the closing of the ritual as described in steps 8–9.

8. Both individuals should take time to express what they experienced or felt. Revelations from the meditations should be shared. Once this

is done, each should place their hands upon the wand and withdraw it from the bowl. Together rotate the wand in a counterclockwise direction, making the bowl sing. This serves to ground the new energy even more strongly, anchoring it around you so that it cannot as easily be dissipated in the days to come. Do this for several minutes. You may wish to visualize the two of you working and playing even more effectively as you make the bowl sing.

9. Chime the bowl like a bell FOUR times. Four is the number of a new foundation. It is anchoring to the creative energy awakened through the ritual.

10. Do not limit yourself to these steps. Adapt them to your own situation. It can be used to awaken a stronger relationship, one that is just forming. It can also be used to work on specific areas in the relationship.

    Placing an affirmation in the bowl and in the wand, as described earlier in the work, is effective as well. The ritual then helps release the energy that can be used to resolve or manifest a particular condition.

    It can also be adapted to those times when the individuals involved are at a distance from each other, i.e., other cities, etc. It is more effective if both have a bowl, but it will still work even if only one does. Set a time for the ritual. Make preparations just as if both are present. Sit at the scheduled time and perform the ritual. Both should visualize the energy entwining. Using a witness, and placing it in the bowl will help link the energies more easily. Perform the ritual just as if the other is present. If possible, make phone calls prior to or just after, to connect and ground the energy more strongly in the physical. If this is not possible, both should write down or record in some way their impressions, responses, etc. This also helps to ground the energy into manifestation into the physical.

You will find, as you work with this, that it is easily adapted to each individual and to even group situations. The bowl is an ideal tool for creating group harmony and rapport. It can be used as a prelude to group meditations.

The more you employ your own creative ideas in working with the crystal bowl, the more powerfully it will work for you.

Exercise 30—
The Song of Peace

The bowl is a tool for higher communication. I have heard stories of individuals and groups of individuals who use the time of the full moon to tone for the entire planet and its peaceful existence and growth.

A good exercise for this is to visualize yourself as part of a worldwide symphony. Your instrument will be combined with all other instruments to send sacred sound out around the Earth. Those who have the bowls, and there are thousands all over the world, are learning to tune in. They are becoming more conscious of their dependency upon, and responsibility for, the Earth.

As you play your bowl and the sound begins to encircle you, visualize it encircling the entire Earth as well. Visualize it touching the subtle consciousness of all life upon this planet. See it touching your individual life, spreading to your community through those you touch, on to the entire country and then to the globe. See it stimulating greater awareness and peaceful co-existence. See yourself as part of a global community at every full moon, a community that promotes and CREATES world peace, first upon the subtle vibrational levels, and then impacting upon the physical levels as well. They can not be separated. One always repercusses upon the other. This is the lesson of the bowl.

Many societies speak of the power of sacred sound in their scriptures and mythologies. The crystal bowl is a tool for the creation of sacred sound, and the directing of it to restore peace within our lives.

Exercise 31—
The Scrying Song

Scrying is the process of opening oneself to higher knowledge. One who scrys in the spirit is also one who learns to control out-of-body experience, to travel and open to the inner temples and the knowledge that lies within.

The crystal bowl is a dynamic tool for opening to this process of scrying in the spirit, whether it is just in the form of higher clairvoyance, or in full out-of-body experiences. It assists us in creating astral doorways that open us to the energies of the more subtle dimensions of life and energy.

There are two steps to the full conscious experience of the more subtle astral realms and energies. First is the activation, strengthening, and energizing of our own astral body. The second is the development of the ability to use the astral band of energy as a separate vehicle for our consciousness, so that it can withdraw from the physical and search out nonphysical knowledge, and bring it back into physical manifestation and application.

The crystal bowl assists in both stages. The sound balances and energizes the entire auric field. The aura is comprised of the energy given off by the physical body as the cells convert our food and air into energy. A byproduct is emitted, called photon radiation, or light energy. It is also comprised of our subtle body energies, which enabled our soul to integrate with our physical body at or around the time of birth. These serve as filters, interpenetrating the physical body and integrating energies from more subtle dimensions and life into physical consciousness.

Most psychic phenomena manifests through the energies of the astral plane and through the astral body in the human. Almost all astral phenomena involves an increased sensitivity to the astral plane, and requires learning to handle and direct them. They can be developed in full consciousness. They should not be treated as an end in themselves, but rather they should be treated as gifts to assist us as we open to even higher planes of consciousness and being.

The simple act of sitting and playing the bowl on a regular, daily basis is strengthening to the auric field and the astral body. It establishes, over a period of time (which varies from individual to individual), a higher vibrational rate which increases overall sensitivity—psychic and otherwise. This will ultimately assist us in higher, more subtle perceptions and impressions; but, as mentioned, it will lead to the use of our astral body as an independent vehicle upon the astral plane.

Sit with the bowl either in front of you or upon your lap. You may wish to set it upon a black cloth. The black cloth will assist you in looking within the bowl for new perceptions. Take the wand in hand and gently chime the bowl as a bell three times. This serves as a call to attention. Begin playing the bowl in a counterclockwise direction. This movement draws you into yourself, to connect with levels of your consciousness that are more in tune with the subtle energies and dimensions around you.

Play the bowl for about five minutes. You may wish to vary the sound. Allow yourself to find your own rhythm and volume in the playing. Playing the bowl at any time balances the hemispheres of the brain, facilitating the attunement to other levels of consciousness.

When you feel yourself relaxing and balancing, becoming a part of the sound, look into the heart of the bowl. The black cloth beneath also helps to draw. As you look within the womb of the bowl, ask questions about things or events with which you are concerned. You may wish to close your eyes—whatever is easiest. Trust your first impressions. Do not try to analyze. There will be plenty of time for that later. Sometimes beginning with yes or no answers is easier. You may find that you are impressed with a particular answer, a color, an image, and so forth. It varies from individual to individual.

Do not worry that you may be imagining. The bowl activates the human ability of creative imagination. This is a good sign. Let the imagination run. We can always filter out later what are true impressions and what is simply uncontrolled fancy. What we consider imagination is a reality in some form, on levels beyond the normal sensory world. With its activation, we create a new awareness, a new kind of experience in color and form—in relation to our physical world. This, in turn, triggers higher forms of inspiration and intuition.

Working with the bowl will activate the creative imagination. Do not be discouraged if it does not immediately occur. If we have ignored our more intuitive and imaginative aspects for a long time, it may take some effort to reactivate them. The crystal bowl can do this for us within a month's time—enough to encourage and reward further efforts.

Exercise 32—
Astral Projection

Astral projection and scrying in the spirit are often used interchangeably. There is a difference, but for our purposes here we will treat them as synonymous. The exercise that follows is easier to accomplish if one individual plays the bowl while another follows the exercise. If you do not have someone to play the bowl for you, you can still perform the exercise, but it will take a little more concentration.

Allow yourself to relax. You may wish to perform a progressive relaxation before hand. Begin playing the bowl in a clockwise direction. We use this direction to loosen and stretch the astral fibers and muscles so that they can be an independent vehicle of consciousness outside of the physical. It helps to draw our astral energies out into greater form and strength.

As the bowl begins to sing, allow the energies to pass through you and around you. Visualize the sound as a color or stream of light that encircles you. As it encircles you, passing through you, imagine it loosen-ing the fibers of your energy safely and gently. Think of it as a tremendous relaxation. Allow the sound to breathe through you, and then to breathe you as it circles.

As you continue playing the bowl, allow your body to move with the sound. You may find it rocking back and forth, or even circling slight-ly. Do not force this, allow it to happen naturally. You may wish to assist it by visualizing your energies loosening in conjunction with the sound. Visualize a second, more ethereal you—like a ghost image—moving and rocking, stretching itself a little at a time away from the magnetic pull of the physical body.

This is the loosening and stretching of the etheric webs which help ground the consciousness to the physical body. Loosening helps to gently open the etheric webs so that the consciousness can be extended out beyond the physical, through what is called the atomic shield. The crys-tal bowl vibrations enable this extension outward to occur without rip-ping or tearing holes in our energy field that other quick forms of development can cause.

After ten minutes of this, slow the bowl playing down and allow the sound to dissipate. Then play the bowl in a counterclockwise direction to draw your energies back into alignment and balance with the physical. See yourself coming into greater awareness of your physical presence with this. Play the bowl only a few minutes in this direction.

Overall, this exercise should only take 10 to 15 minutes. This is a preparatory exercise. After two to four weeks of this we can build upon the exercise. Think of it as adding to our exercise regimen.

Take a few minutes to relax, and then begin the bowl playing as you would normally do. Only do this for a shorter period. By this time it should be easier to feel and experience the loosening and the rocking. When you feel the loosening, allow the sound to draw that ghost image you have been working with up out of the physical body. See the sound as a spiraling magnetic force that gently lifts the body toward the ceiling.

Try to place your awareness in this image that is above you in the ceiling. Look back upon yourself on the floor. Pay attention to the details. Don't worry that you may be imagining it all. Remember that the imagi-nation helps in activating and energizing the astral, so they reinforce each other. Be patient. With practice, you will succeed, and it will hap-pen naturally and safely.

Remember ultimately it is the subconscious WILL which will eject the consciousness with the astral phantom you are energizing. Learn to recognize the symptoms which indicate movement toward success. They encourage us to continue our efforts. This can be a glued-down feeling, a sense of paralysis, a sensation of floating, a whirling or zigzagging motion, jerks and jumps of the body, and dizziness.

If you do not actually feel these sensations, imagine them. Imagine your body vibrating with the sounds from head to toe. Feel the sound rotating and swirling up and down your body. Imagine your body stretching, expanding upward and outward, back and forth, from the head and the feet.

At the end of the exercise, play the bowl in a counterclockwise direction to draw all of the energies back into alignment with the physical body. This also serves to ground us so that the heightened sensitivity will not carry over and interfere with our daily obligations and circumstances.

Other Aids to this Process

- Temperature of the environment can be a negative influence.

- Make sure you will be comfortable.

- Stimulating food or drink prior to the exercise can hinder the process.

- Noises and disruptions will snap the astral energy back into the physical, and can cause discomfort.

- The emotions should be calm and passive, but not the mind. The mind helps us to project the body.

- Practice this in the dark or in muted lighting, as light binds the astral to the physical. Light is a form of nourishment to us physically, and it is a function of the astral to help transfer light to the physical, thus keeping both strongly tied together.

- Persistence breeds success.

The Future of Crystal Sounds and the Birth of the Child Within

The sounds of crystals and their application to our lives have yet to be fully explored. Many societies in the past used crystal and stones as a means of creating sacred sound. In China, stones of jade were cut in different sizes and shapes. They were then played in the manner of a xylophone. These "singing stones" had great application in healing and enlightenment.

It would be simple to construct a set of crystalline chimes. Crystal stones can be cut to various shapes and lengths to be used in a similar manner. We could create our own singing stones. A little creativity and effort is all that is necessary.

Even with the crystal bowls, there are levels yet to unfold. For the past year I have heard rumors of crystal bowls made from rose quartz! Imagine, a bowl that sends out naturally the gentle ministrations of love sounds! I have yet to encounter one, and although I imagine the price at this point in time may be steep if ever found, the benefits may far outweigh it. Imagine crystal bowls made from other stones in the quartz and gem family. Imagine bowls in which precious stones have been set into the bowl itself. Imagine the healing temples and meditations that could be created from their use.

Just the idea of the possibilities awakens that childlike wonder within us. It is that which any crystal bowl stirs. Whenever the male and female are brought into harmony, birth will occur, and it is through the illumined soul—the energies symbolized by the bowl—that the Holy Child within each of us is born!

Bibliography

Andrews, Ted. *The Healer's Manual*. St. Paul, MN: Llewellyn Publications, 1993.

_____. *How to See and Read the Aura*. St. Paul, MN: Llewellyn Publications, 1989.

_____. *How to Meet and Work with Spirit Guides*. St. Paul, MN: Llewellyn Publications, 1992.

_____. *Imagick: Qabalistic Pathworking for Imaginative Magicians*. St. Paul, MN: Llewellyn Publications, 1989.

_____. *Sacred Sounds*. St. Paul, MN: Llewellyn Publications, 1992.

_____. *Simplified Magic*. St. Paul, MN: Llewellyn Publications, 1989.

Baer, Randall N. and Vittitow-Baer, Vicki. *The Crystal Connection: A Guidebook for Personal & Planetary Ascension*. San Francisco: Harper & Row, 1986.

_____. *Windows of Light: Quartz Crystals & Self-Transformation*. San Francisco: Harper & Row, 1984.

Barnard, Julian. *Guide to the Bach Flower Remedies*. England: C. W. Daniel, 1979.

Besterman, Theodore. *Crystal-Gazing*. New York: University Books, 1965.

Chancellor, Phillip. *Bach Flower Remedies*. New Canaan: Keats Publishing, 1971.

Clynes, Manfred, ed. *Music, Mind and Brain: The Neuropsychology of Music*. New York: Plenum Press, 1982.

Cooper, J. C. *Symbolism: the Universal Language*. Northamptonshire: Aquarian Press, 1982.

Cosimano, Charles W. *Psionics 101*. St. Paul, MN: Llewellyn Publications, 1987.

Cunningham, Scott. *Magical Aromatherapy: The Power of Scent*. St. Paul, MN: Llewellyn Publications, 1989.

Denning, Melita and Phillips, Osborne. *Llewellyn Practical Guide to Astral Projection: The Out-of-Body Experience*. St. Paul, MN: Llewellyn Publications, 1979.

Drury, Neville. *Music for Inner Space*. New York: Prism Press, 1984.

Ferguson, Sibyl. *The Crystal Ball*. York Beach, ME: Samuel Weiser, 1979.

FES Society. *Flower Essence Journals*. Nevada City: Gold Circle Productions, 1982.

Frater Achad. *Crystal Vision through Crystal Gazing*. Chicago: Yogi Publication Society, 1923.

Galde, Phyllis. *Crystal Healing: The Next Step*. St. Paul, MN: Llewellyn Publications, 1988.

Graves, Tom. *Dowsing: Techniques and Applications*. London: Turnstone Books, 1977.

Gray, William. *Magical Ritual Methods*. York Beach, ME: Samuel Weiser, 1971.

Harford, Milewski. *The Crystal Sourcebook*. Sedona, AZ: Mystic Crystal Pub., 1987.

Hills, Christopher. *Supersensonics: The Science of Radiational Paraphysics*. California: University of the Trees, 1978.

Khan, Hazrat Inayat. *Mysticism of Sound*. Geneva: International Headquarters of the Sufi Movement, 1962.

Lehrs, Dr. Ernst. *Man or Matter*. Faber and Faber.

Markham, Ursula. *Fortune Telling by Crystals & Semiprecious Stones*. Northamptonshire: Aquarian Press, 1987.

Melville, John. *Crystal Gazing and Clairvoyance*. Northamptonshire: Aquarian Press, 1983.

Nielson, Greg and Polansky, Joseph. *Pendulum Power*. New York: Destiny, 1977.

Raphael, Katrina. *Crystal Enlightenment*. New York: Aurora Press, 1985.

Rea, John D. *Healing and Quartz Crystals*. Boulder, CO: Two Trees Publishing, 1986.

Richardson, Sarah. *Homeopathy: Stimulating the Body's Natural Immune System*. New York: Harmony Books, 1988.

Rudhyar, Dane. *Rebirth of Hindu Music*. New York: Weiser, 1979.

Scheffer, Mechthild. *Bach Flower Therapy*. Rochester: Thorson's Publishing, 1986.

Schwarz, Jack. *Human Energy Systems*. New York: E. P. Dutton, 1980.

Silbey, Uma. The *Complete Crystal Guidebook*. San Francisco: U-Read Publications, 1986.

Smith, Michael G. *Crystal Power*. St. Paul, MN: Llewellyn Publications, 1985.

Stewart, R. J. *Music and the Elemental Psyche*. Rochester: Destiny, 1987.

Tame, David. *The Secret Power of Music: The Transformation of Self & Society Through Musical Energy*. New York: Destiny Books, 1984.

Index

Stay in Touch. . .

Llewellyn publishes hundreds of books on your favorite subjects

On the following pages you will find listed some books now available on related subjects. Your local bookstore stocks most of these and will stock new Llewellyn titles as they become available. We urge your patronage.

Order by Phone

Call toll-free within the U.S. and Canada, **1–800–THE MOON**.
In Minnesota call **(612) 291–1970**.
We accept Visa, MasterCard, and American Express.

Order by Mail

Send the full price of your order (MN residents add 7% sales tax) in U.S. funds to:

Llewellyn Worldwide
P.O. Box 64383, Dept. K026-4
St. Paul, MN 55164–0383, U.S.A.

Postage and Handling

- ◆ $4.00 for orders $15.00 and under
- ◆ $5.00 for orders over $15.00
- ◆ No charge for orders over $100.00

We ship UPS in the continental United States. We cannot ship to P.O. boxes. Orders shipped to Alaska, Hawaii, Canada, Mexico, and Puerto Rico will be sent first-class mail. International orders: Airmail—add freight equal to price of each book to the total price of order, plus $5.00 for each non-book item (audiotapes, etc.). Surface mail—Add $1.00 per item.

Allow 4–6 weeks delivery on all orders. Postage and handling rates subject to change.

Group Discounts

We offer a 20% quantity discount to group leaders or agents. You must order a minimum of 5 copies of the same book to get our special quantity price.

Free Catalog

Get a free copy of our color catalog, *New Worlds of Mind and Spirit*. Subscribe for just $10.00 in the United States and Canada ($20.00 overseas, first-class mail). Many bookstores carry *New Worlds*—ask for it!

ANIMAL-SPEAK
The Spiritual & Magical Powers of Creatures Great & Small
Ted Andrews

The animal world has much to teach us. Some are experts at survival and adaptation, some never get cancer, some embody strength and courage while others exude playfulness. Animals remind us of the potential we can unfold, but before we can learn from them, we must first be able to speak with them.

Now, for perhaps the first time ever, myth and fact are combined in a manner that will teach you how to speak and understand the language of the animals in your life. *Animal-Speak* helps you meet and work with animals as totems and spirits—by learning the language of their behaviors within the physical world. It provides techniques for reading signs and omens in nature so you can open to higher perceptions and even prophecy. It reveals the hidden mythical and realistic roles of 45 animals, 60 birds, 8 insects and 6 reptiles.

Animals will become a part of you, revealing to you the majesty and divine in all life. They will restore your childlike wonder of the world and strengthen your belief in magic, dreams, and possibilities.

0-87542-028-1, 400 pp., 7 x 10, illus., photos, softcover   **$17.95**

HOW TO MEET & WORK WITH SPIRIT GUIDES
Ted Andrews

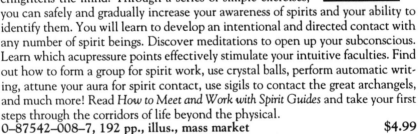

We often experience spirit contact in our lives but fail to recognize it for what it is. Now you can learn to access and attune to beings such as guardian angels, nature spirits and elementals, spirit totems, archangels, gods and goddesses—as well as family and friends after their physical death.

Contact with higher soul energies strengthens the will and enlightens the mind. Through a series of simple exercises, you can safely and gradually increase your awareness of spirits and your ability to identify them. You will learn to develop an intentional and directed contact with any number of spirit beings. Discover meditations to open up your subconscious. Learn which acupressure points effectively stimulate your intuitive faculties. Find out how to form a group for spirit work, use crystal balls, perform automatic writing, attune your aura for spirit contact, use sigils to contact the great archangels, and much more! Read *How to Meet and Work with Spirit Guides* and take your first steps through the corridors of life beyond the physical.

0–87542–008–7, 192 pp., illus., mass market   **$4.99**

ENCHANTMENT OF THE FAERIE REALM
Communicate with Nature Spirits & Elementals
Ted Andrews

Nothing fires the imagination more than the idea of faeries and elves. Folklore research reveals that people from all over the world believe in rare creatures and magickal realms. Unfortunately, in our search for the modern life we have grown insensitive to the nuances of nature. Yet those ancient realms do still exist, though the doorways to them are more obscure. Now, for the first time, here is a book with practical, in-depth methods for recognizing, contacting, and working with the faerie world.

Enchantment of the Faerie Realm will help you to remember and realize that faeries and elves still dance in nature and in your heart. With just a little patience, persistence and instruction, you will learn how to recognize the presence of faeries, nature spirits, devas, elves and elementals. You will learn which you can connect with most easily. You will discover the best times and places for faerie approach. And you will develop a new respect and perception of the natural world. By opening to the hidden realms of life and their resources, you open your innate ability to work with energy and life at all levels.

0-87542-002-8, 240 pp., 6 x 9, illus., softcover $10.00

SACRED SOUNDS
Transformation through Music & Word
Ted Andrews

Sound has always been considered a direct link between humanity and the divine. The ancient mystery schools all taught their students the use of sound as a creative and healing force that bridged the different worlds of life and consciousness.

Now, *Sacred Sounds* reveals to today's seekers how to tap into the magical and healing aspects of voice, resonance, and music. On a physical level, these techniques have been used to alleviate aches and pains, lower blood pressure, and balance hyperactivity in children. On a metaphysical level, they have been used to induce altered states of consciousness, open new levels of awareness, stimulate intuition, and increase creativity.

In this book, Ted Andrews reveals the tones and instruments that affect the chakras, the use of kinesiology and "muscle testing" in relation to sound responses, the healing aspects of vocal tones, the uses of mystical words of power, the art of magical storytelling, how to write magical sonnets, how to form healing groups and utilize group toning for healing and enlightenment, and much, much more.

0-87542-018-4, 240 pp., 5¼ x 8, illus., softcover $9.95

THE HEALER'S MANUAL
A Beginner's Guide to Vibrational Therapies
Ted Andrews

Did you know that a certain Mozart symphony can ease digestion problems ... that swelling often indicates being stuck in outworn patterns ... that breathing pink is good for skin conditions and loneliness? Most disease stems from a metaphysical base. While we are constantly being exposed to viruses and bacteria, it is our unbalanced or blocked emotions, attitudes and thoughts that deplete our natural physical energies and make us more susceptible to "catching a cold" or manifesting some other physical problem.

Healing, as approached in *The Healer's Manual*, involves locating and removing energy blockages wherever they occur—physical or otherwise. This book is an easy guide to simple vibrational healing therapies that anyone can learn to apply to restore homeostasis to their body's energy system. By employing sound, color, fragrance, etheric touch, and flower/gem elixers, you can participate actively within the healing of your body and the opening of higher perceptions. You will discover that you can heal more aspects of your life than you ever thought possible.

0-87542-007-9, 256 pp., 6 x 9, illus., softcover $12.95

HOW TO DEVELOP & USE PSYCHOMETRY
Ted Andrews

What if a chair could speak? What if you could pick up a pen and tell what kind of day its owner had had? What if you could touch someone and know what kind of person he or she truly was—or sense pain or illness? These examples just scratch the surface of the applications of psychometry: the ability to read the psychic imprints that exist upon objects, people, and places.

Everyone is psychic. Unfortunately, most of the time we brush aside our psychic impressions. Now, everyone can learn to develop their own natural sensitivities. *How to Develop and Use Psychometry* will teach you to assess your own abilities and provide you with a step-by-step process for developing your natural psychic abilities, including over 25 exercises to heighten your normal sense of touch to new levels of sensitivity.

With a little awareness and practice, you can learn to use your inborn intuitive abilities to read the history of objects and places ... locate missing or lost articles ... develop intimacy... even find missing persons. *How to Develop and Use Psychometry* gives you all of the techniques you need to effectively "touch" the natural psychic within yourself!

1-56718-025-6, 224 pp., illus., mass market $4.99

HOW TO SEE AND READ THE AURA
Ted Andrews

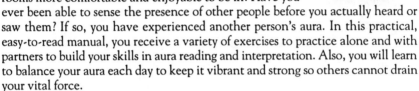

Everyone has an aura—the three-dimensional, shape-and-color-changing energy field that surrounds all matter. And anyone can learn to see and experience the aura more effectively. There is nothing magical about the process. It simply involves a little understanding, time, practice and perseverance.

Do some people make you feel drained? Do you find some rooms more comfortable and enjoyable to be in? Have you ever been able to sense the presence of other people before you actually heard or saw them? If so, you have experienced another person's aura. In this practical, easy-to-read manual, you receive a variety of exercises to practice alone and with partners to build your skills in aura reading and interpretation. Also, you will learn to balance your aura each day to keep it vibrant and strong so others cannot drain your vital force.

Learning to see the aura not only breaks down old barriers—it also increases sensitivity. As we develop the ability to see and feel the more subtle aspects of life, our intuition unfolds and increases, and the childlike joy and wonder of life returns.

0-87542-013-3, 160 pp., illus., mass market, $3.95

HOW TO UNCOVER YOUR PAST LIVES
Ted Andrews

Knowledge of your past lives can be extremely rewarding. It can assist you in opening to new depths within your own psychological makeup. It can provide greater insight into present circumstances with loved ones, career, and health. It is also a lot of fun.

Now Ted Andrews shares with you nine different techniques that you can use to access your past lives. Between techniques, Andrews discusses issues such as karma and how it is expressed in your present life; the source of past life information; soul mates and twin souls; proving past lives; the mysteries of birth and death; animals and reincarnation; abortion and premature death; and the role of reincarnation in Christianity.

To explore your past lives, you need only use one or more of the techniques offered. Complete instructions are provided for a safe and easy regression. Learn to dowse to pinpoint the years and places of your lives with great accuracy, make your own self-hypnosis tape, attune to the incoming child during pregnancy, use the tarot and the cabala in past life meditations, keep a past life journal, and more.

0-87542-022-2, 240 pp., illus., mass market $4.99

THE OCCULT CHRIST
Angelic Mysteries and The Divine Feminine
Ted Andrews

Few people realize that great mystical secrets lie hidden within the teachings of Christianity—secrets to the laws of the universe and their application in our lives. *The Occult Christ* reveals this hidden wisdom and knowledge within Biblical Scripture and presents Christianity as a Modern Mystery School in the manner of the ancient traditions throughout the world.

Within the Christ Mysteries is the cosmic effort to restore the experience of mysticism, power, and the Divine on a personal level. This path not only acknowledges the Divine Feminine within the Universe and the individual, but it also reveals the means to unfold it within your life. You are shown how to access great universal and Divine power through the sacred festivals of the changing of the seasons—times in which the veil between the physical and the spiritual is thinnest. The true Christ Mysteries open the angelic hierarchies to humanity and show the way to attune to them for greater self-knowledge, self-mastery and self-realization.

Breathe new life into your religious foundations with *The Occult Christ*, and learn to walk "the road of shadows where secret knowledge of the soul dwells."
0-87542-019-2, 224 pp., 6 x 9, softcover $12.95

MAGICKAL DANCE
Your Body as an Instrument of Power
Ted Andrews

Choreograph your own evolution through one of the most powerful forms of magickal ritual: Dance. When you let your inner spirit express itself through movement, you can fire your vitality, revive depleted energies, awaken individual creativity, and transcend your usual perceptions.

Directed physical movement creates electrical changes in the body that create shifts in consciousness. It links the hemispheres of the brain, joining the rational and the intuitive to create balance, healing, strength, and psychic energy.

This book describes and illustrates over 20 dance and other magickal movements and postures. Learn to shapeshift through dance, dance your prayers into manifestation, align with the planets through movement, activate and raise the kundalini, create group harmony and power, and much more. Anyone who can move any part of the body can perform magical movement. No formal dance training is required.
0-87542-004-4, 224 pp., 6 x 9, illus., photos, softcover $9.95